All the Rage

A SHAMBHALA SUN BOOK

All the Rage

Buddhist Wisdom on Anger and Acceptance

EDITED BY Andrea Miller

and the editors of the *Shambhala Sun*

Shambhala
Boston & London
2014

Shambhala Publications, Inc.
Horticultural Hall
300 Massachusetts Avenue
Boston, Massachusetts 02115
www.shambhala.com

9 8 7 6 5 4 3 2 1

First Edition
Printed in the United States of America

♾ This edition is printed on acid-free paper that meets the
American National Standards Institute z39.48 Standard.
♻ This book is printed on 30% postconsumer recycled paper.
For more information please visit www.shambhala.com.

Distributed in the United States by Penguin Random House LLC
and in Canada by Random House of Canada Ltd

Library of Congress Cataloging-in-Publication Data

All the rage: Buddhist wisdom on anger and acceptance / Edited by Andrea Miller
and the editors of the *Shambhala Sun*.—First edition.
pages   cm
ISBN 978-1-61180-171-2 (alk. paper)
1. Anger—Religious aspects—Buddhism. 2. Compassion—Religious aspects—
Buddhism. 3. Religious life—Buddhism. I. Miller, Andrea (*Shambhala Sun* editor)
BQ4430.A53A55 2014
294.3'5698—dc23
2014002343

Contents

PART THREE
Going Beyond Blame

PART FOUR
Finding Forgiveness

Introduction

You would never peg me as someone who'd get in a fistfight, and you'd be right. But all the same, there was this one time more than a decade ago.

Urgently needing a place to live, I hastily signed the lease to a drafty apartment with sloping floors and cracks in the walls. I asked the landlord if I could move in on the last day of the month, and he said, "No problem." But twenty-four hours before the scheduled move, the apartment's current tenants apparently had a change of plans and the landlord asked if I could postpone moving by a day. At this point, though, I couldn't; I'd already enlisted movers.

The landlord phoned again. "Okay," he said, "the tenants who are in there now will empty a bedroom for you. You can pile your things into that room. Then the next day, they'll get their stuff out and you can begin living in the apartment." Though not ideal, this was workable.

At the appointed time, I arrived with a load of furniture. The promised bedroom, however, wasn't ready, and the tenants were unapologetic, particularly the woman. Within a hot minute, she and I were raising our voices. All of my irritation with this couple for changing the date, all of my frustration with packing and hefting and organizing—it was all channeled into a heart-thumping electric rage, and I saw the same feeling reflected in the woman's red face. To make matters worse, we were jammed into a tiny kitchen, a space too small for this anger. I sized the woman up. She was my age and small like me. I could take her.

Then suddenly, just before thought became action, my friend came in, breaking the moment. Now the room seemed to spin. I'd gone to a rough high school where I'd often heard the chant "Fight, fight, fight. . . ." Yet I'd avoided those altercations. I'd always seen myself as too mature to get in a fistfight—too sophisticated, too peaceable. Later, when my friend and I were alone in the kitchen, I said, still dismayed, "That almost got physical." "Yeah," she answered. "I could hear it."

Since that day, I'm more sympathetic to people whose anger leads to blows; I know that I have a shard of that behavior in me, too. I also more clearly see the need for understanding where anger comes from, how it manifests, and how I—how we—can work with it most skillfully. This anthology explores these questions from a Buddhist perspective.

The first section, "Understanding Anger," looks at the origin of this emotion and how it impacts our relationships and sense of well-being. Thich Nhat Hanh begins by explaining that in our subconscious mind, we all have negative seeds such as anger, yet we also have positive seeds such as joy, understanding, and compassion. Whenever one of our seeds manifests in our conscious mind, that seed becomes stronger and more likely to manifest again. We cannot eradicate any particular seed, says Thich Nhat Hanh, but we can choose which seeds to water.

Part 2, "Practicing with Anger," focuses on concrete methods. The teachings in this section include Sister Chan Khong's "Beginning Anew," which emphasizes communication. We can learn to listen openly to the grievances others have against us, she says, and likewise we can learn to express our hurt or angry feelings without lashing out. In this way we find solutions to problems rather than add fuel to the fire. "Practicing with Anger" also features lively first-person pieces that provide examples of Buddhist practitioners grappling with anger in daily life. In her inter-action with her young son, Karen Connelly sees that she gets back what-ever emotion she herself expresses. Through his misadventures with irksome members of his *sangha*, Shozan Jack Haubner discovers that the people in our life don't get in the way of our spiritual practice; these people *are* our spiritual practice.

Sylvia Boorstein gets to the heart of the matter: The results of igno-rance—greed, hatred, and delusion—are the real causes of conflict, not particular people, political parties, or countries. So while there may be people who we could name—and blame—as culprits, we would all be better served by recognizing ignorance as the true enemy. Grounded in this understanding, we would then be inspired to right any wrongdoing in a way that is at once firm and loving.

Part 4, "Finding Forgiveness," deals with softening our anger toward those who have hurt us. Moreover, since many of us carry around guilt for past actions, this section also deals with forgiving ourselves. It's important to remember that forgiveness isn't about condoning harmful behavior but, rather, attending to our own hurt and thereby recognizing that the person who harmed us also hurts. Forgiveness, when approached in this way, is an important step in finding resolution, and Judith Toy illustrates this perfectly in her moving story. She lost three family members in a calculated murder, and it was only through forgiving the perpetrator that she was able to heal.

The anthology's final section is about cultivating compassion, especially in the face of anger and aversion. The pieces in this section are full of love, though not the airy-fairy hearts-and-flowers kind. This love is one that can endure the real and often difficult world. The Buddhist teacher Noah Levine looks back on the dangerous years he spent high on drugs and frequently in jail, and he concludes that loving-kindness doesn't protect us from being physically hurt. It does, however, protect us from hatred and all of the suffering that comes with such hatred and in that way loving-kindness does make the world a safer place.

Publishing *All the Rage* has involved the effort and support of many people. I'm grateful to Beth Frankl, my editor at Shambhala Publications, and her assistant editor John Golebiewski, as well as to my colleagues at the *Shambhala Sun* and *Buddhadharma: The Practitioner's Quarterly,* in particular Melvin McLeod, Rod Meade Sperry, Koun Franz, Tynette Deveaux, and my former colleague Liam Lindsay, who came up with the title of this book. On a personal note, thank you to my good friend Rachel for her sharp editorial mind and to my husband, Adán, for all his love and care. And last but not least, thank you to everyone who has ever pushed my buttons. I've learned a lot from you.

By the way, it turned out that the woman whom I so very nearly punched did *not* change her mind about when she was moving. It was the kindly but disorganized landlord who'd gotten the dates confused.

All the Rage

PART ONE

Understanding Anger

Sowing the Seeds of Love

Thich Nhat Hanh

Inside every single one of us there are seeds of suffering—of anger and hatred, despair and depression. But just as important, there are also seeds of happiness—of love and compassion, joy and mindfulness. Which seeds will grow? Those, says Thich Nhat Hanh, are the ones we water.

When we look deeply at a flower, we can see that it is made entirely of nonflower elements, like sunshine, rain, soil, compost, air, and time. If we continue to look deeply, we will also notice that the flower is on her way to becoming compost. If we don't notice this, we will be shocked when the flower begins to decompose. When we look deeply at the compost, we see that it is also on its way to becoming flowers, and we realize that flowers and compost "inter-are." They need each other. A good organic gardener does not discriminate against compost, because he knows how to transform it into marigolds, roses, and many other kinds of flowers.

When we look deeply into ourselves, we see both flowers and garbage. Each of us has anger, hatred, depression, racial discrimination, and many other kinds of garbage in us, but there is no need for us to be afraid. In the way that a gardener knows how to transform compost into flowers, we can learn the art of transforming anger, depression, and racial discrimination into love and understanding. This is the work of meditation.

According to Buddhist psychology, our consciousness is divided into two parts, like a house with two floors. On the ground floor there is a living room, and we call this "mind consciousness." Below the ground level, there is a basement, and we call this "store consciousness." In the store consciousness, everything we have ever done, experienced, or perceived is stored in the form of a seed, or a film. Our basement is an archive of every imaginable kind of film stored on a video cassette. Upstairs in the living room, we sit in a chair and watch these films as they are brought up from the basement.

Certain movies, such as *Anger, Fear,* or *Despair,* seem to have the ability to come up from the basement all by themselves. They open the door to the living room and pop themselves into our video cassette recorder whether we choose them or not. When that happens, we feel stuck, and we have no choice but to watch them. Fortunately, each film has a limited length, and when it is over, it returns to the basement. But each time it is viewed by us, it establishes a better position on the archive shelf, and we know it will return soon. Sometimes a stimulus from outside, like someone saying something that hurts our feelings, triggers the showing of a film on our TV screen. We spend so much of our time watching these films, and many of them are destroying us. Learning how to stop them is important for our well-being.

Traditional texts describe consciousness as a field, a plot of land where every kind of seed can be planted—seeds of suffering, happiness, joy, sorrow, fear, anger, and hope. Store consciousness is also described as a storehouse filled with all of our seeds. When a seed manifests in our mind consciousness, it always returns to the storehouse stronger. The quality of our life depends on the quality of the seeds in our store consciousness.

We may be in the habit of manifesting seeds of anger, sorrow, and fear in our mind consciousness; seeds of joy, happiness, and peace may not sprout up much. To practice mindfulness means to recognize each seed as it comes up from the storehouse and to practice watering the most wholesome seeds whenever possible, to help them grow stronger. During each moment that we are aware of something peaceful and beautiful, we water seeds of peace and beauty in us, and beautiful flowers bloom in our consciousness. The length of time we water a seed determines the strength of that seed. For example, if we stand in front of a tree, breathe consciously, and enjoy it for five minutes, seeds of happiness will be watered in us for five minutes, and those seeds will grow stronger. During the same five minutes, other seeds, like fear and pain, will not be watered. We have to practice this way every day. Any seed that manifests in our mind consciousness always returns to our store consciousness stronger. If we water our wholesome seeds carefully, we can trust that our store consciousness will do the work of healing.

Our bodies have a healing power. Every time we cut our finger, we wash the wound carefully and leave the work of healing to our body. In a few hours or a day, the cut is healed. Our consciousness also has a healing power. Suppose you see someone on the street you knew twenty years ago, and you cannot remember his name. The seed of him in your memory has become quite weak, since it has not had the chance to manifest in the upper level of your consciousness in such a long time. On your way home, you look throughout your basement to find the seed of his name, but you cannot find it. Finally you get a headache from looking so hard, so you stop looking and listen to a tape or a compact disc of beautiful music. Then you enjoy a delicious dinner and get a good night's sleep. In the morning, while you are brushing your teeth, his name just pops up. "Oh, yes, that's his name." This means that during the night while your mind consciousness ceased the search, the store consciousness continued to work, and in the morning it brought you the results.

Healing has many avenues. When we feel anger, distress, or despair, we only need to breathe in and out consciously and recognize the feeling of anger, distress, or despair, and then we can leave the work of healing to our consciousness. But it is not only by touching our pain that we can heal. In fact, if we are not ready to do that, touching it may only make it worse. We have to strengthen ourselves first, and the easiest way to do this is by touching joy and peace. There are many wonderful things, but because we have focused our attention on what is wrong, we have not been able to touch what is not wrong. If we make some effort to breathe in and out and touch what is not wrong, the healing will be easier. Many of us have so much pain that it is difficult for us to touch a flower or hold the hand of a child. But we must make some effort so that we can develop the habit of touching what is beautiful and wholesome. This is the way we can assist our store consciousness to do the work of healing. If we touch what is peaceful and healing in us and around us, we help our store consciousness do the work of transformation. We let ourselves be healed by the trees, the birds, and the beautiful children. Otherwise, we will only repeat our suffering.

One wonderful seed in our store consciousness—the seed of mindfulness—when manifested, has the capacity of being aware of what is happening in the present moment. If we take one peaceful, happy step and we know that we are taking a peaceful, happy step, mindfulness is present. Mindfulness is an important agent for our transformation and healing, but our seed of mindfulness has been buried under many layers of forgetfulness and pain for a long time. We are rarely aware that we have eyes that see clearly, a heart and a liver that function well, and a nontoothache. We live in forgetfulness, looking for happiness somewhere else, ignoring and crushing the precious elements of happiness that are already in us and around us. If we breathe in and out and see that the tree is there, alive and beautiful, the seed of our mindfulness will be watered, and it will grow stronger. When we first start to practice, our mindfulness will be weak, like a fifteen-watt lightbulb. But as soon as we pay attention to our breathing, it begins to grow stronger, and after practicing like that for a few weeks, it becomes as bright as a one-hundred-watt bulb. With the light of mindfulness shining, we touch many wonderful elements within and around us, and while doing so, we water the seeds of peace, joy, and happiness in us, and at the same time, we refrain from watering the seeds of unhappiness.

When we start out, the seeds of unhappiness in us are quite strong, because we have been watering them every day. Our seeds of anger have been watered by our spouse and our children. Because they themselves suffer, they only know how to water our seeds of suffering. When those seeds of unhappiness are strong, even if we do not invite them up from the basement, they will push the door open and barge into the living room. When they enter, it is not at all pleasant. We may try to suppress them and keep them in the basement, but because we have watered them so much, they are strong enough to just show up in the upper level of our consciousness even without an invitation.

Many of us feel the need to do something all the time—listen to a Walkman, watch TV, read a book or a magazine, pick up the telephone. We want to keep ourselves busy in our living room so we can avoid dealing with the worries and anxieties that are in our basement. But if we look deeply into the nature of the guests we are inviting into the living room, we will see that many carry the same toxins as are present in the negative seeds we are trying so hard to avoid. Even as we prevent these negative seeds from coming up, we are watering them and making them stronger. Some of us even do social and environmental work to avoid looking at our real problems.

For us to be happy, we need to water the seed of mindfulness that is in us. Mindfulness is the seed of enlightenment, awareness, understanding, care, compassion, liberation, transformation, and healing. If we practice mindfulness, we get in touch with the refreshing and joyful aspects of life in us and around us, the things we are not able to touch when we live in forgetfulness. Mindfulness makes things like our eyes, our heart, our nontoothache, the beautiful moon, and the trees deeper and more beautiful. If we touch these wonderful things with mindfulness, they will reveal their full splendor. When we touch our pain with mindfulness, we will begin to transform it. When a baby is crying in the living room, his mother goes in right away to hold him tenderly in her arms. Because mother is made of love and tenderness, when she does that, love and tenderness penetrate the baby, and in only a few minutes, the baby will probably stop crying. Mindfulness is the mother who cares for your pain every time it begins to cry.

While the pain is in the basement, you can enjoy many refreshing and healing elements of life by producing mindfulness. Then, when the pain wants to come upstairs, you can turn off your Walkman, close your book, open the living room door, and invite your pain to come up. You can smile at it and embrace it with your mindfulness, which has become strong. If fear, for example, wishes to come up, don't ignore it. Greet it warmly with your mindfulness. "Fear, my old friend, I recognize you." If you are afraid of your fear, it may overwhelm you. But if you invite it up calmly and smile at it in mindfulness, it will lose some of its strength. After you have practiced watering the seeds of mindfulness for a few weeks, you will be strong enough to invite your fear to come up any time, and you will be able to embrace it with your mindfulness. It may not be entirely pleasant, but with mindfulness you are safe.

If you embrace a minor pain with mindfulness, it will be transformed in a few minutes. Just breathe in and out and smile at it. But when you have a block of pain that is stronger, more time is needed. Practice sitting and walking meditation while you embrace your pain in mindfulness, and sooner or later, it will be transformed. If you have increased the quality of your mindfulness through the practice, the transformation will be quicker. When mindfulness embraces pain, it begins to penetrate and transform it, like sunshine penetrating a flower bud and helping it blossom. When mindfulness touches something beautiful, it reveals its beauty. When it touches something painful, it transforms and heals it.

Another way to accelerate the transformation is called looking deeply. When we look deeply at a flower, we see the nonflower elements that help it to be—the clouds, the earth, the gardener, the soil. When we look deeply at our pain, we see that our suffering is not ours alone. Many seeds of suffering have been handed down to us by our ancestors, our parents, and our society. We have to recognize these seeds. One boy who practices at Plum Village told me this story. When he was eleven, he was very angry at his father. Every time he fell down and hurt himself, his father would get angry and shout at him. The boy vowed that when he grew up, he would be different. But a few years ago, his little sister was playing with other children and she fell off a swing and scraped her knee. It was bleeding, and the boy became very angry. He wanted to shout at her, "How stupid! Why did you do that?" But he caught himself. Because he had been practicing mindfulness, he knew how to recognize his anger as anger, and he did not act on it.

A number of adults who were present were taking good care of his sister, washing her wound and putting a bandage on it, so he walked away slowly and practiced looking deeply. Suddenly he saw that he was exactly like his father, and he realized that if he did not do something about his anger, he would transmit it to his children. It was a remarkable insight for an eleven-year-old boy. At the same time, he saw that his father may have been a victim just like him. The seeds of his father's anger might have been transmitted by his grandparents. Because of the practice of looking deeply in mindfulness, he was able to transform his anger into insight. Then he went to his father and told him that because he now understood him, he was able to really love him.

When we are irritated and we say something unkind to our child, we water the seeds of suffering in him. When he reacts, he waters the seeds of suffering in us. Living this way escalates and strengthens the suffering. In mindfulness, calmly breathing in and out, we can practice looking deeply at the types of suffering we have in ourselves. When we do so, we also begin to understand our ancestors, our culture, and our society. The moment we see this, we can go back and serve our people with loving-kindness and compassion, and without blame. Because of our insight, we are capable of practicing real peace and reconciliation. When you remove the conflict between yourself and others, you also remove the conflict within yourself. One arrow can save two birds at the same time—if you strike the branch, both birds will fly away. First, take care of yourself. Reconcile the conflicting elements within yourself by being mindful and practicing loving-kindness. Then reconcile with your own people by understanding and loving them, even if they themselves lack understanding.

The seeds of suffering are always trying to emerge. If we try to suppress them, we create a lack of circulation in our psyche and we feel sick. Practicing mindfulness helps us get strong enough to open the door to our living room and let the pain come up. Every time our pain is immersed in mindfulness, it will lose some of its strength, and later, when it returns to the store consciousness, it will be weaker.

When it comes up again, if our mindfulness is there to welcome it like a mother greeting her baby, the pain will be lessened and will go back down to the basement even weaker. In this way, we create good circulation in our psyche, and we begin to feel much better. If the blood is circulating well in our body, we experience well-being. If the energy of our mental formations is circulating well between our store consciousness and mind consciousness, we also have the feeling of well-being. We do not need to be afraid of our pain if our mindfulness is there to embrace it and transform it.

Our consciousness is the totality of our seeds, the totality of our films. If the good seeds are strong, we will have more happiness. Meditation helps the seed of mindfulness grow and develop as the light within us. If we practice mindful living, we will know how to water the seeds of joy and transform the seeds of sorrow and suffering so that understanding, compassion, and loving-kindness will flower in us.

The World of Modes and Why They Matter

Tara Bennett-Goleman

Anger or despair, equanimity or optimism, we each have certain emotions or modes that we tend to manifest. Our modes, explains Tara Bennett-Goleman, are unconscious habits, the result of countless choices that we made sometime in the past and have long forgotten. But we are not doomed to fall forever into the rut of our toxic modes. Since they're learned habits, we can alter them with reparative learning. The first step is compassionately accepting ourselves and our modes. We gently nod to how our toxic modes originated as adaptations to difficult situations and acknowledge that these early survival mechanisms have persisted past their time.

My stepson Hanuman went on a vacation with a girlfriend some years ago. A longtime musician and songwriter, he was accustomed to bringing a guitar along on trips, to take advantage of the open time when inspirations might come.

His smallish travel guitar, a bit beaten up, has never been a problem; it's fitted into overhead luggage compartments wherever Hanuman has gone in the world. He once took it to India and back. But this one time a guy at airport security refused to let him take it through, saying, "The rules don't allow it. You'll have to check your guitar as baggage"—a recipe for disaster, since the guitar had no case.

Hanuman tried to explain that he'd always been able to take it aboard and store it in the overhead with no problem. But the guy wouldn't budge.

This triggered a rebellious streak in Hanuman, and the two locked horns. Neither of them would give in, and their encounter spiraled downward. Hanuman was angered by how the security guard was fixed in his attitudes and couldn't be open to considering other possibilities. But Hanuman, too, was feeling so reactive that he couldn't either.

Just at the low point, his girlfriend stepped in, and with utter calm and lots of charm politely said to the security guard, "I have a suggestion. How about if we take the guitar to the gate and ask them if we can take it on board? If not, we'll check it."

Completely disarmed, the guard responded, "Well, I guess that would be all right."

They got the guitar on board and stowed with no problems.

I asked Hanuman what he had taken away with him from that encounter. He said he was amazed that, in the grip of his reactivity, he'd seen absolutely no solutions. And how his girlfriend had seen right through the conflict to a simple answer, coming up with a creative alternative. The critical difference lay in the mode from which each person was operating.

If ten different people confront the same difficulty, you'll see ten different responses. How we react to any given situation depends on our outlooks, our attitudes and assumptions, and our emotional habits—our modes.

Our mode of the moment organizes our entire state of being, shaping what we seek out and notice. Modes dictate our feelings and even what we can most readily bring to mind from memory. Some are toxic ruts; others let us flourish. In either case, they fuel our drives and determine our goals, just as they dictate our moods.

"You can't solve a problem from the state of mind that created the problem," Albert Einstein said. Recognizing when we're in a mode-driven mind-set gives us a chance to see more clearly and take the steps needed for change.

Most models in both East and West agree about what our unhealthy modes look like, though they apply differing labels: maladaptive, insecure, distorted, dysfunctional, unwholesome, or even deluded. These unhelpful modes are all contrasted with those that make us more adaptive, secure, wholesome, or wise. Each of these modes, importantly, can move from a negative to a positive way of being.

Our modes of being can be sorted into two main categories: wise or deluded. In our bewildered modes, our perceptions twist in ways that throw us off-kilter emotionally, and we focus on our small-minded world. Such modes bias how we see the world and limit our decisions. But in our wiser modes, we see clearly—without distorting lenses—which spontaneously enhances our empathy.

So for our thinking to be clearer, it is vitally important to learn how to recognize our modes and clarify our perceptions, our feelings, and the actions we take. Our choices can lead us toward the mud of confusion, clouding our perceptions, and toward the murkiness of unknowing; or they can lead us toward the lotus, with its petals unfolding in the light of wisdom, awakening and blossoming, connecting with the nutrients within the mud that allow the lotus to bloom. Rather than succumbing to confusion, mired in the murkiness of blurred perceptions, there's always the opportunity to turn toward *sanje,* the awakened quality that allows the lotus of wisdom to blossom through the mud of confusion.

Buddhist psychology sometimes uses the term *bewilderment* to refer to a haze of confusion in the mind (another term used is *delusion;* Western models speak of *cognitive distortions*). Once we correct the underlying misperception, we can gradually allow a clearer awareness to be revealed.

THE NEUROSCIENCE OF HABIT

East and West psychologies agree: a dysfunctional mode does not doom us. These are learned habits; so with reparative learning, we can alter them.

The neuroscience of habit formation and change tells us habits arise because the brain needs to conserve energy. When we first learn any of the endless habitual routines that get us through each day, the brain pays a lot of attention and exerts a lot of energy. But the more we repeat these routines, the less energy and attention is required.

As we practice a routine to the point of mastery, its execution transfers from the higher, conscious part of the brain to the basal ganglia near the brain's bottom. This golf-ball-size brain network guides us as we transfer toothpaste to our toothbrush or change lanes on the freeway while we think about other things—a sign not only that the brain uses little energy for habits but also that they operate outside our awareness. The advantage of habits, of course, is that we don't have to think about them as they guide us through our days. The downside is the same: we don't realize how habitual routines lull us into complacency, into going through the same motions over and over mindlessly. While it's great to be able to type without a second thought of where the Z key might be, when those habits are the recipe for our negative modes, complacency hurts. For one, every time we act on these habits, we give them more power, actually strengthening the brain's circuitry for them.

Our modes are complex sets of unconscious habits, the result of countless choices that we made sometime in the past and have long forgotten. Our habits may seem the result of thoughtful reasoning, but in truth they were established by forces in the mind that we do not notice, let alone understand.

Mindfulness can bring into our awareness workings of the mind that ordinarily are unconscious. When it comes to changing the bewilderment of blind habit into a wakefulness that gives us choice once again, mindful awareness is the key. Recognizing modes in our minds, in our relationships, and in our lives takes our full attention. Lacking that, we are helpless to detect the emotional habits that work invisibly to wield their power over us.

So the first step in changing our mode habits requires that we bring those habits into our awareness, which leads to what I call mindful habit change. The fundamental change that mindfulness brings is one of waking up rather than of being lulled by habitual complacency.

It's a bit like that scene in *The Wizard of Oz* when everyone trembles as a mighty voice booms, "I am Oz!" The little dog, Toto, goes over and pulls back a curtain, revealing an old man stooped over a control panel and saying into his microphone, "Pay no attention to the man behind the curtain." Our modes have an Oz-like power over us, one that deflates the moment we bring a bold and honest introspection to bear. That true seeing disempowers the invisible grip of mode habits, restoring choice. The clear discernment of mindfulness is like an inner Toto!

Through increasing our awareness of our habitual mode responses and educating the emotions that drive them, the choices we make become less automatic and unthinking, less driven by sheer habit, and more adaptive. Plus, each choice is made with discerning awareness.

PHASE TRANSITIONS

A friend told me about a time earlier in his life when he was very cynical and negative. He was severely depressed, to the point—though he never tried to act on it—of focusing on thoughts of suicide. His life was falling apart; his wife had left him, taking their young daughter. He felt there was no reason to go on.

An environmentalist by nature, during this gloomy time he went with some friends on a long camping trip to commune with the wilderness of Washington State. On that journey his bitter mode completely shattered and was replaced by a far more positive mode.

One day he was at the top of a waterfall looking out over a gorge at a great expanse of natural beauty. Feeling exuberant, he decided to climb a bit farther down the hill while holding on to a large root sticking out of the ground, but the root snapped and he went tumbling. His body rolled over and over down the hill toward the edge of the cliff above the waterfall. His friends watched his tumble in horror, seeing that in just a few more feet he would be gone. But somehow something on the hillside snagged him and kept him from rolling over the cliff.

Perfectly conscious, with only a few scrapes, he jumped up and shouted to his friends, "I'm okay!"

"From that moment on," he told me, "I never had a suicidal thought. Everything felt like a gift." He said that during those terrifying moments he thought mostly about the love he felt for and from the people in his life—and that was the real gift. In the face of death, his mind shifted into a positive mode where he felt filled with love.

Amazed by this miraculous turn of events, I asked him if there was anything else he had learned from this experience that had been life changing. He reflected for a moment, then said, "I clearly see how the choices we make—motivated from the place we're in at a particular moment—can turn us toward the negative or the positive."

In the years since, he said, he has rarely fallen back into his cynicism, anger, and negativity—at least not for long. When once he had been motivated by anger, he was now more interested in positive solutions. Where once he had seen only disconnection and hopelessness, he now found connection and possibility.

Negative thinking originates in a self-centered focus on what's wrong. The more we focus there, the more we suffer. But if—like my friend after his brush with death—we shift from "my pain, my desires, my attachments" as a central focus, the habit of self-referencing starts to fall away.

We all have a handful of favored modes we enter at one time or another. Their transitory nature allows for growth and change if we spend more time in adaptive modes and visit our unhelpful ones less and less.

No matter how firmly a negative mode grips us or how unhappy it makes us, we always have the potential to shift into a better one. Physicists call such a change in state a "phase transition." Phase transitions occur everywhere in the world of matter, as well as in our minds. Heat a wet glob of clay sufficiently and it hardens into a brick. Heat sand along with a dash of chemicals at high temperatures and behold: glass.

Like water changing to ice or steam, our minds can transmute modes. A confused and agitated mode, when the right interventions are applied, can morph into one of discerning calm and clarity: pick up a baby having a tantrum, hold her lovingly while singing softly, and she just might fall asleep in your arms. . . .

The secure, or integrated, mode fosters a range of positive, adaptive ways of being in which we seem to flow through life and blossom in our relationships, health, productivity, and creativity. The secure mode is pivotal in this progression, an emotional safe harbor at the core of mental well-being, which fosters wiser choices in our lives and stronger bonds in our relationships.

Eastern psychology details a mode range beyond such day-to-day well-being: with a wise heart, we undergo a transformative inner evolution toward compassion, wisdom, and equanimity, where life's hassles can leave us unperturbed. Most spiritual paths aim toward some version of this mode.

The spectrum of modes resembles a ladder of inner phase transitions, from heavy to light. At the lower rungs are our more distressing and self-defeating ways of being; like the atoms in steam, our thoughts can be chaotic and our feelings turbulent. As we shift into more healthy modes, we calm down and gain clarity. And the positive range of modes goes into states of mind where our lightness of being transcends the weight of our ordinary ways of being.

Wherever we tend to be on this ladder, we would do well to remember what the Zen master Suzuki Roshi wryly observed: We are perfect just as we are—and we could still use a little improvement.

PERCEIVING ANEW

... When seeing Monet's paintings, we may marvel at how an innovative way of seeing can be catalyzed by a single gifted person inviting us along to see things in a fresh manner.

Art historians tell us Monet's remarkable Impressionist works were partly an expression of the distorted perceptions induced by cataracts. As his vision became increasingly blurred, he went on painting through the years, depicting what he saw.

Monet took great care in his study of the nature of light and the ways it subtly alters what we see. The point for him seems not to have been whether the landscape was foggy or clear but rather the particulars of light that could be captured on the canvas. Monet's fuzzy vision shifted our own from the specifics of objects to the qualities of light cast on them.

Can we allow ourselves to perceive anew, even when our vision is blurred? Can we find wisdom—or at least clarity—in the thick of confusion? Can we miss significant meanings amidst the mind's muddy waters? And could reperceiving help clear the haze?

A children's book about the senses has inserts to touch, see, smell, feel, and taste, each instructing kids on how we perceive. One of the inserts is a card with transparent strips of colored plastic. The book tells the child to look at an object through one of the colors for ten seconds and then take the strip away and see how that object looks now.

For a brief period there's an afterimage, a haze of the color complementary to the one you were looking through; if you used the green, you see the world as if through a rose-colored lens, with a reddish patina. But the colored afterglow eventually fades, giving you the ability to see things clearly again—that is, if you don't keep gazing though the colored lens.

How are our perceptions affected by the lenses we see through? What are the lenses we put on time and again? And how can we learn to see our world clearly, free of the bias of our lenses?

Modes color our perceptions. They define how we perceive, and that defines our world. It's not so much the ways life tests us that define us but our outlooks as we meet those tests. "We are disturbed not by things," Epictetus, a Greek philosopher, observed, "but by the view we take of them."

Aaron Beck puts it a bit differently: "The question comes down to where we focus our attention. If you focus on the negative, that's all you're going to see. If you focus on the positive, you see things very differently." Those who habitually see the glass as half empty are not just more pessimistic; as Dr. Beck has found, they actually are more susceptible to a depressed mode.

Our modes are like obscuring veils. You see a veil as it is, but you also see the world through it. As you become more settled and present, the veils become more and more transparent, like the mud that settles to the bottom of a pond, revealing the crystal clarity of the water above. . . . You can allow the light of awareness that is always there—though temporarily obscured—to illuminate the mind.

RECOGNIZING OUR MODES

To begin to understand the unique sensory universe of a horse, put your open hands together in front of your face so that you can't see straight ahead but only to the sides. "That's how a horse sees the world," horse trainer Bob Sadowski explains. "Each eye talks to only one half of the horse's brain. Watch a horse approach something it's trying to understand, and you'll see that the horse turns its head from side to side so that both eyes can take in the image."

Because their eyes are on the sides of their heads, horses have a huge blind spot directly in front of them. But we humans are used to eyes oriented in front, and we act as though horses are like us—we come at them head-on, or we bring our hands or a halter up from below, another horse blind spot. This can be unnerving or even threatening to a horse. It's even seen as predatory.

So instead, Bob approaches a horse from the side, slowly, the way other horses do. He shows a horse its halter, putting it within sight to the side of the horse's head, and then gently rubs the horse with it, so the horse feels safe. Contrast that with the typical way people approach a horse and put on its halter, and you see that things have been off track between humans and horses for a long time.

Recognizing our modes is a bit like getting to know how another species, like a horse, experience the world. Every mode has its own reality. We can begin to recognize when the distinctive signs of a mode arise in our bodies and minds—a flash of anger, the clench of fear, the numbness of avoidance. We might not even realize what mode we are in, but we feel a negativity coming over us, an all-too-familiar knot of unpleasant feeling or a mental fog distracting us from the present.

While we're caught up by a mode, we see our world through those lenses, without realizing that we're seeing through them. But there are some telltale signs that we're in the grip of a maladaptive mode. Our thoughts tend to follow a rut, and our feelings are often way out of proportion. Or our responses are knee-jerk rather than well-considered choices.

What we pay attention to defines our subjective reality at every moment; the more adaptable our attention, the more aspects of reality we can consider. On the other hand, the more we freeze our focus, the smaller our range of choice, and we become self-absorbed.

Three elements of self-absorption all operate while we are in the grip of an unhealthy mode. First, attention fixates on thoughts and feelings typical of the mode itself; we have little or no ability to see other than through the mode's lens, and we ignore what does not fit that view of the world.

Second, we skew the meaning of events (even irrelevant ones) by interpreting them as references to ourselves. We are trapped by egocentric thinking and create distorted personalized interpretations that exaggerate how much an event actually has to do with us.

Finally, we cling to the goals and desires the mode imposes for us, sometimes even at the expense of the well-being and rights of other people—and, sometimes, at our own expense.

Getting to know the signs that a negative mode has begun is the first step in changing that set of habits toward a better direction. Once we recognize the mode, we can remember that these are like changing weather patterns, passing states of mind.

While a group of my workshop students studied this together for a year, one of them realized how her lifelong history of repeated relationship difficulties signaled a mode pattern that she had not until then recognized. As she put it, "I see how I have distorted perception. I never thought of it so much as a warped view. I just thought of it as me!"

ACCEPTANCE

A man in his late seventies said to me that as he looked back on his life, one thing that he'd found important was "being seen." An attunement to the unique reality of another person lies at the heart of compassion, and a first step in compassion is being able to truly see and understand people, so you can help them effectively.

Life is full of moments when we can practice compassion if we're attuned to these opportunities. Sometimes it's quite subtle; it may be simply sitting in silence with someone who is going through a difficulty and being available when needed. It may be giving our full attention. Or connecting in a way that allows difficult feelings to rise to the surface and perhaps even melt in our loving presence.

It's the same when we approach our modes: we need to attune to the unique reality of the mode and understand how it leads us to think and see the world. . . .

Listening and empathizing help attune us to the genuine essence of people. Once we know that negative modes are part of everyone's packaging, with compassion we can give a nod of acknowledgment yet not get distracted or defined by another person's modes. This applies to our own modes as well.

We each tend to gravitate toward favored modes that have become habitual—they feel like "me." That's one challenge in changing our habitual modes: it can seem as though these habits are just the way life is. If we do not see that we are stuck in a problematic way of being, then we're unlikely to consider changing things.

. . . Practicing loving-kindness and compassion toward ourselves and others opens our hearts and counters harsh judgments. In investigating our modes, for instance, we might gently nod to how our toxic modes originated as adaptations to difficult situations and acknowledge that these early survival mechanisms have persisted past their time.

Even in the midst of our mode blowups and meltdowns we can tune in with empathy for ourselves and with compassion for the mode's perspective. Empathy also helps us be forgiving with ourselves about lapses rather than being harshly judgmental or feeling dispirited and giving up.

Empathy and acceptance are vital in this mode alchemy. When in the grip of a distorted mode, it's as though we're the little kid who's been frozen at an early developmental stage. To melt this frozen state, we need warmhearted understanding.

Compassion melts inner barriers, while insight releases them, as we integrate fragments of our beings into a larger dimension of our nature. Just as the caterpillar thought the world was over, as a saying goes, it became a butterfly.

Five Habits of Mind That Are Obstacles to Waking Up

Toni Bernhard

According to traditional Buddhist teachings, desire for sense pleasure, anger or ill will, lethargy, restlessness or worry, and skeptical doubt are the five habits of mind that are obstacles to awakening. Frequently, says Toni Bernhard, one obstacle can arise on the heels of another, and the usual culprit is anger, because it shows up as aversion to whatever obstacle has arisen. Yet we can work with obstacles. The key is awareness.

The Buddha identified five habits of mind that are obstacles on the path of awakening because they hinder or cloud our ability to see clearly the three marks of experience—impermanence, no fixed self, and *dukkha*. Called the five hindrances in Buddhism, they are collectively known by other names—demons, negative energies, temptations—in almost all spiritual and religious traditions.

All five hindrances are familiar to us, but each of us seems to have our own "areas of specialization," meaning that, as a result of our past conditioning and our unique life experiences, some of the hindrances have become more individually entrenched as mental habits than others. We'll look at each of the five in turn and then practice working with them.

DESIRE FOR SENSE PLEASURE

There's nothing wrong with having a good time, but when we're caught up in this hindrance, we actively, sometimes obsessively, pursue pleasurable experiences through our sense doors. In Buddhist thought, the mind is considered to be the sixth sense, so the sense doors would be sight, sound, smell, taste, bodily sensations, and thoughts and emotions. This hindrance takes the form of desiring to please those senses to the exclusion of other experiences. We want to hear our favorite music, eat our favorite foods, experience pleasurable body sensations, have only pleasant thoughts and emotions.

Desire for sense pleasure becomes an obstacle to awakening when it leads us to continually chase after pleasant experiences. We can easily come to desire and even expect that everything we encounter will please us. This clouds our ability to see that life is an ever-changing mixture of pleasant and unpleasant experiences—joys and sorrows. And so we're setting ourselves up for suffering when we continually pursue pleasant experiences, because an unending parade of pleasantness is not possible.

True happiness is an inner peace not dependent on all of our experiences being pleasurable.

ANGER OR ILL WILL

When we're caught up in this hindrance, we're quick to criticize and judge. Nothing meets the standards we set up and then cling to as "right." No wonder we're unhappy! Anger or ill will can range in intensity from mild irritation to resentment to destructive outbursts of rage. We may criticize others: "She doesn't know what she's talking about"; "He's full of crap." We may criticize ourselves. When I became chronically ill, I used to be angry at myself for not recovering my health. The anger took the form of self-blame and recrimination. It added an extra layer of misery to the symptoms of the illness. It took me years to realize that this anger was just a way to keep me from experiencing the deep sorrow I was feeling.

When our wisdom mind is clouded by this hindrance, we don't see that life's mixture of joys and difficulties, successes and disappointments, applies to us too, and so we get angry when circumstances and other people don't conform to our liking. But anger gives rise to suffering. The Buddha said that when we direct anger at another, it comes right back to us—like fine dust thrown against the wind. In my experience, when I direct anger at myself, it also comes right back at me, in the form of suffering.

TORPOR OR LETHARGY

This hindrance doesn't refer to bodies that are sick or in pain or simply need to rest; the hindrances are mental states. This one is characterized by apathy and lethargy—a feeling of staleness and lack of enthusiasm in the mind. Everything is too much effort, as in, "I can't be bothered," or "This is too much of a hassle." If you've raised teenagers, you've experienced this hindrance in action. If you ask them to clean their room, they'll say, "I don't have the energy." If you then say, "Okay, then you must not have the energy to go for an ice cream," they'll perk right up and say, "Sure I do," and this hindrance will disappear from their minds!

More seriously, torpor and lethargy can take hold of us at a deep level. The lack of enthusiasm in the mind can permeate our whole day. We can't be bothered to keep an engagement. It's too much trouble to fix a meal. We couldn't care less about life. This hindrance is a painful obstacle to awakening because we don't have the energy to engage life.

RESTLESSNESS OR WORRY

When this hindrance arises, we're anxious, agitated, and often fearful. Both restlessness and worry stem from an uneasiness about life. Restlessness reflects an uneasiness about the present, and worry reflects an uneasiness about the future. When we're restless, we have difficulty being still in the moment. We want to be moving all the time—do this, do that, do anything but be still because something better than whatever is present must be right around the corner.

When we're worrying, we're afraid that things are going to go wrong. We think that if we could only anticipate what's going to happen in the future, we could prepare for it. As a result, we obsess over every imaginable possibility. I know, because this is my particular area of specialization, and storytelling dukkha is its primary feature: "If I'm in an accident and taken to the hospital, will they understand that I'm already chronically ill?" "What if my husband, Tony, gets sick or injured and suddenly needs me to be the caregiver?" These worst-case scenarios are a great source of suffering for me—unnecessary suffering, since it's impossible to predict the future.

The words *worry* and *fear* are often used interchangeably, and I'll be doing so here. Fear can arise without worry—and be constructive— such as when an immediate danger triggers fear that results in a fight-or-flight response. But worry and fear usually go hand in hand.

They can arise over mundane matters—"If this traffic doesn't start moving, I'm afraid I'll be late for lunch." Or they can arise over profound concerns—"If my parents' health deteriorates and they can't live independently, who will take care of them?" Both worry and fear focus our attention on some imagined event or experience in the future. Of course, skillful planning for the future is a wise use of our time and can prevent much suffering in the years to come. But there's a difference between thoughtful planning and persistent worrying about the future. The latter is the hindrance that we'll be working with.

Both restlessness and worry cloud our ability to wake up to the moment because they keep us from being at peace with our life as it is right now. When we're restless, we're always thinking something better must be around the corner. When we're worrying, we're too lost in fearful thoughts about the future to be able to embrace the present moment.

SKEPTICAL DOUBT

There is skillful doubt—not believing something just because we've heard it somewhere else but instead seeking to verify it ourselves—and there is skeptical doubt. Skeptical doubt is characterized by the constant wavering between belief and disbelief.

With skeptical doubt, we find ourselves skipping from this belief to that one and from one spiritual practice to another when, in fact, any number of paths might be to our benefit. I once had myself enrolled in three overlapping meditation retreats—one Zen, one Tibetan, and one Theravadin—because I couldn't decide which one held the magic key to the peace and well-being I was seeking. This served only to increase my suffering as I directed negative self-judgment at myself: "You can never settle on anything!"

When our wisdom mind is clouded by this hindrance, we can't see clearly that this relentless questioning of our assessments and decisions is keeping us from embracing wholeheartedly what we're doing right now, in this moment.

WORKING SKILLFULLY WITH THE HINDRANCES

As if we don't have our work cut out for us when only one hindrance arises, it's very common for one hindrance to arise on the heels of another. Buddhist teachers often lightheartedly refer to this as a multiple-hindrance attack. The usual culprit is the second hindrance, anger. It shows up as aversion to the presence of whichever hindrance has arisen.

The aversion takes these forms: "I hate this desire"; "I don't want to feel this lethargy"; "Worry is ruining my day." And because aversion usually carries a negative judgment about ourselves along with it—"I shouldn't feel this way"—the result is suffering in abundance. I'm quite sure that no one is a stranger to feeling aversion to these five habits of mind.

Learning to respond skillfully to the hindrances minimizes their impact on our lives. For most of us, each of the hindrances will arise from time to time. When they do, how we respond to them will affect the depth of suffering that results.

To work skillfully with the hindrances, we'll use a four-step approach. I'll go through the four steps and then we'll practice with several of the hindrances.

The first step is to recognize it—become aware that a hindrance has arisen. This can be a challenge because our attention can become so focused on the object of the hindrance—the chocolate brownie, the person we're angry at, the appointment we're worried about, the spiritual practice we're doubting—that we don't even recognize that we're in the throes of the hindrance itself. Good mindfulness skills can help here. With practice and patience, we can become adept at recognizing that a hindrance is present in the mind.

Having recognized the presence of the hindrance, label it. Giving it a name helps us hold it as an object of our awareness so that we can investigate it. In the written record of the Buddha's teaching, he often used the words "I see you" to label the various mental states that were obstacles to awakening. When I imagine the Buddha speaking this phrase, I hear him saying it in a friendly tone, not a frustrated or hostile one. This is because I've discovered that a friendly tone keeps aversion to the hindrance from arising or, if it's already arisen, keeps it from intensifying. I call this attitude of friendliness toward the hindrances treating the hindrances as guests.

I started treating them as guests when I realized how often I was adding to the simple presence of a hindrance thoughts about how much I disliked it, followed by a negative self-judgment for feeling this dislike. Call it suffering upon suffering upon suffering. How we can make ourselves miserable over a simple arising and passing event in the mind!

So try treating the hindrance as a guest, even if it doesn't feel genuine at first. If you like, you can say something like the Buddha did: "I see you." Being friendly has the most disarming effect on the hindrance in question. It stops aversion to it from arising or, if aversion has already arisen, it steals its thunder. We're friendly to our guests when they show up unexpectedly. Well, when we're friendly to the hindrances, aversion to them never gets a foothold.

Because we've labeled the hindrance in a friendly manner, we can investigate it (step 3) without aversion. Start by noticing how the hindrance feels in the body. Pleasant? Unpleasant? Are there areas of tension or discomfort? Just as our physical condition can affect our thoughts and emotions, what's going on in the mind can affect the body. The mind and the body are interconnected, so noticing the bodily sensations that accompany a hindrance increases our overall awareness of it.

Then we can begin to investigate how the presence of the hindrance makes us feel mentally. Does it feel pleasant? Unpleasant? Once again, mindfulness is an important tool: it's one thing to be aware that we're angry; it's quite another to be aware of how that anger makes us feel.

We can check to see if we're treating the hindrance as a fixed part of who we are—"angry person," "worrywart," "always indecisive." Identifying with it as a fixed self inclines the mind toward the hindrance in question, and this creates the causes and conditions for it to become a repeating pattern in the mind. It also feeds any feelings of unworthiness—that inner critic that so many of us carry around. So instead of identifying with the hindrance, try treating it as an arising and passing event in the mind.

We can also look for the want/don't-want that's behind the hindrance. In other words, what is it that we want but aren't getting? What is it that we're getting that we don't want? It's also fruitful to examine any stories we're telling ourselves in relation to the hindrance. Are we spinning exaggerated tales and worst-case scenarios and then believing them without question? This is storytelling dukkha. If it's helpful, recall Ayya Khema's assessment of thoughts: Most of them are just rubbish, but we believe them anyway.

This investigation holds the promise for transforming these deeply ingrained habits of mind. For example, we may know from the law of impermanence that if restlessness arises, it will eventually pass out of the mind. But unless we investigate the restlessness—how it feels physically and mentally, the nature of the desire that's behind it, whether we're identifying with it as a fixed self, the stories we tell ourselves about it—it's likely to pop right back into the mind again. With mindful investigation, we're gradually coming to know our own mind—what makes us tick! And the better we know our mind, the better able we are to incline it toward kind and nonharmful thoughts, speech, and actions.

Finally, having investigated the hindrance as best we can (sometimes we'll be more successful than other times), we just let it be. Recoiling from it or trying to force it out of the mind with a "let it go" command may only strengthen it and is likely to lead to self-blame if our efforts fail. Instead, with compassion toward ourselves for any suffering the presence of the hindrance is causing, we patiently let it be, knowing that it will eventually yield to the law of impermanence and pass out of the mind. Letting it be can be a moment of awakening because we're accepting unconditionally—without aversion—that this is how we feel at the present moment.

When working with the hindrances in this way, be content to take baby steps and be ready to lose your way sometimes. If you get lost in the throes of anger or worry or another hindrance and you're not able to go through these four steps, that's fine. Take a deep breath and know that in the next moment, you can start the practice anew. We can go from dukkha to no dukkha—from suffering to no suffering—over and over again! And if you can't concentrate on the four steps at this moment, that's okay too. Wrap yourself in a cloak of compassion, safe in the knowledge that the law of impermanence is on your side and that the hindrance will eventually weaken and pass out of your mind.

Practicing with Desire for Sense Pleasure

Many years ago, I was at a daylong retreat with the Buddhist teacher Ruth Denison. Everyone had brought a dish to share for lunch.

When the time came to eat, we lined up at the front of two long tables that were filled with food. Then Ms. Denison took us by surprise. She said, "Before you take a dish and start serving yourselves, everyone is to walk slowly by the tables—twice—and notice your desire for the food." As I walked past the food the first time, if you'd asked me if I was caught up in the desire for sense pleasure, I'd have said "No!"

But as I began to walk past the food the second time, suddenly the sensory pleasure I was experiencing from seeing and smelling the food was overwhelming. I wanted her to call off this silly exercise so that I could get those mouth-watering morsels into my body as soon as possible! I knew I couldn't very well start grabbing at the food. So, not without irritation, I decided to give in to her instructions and simply notice the presence of desire in my mind and body and see if I could feel its pull on me.

Amazingly, recognizing and investigating the desire in this fashion became more interesting to me than the food itself. I noticed that being hungry was a sensation in my body but that wanting to eat was a mental state. It was a thought I could label: "Desire to eat this food." By the time I walked down the line the third time, the desire had subsided. I filled my plate slowly, with a feeling of gratitude toward those who had taken the time to fix such delicious food to share.

I learned so much from Ms. Denison about how desire for sense pleasure works that I've tried her exercise at home. I choose a meal that contains some of my favorite food. Instead of picking up my utensil and diving right in, I stop for three to five minutes and notice everything I can about the food—how it looks, how it smells, how I feel about it. Recognizing that desire for sense pleasure has arisen, I label it: "Wanting this food"; "Desire has arisen for this food."

Sometimes I realize that I'm telling myself stories about how I've learned the lesson of the exercise already: "I get the point—desire for sense pleasure can be powerful—so there's no good reason not to eat right now!" When this happens, I note the thoughts and then let them be, knowing with my wisdom mind that they're just arising and passing events in the mind.

I encourage you to try this. The idea here is not to take a negative view of wanting delicious food but to begin to make the hindrance of desire for sense pleasure a more conscious part of your everyday life. When you do this, you'll begin to recognize how often you chase after sense pleasure and how this can lead you to expect all of your experiences to be pleasant—a surefire setup for suffering!

Practicing with Anger

When anger arises, we tend to get so caught up in the object of our anger—"How can she get away with that?" or "He's dead wrong"—that our ability to see clearly is hindered. Specifically, we don't realize that it's the anger in our own mind and not the object toward which that anger is directed that's making us suffer.

But we can learn to handle anger skillfully. First, of course, we work on recognizing that it's arisen. Then we label it: "Mind filled with anger"; "I see you, anger." If we label it with a nonjudgmental attitude, as if we're hosting an old friend, we can keep it from intensifying.

Investigating the anger, we can ask ourselves how it feels physically and mentally. Does it tend to arise in the presence of certain people or at certain times of day or when we're too busy or feeling tired? Can we pinpoint the desire behind the anger—what it is that we want that we're not getting, or what it is that we're getting that we don't want? Are we making the anger worse by telling ourselves stories about it? If so, can we dispassionately ask ourselves, "Am I positive this is a true reflection of how things are?"

With increased awareness and a better understanding of how anger works in our minds, we can develop the skill of refraining from speaking or acting out of anger, so that we don't harm ourselves or others. This refraining is how we let the anger be, patiently waiting until it passes out of the mind.

Many years ago when I was in law school, I was in a study group with six other students. One evening, I got into an argument with another student over how to interpret a case that we'd studied in class. He and I disagreed, and neither of us was willing to budge. The more we argued, the deeper each of us dug our heels in. "I'm right; you're wrong" is a common story underlying anger.

Now I look back on the incident and realize that I thought I was angry because he refused to acknowledge that I was right and he was wrong. But if I'd had the skills to bring that anger into mindful awareness and investigate it, I would have seen that my anger wasn't due to what he did or didn't believe. It was due to my own self-focused desire—my perceived need—to be right (and the accompanying fear that perhaps I wasn't).

This desire was then compounded by two more desires—to impress the other students in the group and not to be embarrassed in front of them. (He probably felt the same way.) As I kept arguing, I was also silently spinning stories about what I perceived my fellow students to be thinking about me, even though, of course, I had no idea what was going on in their minds. These stories only served to increase the high level of stress I was already feeling. And so the two of us continued with this fruitless argument—fruitless partly because, as it turned out, the interpretation of the case wasn't clear to the professor either! All I got for my time and effort was a lot of suffering.

Because of my Buddhist practice, if this same scene were to play out today, I'm confident that I'd recognize early in the process that what started out as a disagreement over a legal issue had degraded into a battle of one anger-filled mind against another, and that nothing but dukkha was going to come out of it. Once each of us made our points, I'd say something like: "Let's agree to disagree. We can ask the professor about it in class."

Another example. A few years ago, I was referred to a specialist to find out if he had any ideas for treating my mysterious chronic illness. He exuded confidence and told me emphatically that he'd find out what was wrong and then treat me. He ordered a battery of tests. But when the tests came back negative, he was curt and dismissive, simply telling me to go back to my primary care physician.

When I left the follow-up appointment, I was angry. I could feel the anger in my body. My chest was tight, my face was flushed, and I started sweating. Then I began to spin stressful stories that served only to feed the anger: "He had no business making promises he couldn't keep"; "That's the last doctor I'm going to trust." My suffering over this incident lasted for months.

Looking back on it, I see how I could have handled it more skillfully. It's not that I was wrong in thinking that the doctor shouldn't have made those promises. But it wasn't the doctor's behavior that was making me suffer. In other words, my suffering wasn't due to the object of my anger—the doctor. It was due to what was going on in my own mind. Behind the anger that I was directing at him was an intense desire to recover my health. And that was the source of my suffering: my inability to get what I wanted.

As for the doctor, yes, he probably shouldn't have acted so assured at that first visit (although maybe he really did think he could cure me), and it would have been nice if he'd been more compassionate at the follow-up. But as I like to say about the medical profession: some doctors come through for us and some don't. Just like everything and everyone else in life.

Since this incident, I've had two similar experiences with other doctors, and yes, I was disappointed each time. But I didn't get angry. Now I know that anger only harms me. It doesn't get me better medical care, and it doesn't help me regain my health.

PRACTICING WITH WORRY AND FEAR

Now we come to my own special hindrance. As I mentioned, one of my recurring worries is that Tony will get sick or be injured. I conjure up stories where I'd need to be at his bedside in the hospital, navigating the health care system and providing him with love and support. These stories trigger worry and fear because, right now, I'm too sick to be able to do this.

If I resist feeling these two painful mental states when they arise, they get more intense. So I work on being mindfully present with them. When I recognize that worry and fear have arisen, I hold them in conscious awareness by gently labeling them with a friendly voice. I use phrases like these: "Worry and fear"; "Worry is present"; "Mind filled with fear." Sometimes I use the Buddha's label: "I see you, worry. I see you, fear."

Maintaining friendliness is important because otherwise I slip into aversion, and that invariably carries with it a negative judgment about myself in the form of commentary like "Can't I stop this constant worrying?" or "I shouldn't feel this way." So I throw aversion off guard by treating worry and fear like old guests.

Then I investigate how they feel. I experience worry and fear as a heaviness, both mentally and physically, as if I were carrying an extra weight around. When I investigate what gives rise to worry and fear, I find that it's my desire to control the future. That realization loosens their grip because I know with my wisdom mind that controlling the future is impossible. Peace is only to be found by acknowledging the truth of those two corollaries of impermanence: uncertainty and unpredictability. This means there's no more reason for me to assume that Tony will get sick or be injured than there is to assume that he won't. All of those stories I spin in which I project this medical crisis and that medical crisis serve only to increase my stress and suffering.

Fear and worry are habits of mind, and habits can change. As Aung San Suu Kyi courageously asserts, "Fear is a habit. I am not afraid." Continually questioning the validity of these stressful scenarios that I spin is one of the ways I'm changing this painful habit.

Working this way with worry and fear weakens them. Then, evoking compassion for myself over the suffering that accompanies these painful mental states, I let them be, knowing that they'll eventually yield to the law of impermanence and pass out of my mind.

It takes time to learn how to respond skillfully to the hindrances, but by practicing in this way, we can gradually transform our responses to these painful and disruptive mental states. The hindrances arise as a result of various causes and conditions in our lives. By maintaining a non-judgmental attitude toward these habits of mind, we can coax them out of the darkness so that we can shine the light of mindfulness and investigation on them. If we're self-critical or judgmental about their presence, they may retreat back into hiding, where they'll only intensify, along with our suffering. So investigate these mental states with curiosity and with patience.

We can reach a point where we know our minds well enough that we can catch a hindrance right when it arises and then consciously choose not to take it up. Sometimes just treating the hindrance as a guest is all it takes to stop it in its tracks. And when this happens, we experience the peace of mind that comes with relief from suffering.

Anger Is a Poison

Carolyn Gimian

In traditional Buddhist teachings, anger, greed, and ignorance are known as the three poisons. Because they wreak so much suffering, we try to get rid of these emotions. Yet we can never succeed in making them go away—they are at the very center of this wheel of life. Here Carolyn Gimian offers us another approach. Instead of rejecting our emotions, we can work with them, she says. And, ultimately, we can tame and transmute them.

Maybe Copernicus and Galileo were right about the Earth orbiting the Sun, rather than the other way around. I don't know about the universe, but in my little world, it all revolves around me! Thoughts and emotions are the planets and asteroids that rotate around the core of me-ness. Whoa, a whole bunch just zoomed past. And here comes another cloud of them. . . .

Our thoughts and emotions go around and around in confusion, and this experience is depicted in the Wheel of Life, an ancient visual teaching. At the center of this wheel are three animals: a rooster, representing passion, grasping, and desire; a snake, representing aggression, anger, and hatred; and a pig, representing ignorance and delusion. They are at the hub of the wheel, the central point or focus. Around this hub, complex realms of experience develop, and on the rim of the wheel, we find the dramas that make up cause and effect. All of this complexity is generated from that core of three confused emotions, which are often referred to as the three poisons.

Another analogy for passion, aggression, and ignorance might be atomic particles. I'm thinking here of the prevailing view of the atom as I learned it in grade school. The atom in those days was thought to be composed of combinations of three particles that had positive, negative, and neutral charges. Emotionally speaking, the rooster of passion has the positive charge, which is trying to suck everything into its orbit. The snake of aggression has the negative charge and is trying to push away or destroy things. The pig of ignorance is just there neutrally snuffling around in its blind vagueness, neither repelling nor attracting. By combining in various ways, the three can generate myriad emotional states of mind: envy, jealousy, depression, exhilaration, and many more—all of which are trying to hold the fundamental atom of ego together. The model of the atom that I learned as a child was limited and simplistic. Likewise, the idea of ego as a truly existing entity is full of holes.

Sometime in the 1980s, I went with Chögyam Trungpa Rinpoche and a group of people to a revolving penthouse restaurant in San Francisco. You could see the whole city move past you as the restaurant turned. It was the restaurant that was turning, but it seemed as though it was the city. Later that evening, Rinpoche asked me, "How are you?"

"I'm still dizzy," I said, referring to the restaurant experience. "I still feel as though I'm going around and around."

He looked at me intently and said, "Yes, you are."

Hmmm. Point taken.

In contemplating the Wheel of Life, I feel a little guilty about maligning the animal kingdom. We can imagine a hub for the wheel that substitutes human stereotypes for the emotions. We could replace the ignorant pig (and pigs are actually quite intelligent, by the way) with most teenagers, all couch potatoes, and everyone disappearing mindlessly into their computer screen or mobile device. For the rooster, I am seeing Imelda Marcos, Donald Trump, and a host of movie stars dressed for the Oscars. For the snake, I can picture drivers struck by road rage, a host of intellectual snobs, terrorists, assassins, and the passively aggressive Nurse Ratched. I know all of these people quite well, because I regularly invite them on retreat with me. They all arrive, and then it turns out I'm the only one there. They're all a part of my projections.

I wonder about people who talk about their emotional upheavals in the past tense, as things they used to experience when they first started meditating. The Buddha was visited by the daughters and armies of Mara on the night of his enlightenment. He'd been meditating for many years at that point, so this shows us that, on the path to liberation, these characters show up for a long time—even if you're the Buddha. If you haven't seen any of them in your meditation practice in quite a while, you might wonder, too. Maybe you're bull-poohing yourself. (Insert stronger term for bull pooh, if you wish.) Or maybe you're using your meditation practice as a tranquilizer. Either way, this probably won't last forever. Sooner or later emotional upheavals will undoubtedly and undeniably crop up.

Think about a garden in summer. Then think about a garden in winter. Where did all the foliage go? Where are all the fruits and flowers? If your meditation is like the garden in winter and you think you've eradicated all the weeds of negative emotion, just wait for the spring. Turn your back for one minute and there are all of those thousands of weeds waving at you, mocking you: "We're back!" There is not a weed killer in the universe that will instantly vanquish these invasive thoughts and emotions. So until that magic weed killer does hit the market, the practice of meditation is an excellent tool to work with the poison of our emotions. It's an ancient approach that is still totally up-to-date.

There are a number of meditative techniques that develop mindfulness and awareness. Most of them involve assuming a dignified or deliberate posture, working with the breath, and acknowledging thoughts and emotions as they arise. It sounds simple, and it is—devilishly simple. It's a little like golf, I imagine, a game I don't really play but watch on television. The simple description of golf is that you have a little ball and you have some sticks, or clubs, and you hit the ball with the clubs until it lands in the hole. Simple. Devilishly simple. But think of all the clinics, lessons, hours on the driving range, equipment, clothing, shoes, greens, fairways, caddies, sand traps, tournaments—it's a whole world, just to put that little ball in the hole.

Meditation may also involve extensive preparations and procedures: special clothing, choosing a cushion or chair, arranging the space, and even deciding what time to sit. And meditation involves technique. Are your eyes open or closed? Where do you rest your gaze and what do you do when you fall asleep on the cushion or your mind takes off like a runaway train?

Sitting in a dignified posture, identifying with the breath, and label-ing your thoughts—this simple act often seems simply impossible to achieve. As we encounter the complexity of thought and emotion on the cushion, we may recognize that the seemingly singular act of meditation is actually an evolving experience. Meditators often call this "the path." It involves difficulties, challenges, and discoveries, like all good journeys.

In my own experience, the first discovery I made on the cushion was that I was not my thoughts. Or to put it in positive terms, I discovered space or a gap between my thoughts. It was quite shocking. Having dis-covered that there was more to me than thinking eventually allowed me to see thoughts more clearly. That doesn't mean I could do anything about them, but I could see them. And I could return to the breath, again and again. Because of the instructions I was given (to simplify everything into thinking, not giving special status to emotions), I was also able to look at my emotional states of mind as part of my thinking process and see that the emotions were much less solid and less defining of me than I had previously believed. Because I was also given the instruction not to ignore my emotions, I began a rather painful process of relating with them, which is sometimes called "making friends with yourself." This is the time when the three poisons show up in your meditation and make their displays and pitches. In your practice, you are making friends with all of that! Quite a tall order.

I spent most of one meditation retreat silently lusting after a man I had recently met. Many people have the passion retreat, where they ob-sess about someone or something they want. I also have had the aggres-sion retreat, where I fumed for days over someone who had "wronged" me. The intense feelings of anger were shocking to me, but illuminating in another way. And I have had the ignorance retreat, where I ignored something looming in my life, trying to rest in some kind of manufac-tured peace, only to leave the retreat and realize my ignorance when I ran full tilt into what I was trying to ignore.

I know this may sound odd, but these are the precious occurrences in life: discovering one's preoccupations and self-deceptions, silhou-etted in the open space of practice. Though they are often not appreci-ated as such, these are the golden opportunities.

Through practice, we see how much we invest in our emotions and how much energy we give to them. We may also begin to see how small things, small thoughts, and small feelings can grow into gigantic monsters that fuel hatred, traps that lure us, or foam pads that prevent us from feeling. As Sir Walter Scott wrote: "Oh what a tangled web we weave / When first we practice to deceive."

When we start to recognize that we are creating this jungle of confusion, the hard work of practice really begins. Meditation is a lifelong path of practice, and if not an endless journey, then a journey without a lot of immediate gratification. This is probably quite different from what we imagined when we began.

The naive approach is simply to try to get rid of our negative emotions. Emotions do not disappear, but—when tamed and transmuted—they can shine like a jewel in our lives. As many great teachers of meditation tell us, we should be delighted that we have our thoughts and emotions; they are the marks of being alive.

At the same time, we don't want to be dizzy for eternity, spinning the wheel of life ever faster within this existence and from one existence to another. Thus, we return to the image of the Buddha, the one who woke up from the dream and stopped spinning the illusions that drive our suffering. He made it possible for others to do the same, by sharing his example. Shakyamuni and other buddhas may be naked or dressed in rich brocade. There are some who wear monastic robes, some who sit on elephants or stand on tigers, and some who wear their emotions as diadems or jeweled necklaces.

These displays of awakened mind may be inspiring, but there is a difference between imitating the outer trappings of the buddhas and emulating their state of mind. We may think that if we sit up really tall, tuck in our chin, and either close our eyes or lower our gaze and rest our hands in a meditative gesture, this is all that's required. Well, it will help, actually. But if we have a self-satisfied internal grin, then our peaceful pose may be more deceptive than liberating. We have to open to ourselves, and rather than trying to cage our emotions and calling this a spiritual achievement, we have to work with them.

For me, for now, I'll continue to invite all my rampant thoughts and emotions to join me in retreat. At least for the duration of the retreat, I'm not inflicting them on anyone else! And who knows, maybe one day the Buddha will also show up. I'm sure he or she will. I've had glimpses.

The Other Side of the Fence

Dzigar Kongtrül

The people who have the most aggression are the most paranoid. Fear and paranoia come with aggression because when we have made a separation between ourselves and others, we have, in effect, created enemies. This, says Dzigar Kongtrül, is a form of violence. Of course, we can come up with all sorts of reasons to justify our aggression. We may even be "right." After all, one hundred people back us up. But this so-called logic does not just harm the people we view as our adversaries; we also get hit hard with our own fear and aggression.

Yₒu are at a party and there are beautiful people, surroundings, and laughter. The music is good too. Suddenly someone gets angry and throws a glass of champagne. It ruins the whole show—even the dog leaves the room. When someone gets angry, it effects the whole environment like an unpleasant odor that everyone has to smell. And as our mental states are often quite fragile, it disturbs people's minds. But it disturbs the person who gets angry more than anyone else.

When we get angry, we lose the dignity of our intelligence. We become a stranger to pleasure. Others stay away from us, and we are left alone with our mind and all the residue that comes from our angry reaction. We feel vulnerable to the core, not because something happened outside but, rather, because we've lost trust in our ability to respond to situations in a sane and reasonable way.

Most people don't consider themselves violent or aggressive. Moreover, most of us condemn the violence we hear about in the news or witness around us. But aggression expresses itself in many, often subtle, ways. We may not necessarily lash out when we are aggressive. We may just have a sour or distrustful attitude toward others in such a way that we no longer keep them in the realm of our care. We may suspect someone is angry at us: "He didn't say a word when he saw me. What did I do to deserve that?" The imaginary scenarios we create seem to proliferate on their own. Because we no longer trust this person, we take away their "ally status" and put him or her on the other side of the fence. Whether we are "spitting fire" or quietly harboring animosity, aggressive mind is always engaged in rejecting with a sense of aversion.

We may even have an external reason for our suspicion that someone is against us or wants to bring us down. Someone we considered a friend may no longer back us in some way. This happens. We may need to use our critical intelligence and remove ourselves from a harmful situation or take care in terms of relating to certain individuals. We may even need to speak out against something that has potentially harmful consequences for a larger group of people, a nation, or the world at large. But proceed with caution: Sometimes aggression moves in. And when it does, we often mistake it for discerning intelligence or our instinct for expressing generosity and care or our longing to better the world around us. The reason for this is that anger gives the illusion of clarity. A certain strength arises when we have an opinion and we know where we stand.

The difference between the clarity we believe we have when angry and the clarity that results from actually seeing clearly is that aggression has its own narrow logic, which does not take into account the deeper level of causes and conditions that surround each situation. Because it has no foresight or perspective, the aggressive mind doesn't see any reason to hold back; it is only concerned with preserving the sense of self it seems to be working for. It doesn't think about peace or disturbance, benefit or harm, so it does not try to reroute itself in an emotionally positive direction. Aggression fixes its logic on the wrongness of the other and always possesses the distinctive feature of aversion. We see that aggression results, to some degree or another, in our not responding well to situations. We lose our poise and dignity and get all keyed up like a nervous little dog barking and jumping around, trying to intimidate others. We lose our ability for reasonable discernment, which we regain only after our anger has subsided. But by this time it is too late. We've created a mess, and we feel shredded.

Needless to say, when we expel others from the realm of our care, we ignore our bodhisattva vow. When we take the bodhisattva vow, does it say, "May all beings find perfect happiness . . . except all politicians and my ex"? Do we leave out terrorists; dictators; big, hairy spiders; and everyone that irritates us? When we put anyone on the other side of the fence, we lose our foundation for seeing clearly and acting for the welfare of self and others. Instead, we begin to experience a lot of anxiety and fear. We can see that the people who have the most aggression are the most paranoid of all. Fear and paranoia come with aggression because when we have made a separation between ourselves and others, we have, in effect, created enemies. This is a form of violence.

Of course, we can come up with all sorts of scenarios to justify our aggression. They may be logical and fair. We may even be "right"; after all, one hundred people back us up on this! So we throw in the towel and say, "I can't take it anymore—I've had it!" Anger seems reasonable when we feel threatened. As it's said, "anger comes in the guise of a friend"— righteous and protective and with airtight logic. Someone or something else is always responsible. But this logic only blinds us, and we get hit hard with our own fear and aggression instead. So what good does this do even if we win?

Ego's Empire

The pain and anxiety we experience in our lives are in equal proportion to the size of our self-importance. Our attachment to self is at the center of ego's world—ego's empire. We want the best for ourselves and all of those we associate with ourselves. All that we include as part of me and mine is ego's domain. Of course, this is unstable and changing all the time. Someone might say, "Oh, I love your children," so they're in. Someone doesn't back you on a project or puts down your country— they're out. In the traditional Tibetan Buddhist teachings, those we associate with ourselves usually include our friends and family. When a loved one is ill, we may find it more unbearable than if we fell ill ourselves. But oddly, we often have less tolerance for those closest to us. This shows how bewildered our mind can be.

Meanwhile, we want happiness and do everything we can to avoid suffering. We long for the material goodies this world has to offer but then fear losing or not being able to obtain them. We hope for sweet praise to reach our tender ears but fear criticism and disapproval. We want recognition and fame, and dread ordinariness and obscurity. The preoccupations we have with our various hopes and fears fill our whole day. We have anxieties of not getting what we want, with so many people in the way, and a readiness to leap into aggression when we don't. Let me tell you, this is not helpful! We hold tight to our empire, which only means more aggression for us.

As for our adversaries—those we put on the other side of the fence—we secretly wish for them not to succeed or accumulate wealth or do well. When we hear they are happy, we might say, "What wonderful news!" but it does not sit well inside. When something unfortunate happens to them, we feel a sense of relief. Conversely, when we hear, for example, that the stock portfolio of someone we don't like has gone up, it hits us hard in the gut. If someone likes this person, we make a special point of exposing all of our adversary's faults by saying something negative. We try to give our naive friend a little bit of "truth."

In our attempt to secure ego's empire, we must wrestle with the world and all of its unpredictability. We have so much less control than we would like. All of our hopes, fears, and preferences stir up feelings of insecurity within us and feed our mental unrest and aggression. The way we feed our mental unrest is often subtle. We may find ourselves sitting across the dinner table from our spouse, casually venting some insecurities about the day's events: "He is mad at me. . . . She is not behind me. . . . I don't like the way he . . ." Letting our minds wander into negative thinking ruptures our peace of mind. It's a dangerous direction to let our minds move in.

SELF-AGGRESSION

Our aggression can point outwardly toward external objects, or it can fix on our inner life of thoughts and emotions. When we sit to practice meditation, we may find it hard to face what's "in there." All sorts of undesirable sensations and thoughts arise. Our response? "This is bad . . . very bad indeed. I need to cut this. I need to get rid of this. I'm so intense!" Our inner life does not often fit the image of ourselves that we try to maintain. Sometimes we doubt the possibility of ever having a positive relation to this self at all. Guilt and aversion arise as yet another form of aggression—the rejection of how we see ourselves, how we feel, what we think.

The world is what it is; we have to face what is happening around us, our relationships, or just whatever goes on in our own mind. We cannot expect it all to go away. We have to be practical; otherwise, we just create further suffering for ourselves. Much of the time, we can't resist the temptation of sorting things out with our emotions. When neuroses and negative thoughts arise, we react by either suppressing or venting them—both responses, of course, aimed at trying to get rid of unwanted experiences.

THE PRACTICE OF NONVIOLENCE

On the Buddhist path, rather than trying to protect ourselves from our own mind, we actively investigate mind in order to understand how it works. We often have to be quite critical of our habits. We have to look at our faults, including our aggression. We have to examine our neuroses. There is research to be done. If we respond with revulsion toward our mind and its activities, this inquiry cannot take place. We need to understand the mechanics of aggression and learn to reflect in a nonjudgmental way. We may be hard on ourselves, thinking we have "anger-management problems" or calling ourselves "a lost cause." But in this way, we just sidestep really looking. We need to look at the mind without judgments of good or bad. At the same time, we need to understand how both good and bad are defined by virtue of how they function to create happiness and pain. In other words, we need to sort things out with wisdom mind and bring them into review.

There is much to appreciate in ourselves and our minds—even in being "messed up." The more we know, the more we can resolve; while the more we reject, the more we alienate ourselves from our experience. If we are truly to abandon something, we should do so with wisdom rather than aggression or fear. If only we knew how to bring our difficulties into the light of our intelligence.

All the Buddha's teachings find roots in nonviolence: nonviolence toward others, nonviolence toward ourselves, and nonviolence even toward negative emotions. It is important that we have a taste of the peace that comes from nonaggression. The dualistic tendency to push things away poses the biggest problem for us. We have so many wants and "unwants" . . . but how wonderful—there is room for all. When we begin to understand our mind's habits, we have the leverage to slowly and steadily outsmart them.

The famous Tibetan meditator Geshe Ben said that his only practice was to watch his self-importance bloat up and then crumble down again and again. Seeing how it made his mind freer and freer every time it crumbled brought meaning and pleasure to his life. In fact, it was his life's passion. His is an example of a genuinely nonviolent attitude toward his own mind and experience. We should study such examples and let them rub off on us. Even just admiring someone who lives this way can undermine our addiction to our emotions. We can study his or her attitudes, wisdom, and broad-mindedness. Bodhisattvas engage in the practical discipline of nonviolence toward their own minds and the world around them. They have simply decided to resort to wisdom instead of aggression.

His Holiness the Dalai Lama, I'm certain, considers all the people of the world as his friends. We often see pictures of him in books and magazines holding someone's hand tightly—as if they have been buddies for his entire life. When we listen to his speech or see him with others, his compassion and inclusiveness strike us. Although China still occupies Tibet, it is hard not to notice that His Holiness continues to refer to the Chinese people as his brothers and sisters rather than putting them on the other side of the fence. His example alone teaches us how to practice nonviolence. It shows us that whoever practices nonviolence pacifies not only his or her own mind but also that of everyone around him. Kindness naturally provides others with a way to respond that is free of aggression and hatred. Mahatma Gandhi said that when you are able to respond to another's aggression nonviolently, that person softens and they are able to self-reflect. Acting upon these principles, the Indian people won independence from the British Empire.

Through the practice of nonviolence, we can surely gain independence from our own afflictions.

We may think that nonviolence is a meek, passive, or naive response to the wrongdoings in the world. In relationships, we fear that if we don't respond aggressively, we will be victimized or taken advantage of. We would rather settle our scores through fighting back in order to preserve our sense of dignity and strength. But nonviolence does not fall into the extremes of either aggression or passivity. Nonviolence is a path of total engagement.

The great practitioners of nonviolence have never turned their heads or shrunk away from their own or others' suffering. Knowing the downfalls of aggression, they have been able to respond with wisdom and broad-mindedness. This type of wisdom and courage grows from our commitment to understanding our own mind and reactions and the causes and results of our actions. We develop the ability to accurately read and respond to the world around us without rejecting it. This is the practice of nonviolence. Of course this takes some maturity. We really need to cultivate this kind of maturity.

POSITIVE DISGUST

Normally we have so little control over our emotions—and we feel our vulnerability as a tight knot in our chests. People talk about needing armor, particularly around their chests, to protect themselves when they go to war. Even bugs have shells to protect themselves. But no physical armor can protect us from what disturbs us inside. We cannot hide ourselves in a box in order to insulate ourselves from our own minds. The only real protection we have is the practice of nonviolence.

In Tibetan, the term for nonviolence is *tseme zopa*. *Zopa* is translated as patience, tolerance, or endurance. Inherent in zopa is a feeling of positive disgust, or renunciation, that comes from knowing the negative result of anger. This disgust is similar to the disgust we might experience from eating the same greasy food again and again, day after day. Through constantly getting burned by our own aggression, we will lose our taste for anything that feeds it and instead turn toward the virtues of practicing patience. With this kind of intelligence, we can endure anything. But more important, as we establish patience, we cultivate merit in this life and the next.

It's good to be a little afraid of aggression. Many think that being motivated by fear is not good. But we all get insurance, and we pay our premiums. If we were not afraid of tickets or getting in an accident, we might go through red lights. But due to our fear, we restrain ourselves. Studying other realms as described in the Buddhist scriptures informs us of the future consequences of our actions. For example, those who have a propensity for killing and harming others experience a paranoid hellish existence. However, we don't need to go to such extremes to observe the cause and effect of aggression. We see it in ourselves, in those around us, and even in movies and television. Sometimes it helps to have something visual to relate to. I have a friend whose son was stealing, so she sent him to a prison in order that he could see what his options were. He saw that prison was not just a place where inmates relaxed in cells and watched TV. It put everything in perspective for him right away.

I read an inspiring story about a man in Tibet who had all the markings and characteristics of a demon. In fact, Padmasambhava, the Indian *mahasiddha* who brought Buddhism to Tibet, predicted this man's coming in the Buddhist scriptures. This man knew about this prediction and recognized in himself his affinity for war and violence and all the signs described in the text. He recognized that his own weaknesses could harm both himself and others. So he sought out the great fourteenth-century meditation master and scholar Kunkhyen Longchenpa. How unusual this is! Generally people don't want to identify themselves as demons! This is very touching, I think. It demonstrates how recognizing the qualities of aggression can turn our minds in the direction of peace. This is why in Alcoholics Anonymous people say, "I'm an alcoholic." People need to acknowledge that they need help, without feeling bad, and then seek an antidote.

Simmering Practice

Once we have identified our aggressive tendencies, we can apply the principles of nonviolence. We will need to make a firm decision not to feed our aggression. If we were to go on a diet to slim down, for instance, we would need to refrain from old patterns of eating that don't support weight loss. Of course we would be able to eat—but no brownies! We would need to decide beforehand that brownies would not support our weight loss. Then, if a craving for brownies were to arise, we would need to practice abstinence—we would refrain from eating that brownie. It may seem natural to just go ahead and eat one, because that's our habit, and it might seem artificial to refrain. But our wisdom tells us that "the no-brownie way" provides the only path to weight loss. If we were to stick with this wisdom, we would have to simmer in the discomfort of not having our brownie. We would have to starve our brownie-eating tendency . . . and maybe go get a carrot stick instead. But in the end we would feel lighter and more confident about having moved forward with our aspirations.

Similarly, when we decide to practice nonviolence, we make a deliberate choice to simmer with our aggression. Simmering doesn't mean you boil in your aggression like a piece of meat cooking in a soup. It means you refuse to give in to anger because you know the result of aggression and you want to experience the confidence that comes from patience. So you summon up all of your strength and let yourself feel how strong the tendency is, without rejecting it or giving in to it. In other words, simmering wears out the tendency to react habitually. Athletes do this in their own way. They love the pain of burning muscles when they exercise. They appreciate that kind of burning sensation because they know it makes them stronger and builds endurance.

Through the nonviolent practice of simmering, we can work to change our basic reactions to the world around us, and this has a positive effect on others. Then we can feel good and safe in the world of unpredictability, and we will not feel so intimidated by various states of mind, such as anger. In fact, when we simmer with our aggression, we not only burn the seeds or latent tendencies that give rise to further aggression, we also make good use of those seeds as an opportunity to cultivate patience. We might begin to question the nature of anger: What is anger, really, when we don't react to it? You might be surprised to find it isn't as substantial as you thought.

Many people consider reaching the peak of Mount Everest a great accomplishment. But imagine accomplishing the practice of nonviolence. Through simmering in the raw discomfort of our tendencies, we can gain victory over our aggression and experience the confidence and well-being that come from patience. When you climb Mount Everest (and this is no insult to climbers), you still have to climb back down, but, accomplishing the practice of nonviolence, we just keep moving forward, building our confidence and sense of freedom. We move from one good place to an even better place. Because of the peace that comes from nonviolence and the pain that we experience from aggression, Shantideva, the eighth-century Indian master and author of *The Way of the Bodhisattva,* says that patience is the noblest austerity.

Most of us know at least one person who is really patient. Patient people seem to have a jovial mind, a mind that is happy at the root. Some people seem naturally patient, and we marvel at how lucky they are. But in most cases, a patient, jovial mind needs to be cultivated through the practice of tolerance and nonviolence. So much of this has to do not just with calming irritations but with how we shape our minds—how we replace aggression with patience. It requires a sense of broad-mindedness that comes from seeing the effects of aggression and, conversely, the effects of patience. This takes some contemplation. Someone told me recently that through simply contemplating the ways in which she feeds her mental unrest, she had the first good night's sleep she had had in a long time. That is what we all want, isn't it? A good night's sleep: a mind that is not reactive, a restful mind, a mind free from struggle.

Harnessing the Energy of Anger

Pat Enkyo O'Hara

Anger will always hover as a potential energy within us. How we use this energy is the key to how we affect our own life and the lives of others. As Pat Enkyo O'Hara teaches it, anger develops in three phases: our physical reaction to a perceived threat, our thoughts about what's making us feel that way, and our conduct, that is the expression of our anger. It's our conduct that determines whether we move toward wisdom or toward more suffering.

I have struggled with anger most of my life. From a childhood in a chaotic and brawling family, one that idealized a "hotheaded" woman, I found it grueling even to try to manage my anger. All it would take was a trigger, and I would go off. "Going off" usually meant making a fool of myself by snapping at someone, walking away and denying myself what it was I wanted in the first place, or muttering under my breath at the stupidity around me.

What to do?

On my computer desktop is an image from an old Japanese handscroll showing a monk sitting calmly facing a giant demon who is spewing hot flames. This is kind of how I feel these days: I can sit here and watch my demon spit out its flames. I can ask the demon, "What is it now?" And I can begin to find a way to work with what it is that has triggered me once again.

Not that I am without anger now. But through the years, somehow, something has changed. The explosions last but a few seconds, and then the question arises, "What was that? Oh, another gut-level response to something I don't want to let in, some unwelcome challenge to my sense of who I am, my values, or even my rights."

Anger is such a difficult energy. It often thrives on the muck of life (our resentment, fears, neediness, etc.), then it bursts forth, often creating even more of a mess for us. Sometimes our anger can propel us to do something we need to do or say something that needs saying. Too often, though, anger blunts our skillfulness, and we wind up hurting ourselves and others, creating unnecessary discord and acting a bit like fools.

An old Indian myth tells of a great battle among the gods, during which the angry spirits are defeated and escape, diving into the holes of the lotus flower and hiding in the threads of the stem. I have always found this image provocative: the idea that my angry demons are hiding in the lotus at just that point that connects the beautiful flower to its roots in the muddy water. What this means for me is that my anger hovers as a potential energy within my being. It sits between the muddy everyday reality of my life, with all of its demands and frustrations, and the blossoming and unfolding of my wisdom and compassion. How I use this energy is the key to how I affect my own life and the lives of others.

We can think of anger as developing in three phases: our physical reaction to a perceived threat, our thoughts about what's making us feel that way, and our expression of the anger.

Recently, I was in an airplane—in one of those increasingly smaller economy seats—and just as I was treasuring my little cup of coffee, the person in front of me suddenly reclined his seat, thrusting the tray and the coffee into my body, seemingly impaling me in my seat. My body said, "Alarm! Here comes adrenaline!" This is the first in the cascading physical responses to a threat: the heart starts beating fast and the muscles tighten. Often when we speak of anger, we are only thinking of this transitory reaction; yet this is the one that comes and goes, not the one that stays.

What we do next is pivotal. My mind starts with, "How dare he invade my space?" Then it indignantly asks, "What is this person thinking?" and I notice an impulse to kick the seat. Then I take a breath:

"Whoa! There's a lot of feeling in my body right now." After several more breaths, looking at my reactions, I recognize that I'm thinking the person in front of me is invading my space, not considering me, and that I'm beginning to make a lot of judgments about him. This is the second part of anger: how we think about what's happening and what has triggered our physical feelings.

How will I react? Will I kick the seat or politely request that the person move his seat back forward a bit? Will I look to see if it is a demon, a child, or a physically compromised person sitting in front of me? Or will I "stuff it" and hold the energy inside until it shuts me down or is unleashed at another time? This is the third aspect of what we call anger: our actual conduct, or expression of what we're experiencing.

That expression of our anger is what determines if we are moving toward wisdom or more suffering. On the one hand, anger can be a positive force that signals danger; it gives us energy to react and a sense of control over our situation and response. On the other hand, anger can lead to impulsive aggression, confusion, or even complete shutdown.

What can we do when the volatile winds of anger shake us? In some spiritual circles, anger gets a bad rap and is smothered. In Zen, however, there is a long tradition of investigating the mind of anger. Regarding the precept of not indulging in anger, Zen master Dogen counseled, "Not advancing, not retreating, not real, not empty. There is an ocean of bright clouds. There is an ocean of solemn clouds."

In these words, Master Dogen urges us to stay right smack in our experience: to be intimate with what we are feeling in our body, with our racing thoughts, and with what is actually happening in front of us. By not advancing, we stay with the feeling and sensations we are having. We don't jump—advance—to action. We take a breath and give our mind a chance to catch up with our feelings. By not retreating, we stay in the midst of what has come up; we do not hide nor stuff our feelings. We don't go back over the story again. Neither real nor empty, the energy of our anger is like a strong wind. These are our feelings, our responses to a trigger, and they are not "real" in the sense that they are constantly changing impulses that rise and fall. However, they are not "empty" in the sense that they do have an effect on us; they are present to us just as our lives continuously shift from the bright clouds to the solemn clouds in the sky of our feelings and thoughts.

Not advancing and not retreating prevents us from jumping onto a succession of thoughts that can lead to "my" story.

Often these stories are "trueish." There is an element of truth, but there are also elements of past stories—things we've thought, things we've heard, things we've imagined. In the example of the reclining seat, I might unconsciously attach the other times I've felt ignored or disrespected to the action of the person in front of me.

This is even more evident when the incident involves someone we are in relationship with in our family, workplace, circle of friends, or community. Stories are the way we make sense of disparate events in our lives. We all know how easy it is to even slightly shift the emphasis in order to make ourselves the hero or the victim—and to believe the story we've made up. Even if many of the facts are true, the story can crystallize the feelings and ideas around the story, essentially creating a static solidity that does not allow other views of what happened. In this way, we form unmovable judgments and grudges that develop into long-standing hatred of others.

Once I had a strong disagreement with a spiritual teacher I'd studied with for many years. There was no flash of volatile anger but, rather, a long escalation of difference of opinion leading to little slights that grew to what felt to me like shunning. Finally, I felt it necessary to leave and find another teacher and community. There was a deep sense of loss, of not being heard, of not being respected.

Not surprisingly, I felt very angry with him for several years afterward, and it was extremely difficult for me because I didn't want to be angry. I wanted to be kind and good-hearted with him, but basically I was angry. It was a difficult, complex situation. Fortunately for me, I was able to sit long periods of meditation during this time and find a still point in my heart and mind. Many possible stories about our rupture rose to the surface of my mind: some were wildly off base, and others were more or less in the realm of reality. But I remained with feelings of hurt and anger. I sincerely didn't want to be angry, yet anytime anybody would mention this person or this place, a fire would envelop me; it would lick up at my ears. I would try my best not to say something mean-spirited, but I failed a number of times. Nasty little remarks came flying out of my mouth.

I resolved not to make a solid story about what happened. When I was asked to write or talk about it, I knew that it would be impossible. I knew that I would get carried away with one story or another, with a grain of truth here or there, and embellish the situation.

So instead, I spent a lot of time—years, actually—questioning my anger, experiencing my anger, dropping my anger, picking up my anger, and checking my anger. It would fall away and be gone; I wouldn't notice it for months. Then all of a sudden, something would be said, or I would even be in the middle of my meditation, and this thing would come lashing out.

It was difficult to avoid falling into some old story without toppling into a hardened grudge or, worse, hatred. I wanted to be at the center, to allow the feelings that came, neither retreating nor advancing, neither diminishing nor enlarging. The years of sitting meditation and Dogen's words strengthened my resolve to experience both the dark clouds of sadness and the bright clouds of letting it go.

What was that about? What did my anger want? What did I need that made me want to feel angry again?

I realized that what I had wanted originally was to be acknowledged as a sincere practitioner. So I began the practice of recognizing myself, of giving myself the acknowledgment, thinking, "You are really a whole-hearted dharma student." You are really giving it your all, and I really appreciate you. Through this practice, I found that by addressing my underlying need, my reactive anger was transformed into free energy; then I was able to make use of that energy to take care of myself.

Sometimes, when the hurt is so deep or the violation heinous, the work of breaking down our internal hatred requires even stronger measures. Bernie Glassman, at one of his annual retreats at the Auschwitz concentration camp, was asked how we handle the deep hatred we feel when we witness such utterly vile human horror. Bernie said we have to take the hatred out of our hearts, put it on our altars, and take really good care of it. By "putting it on our altars," we bring our wrath and need into our consciousness, and we nourish what it is that has been defiled. In the case of the Holocaust, we recognize that our need for humanity and compassion and caring was horridly violated and that we must care for these needs so that we don't also turn toward violence and hatred.

Whether your altar is within your mind or actually in your room, you can use this as a way to feed those parts of yourself that need safety, compassion, respect, and care.

Of course, there are definitely times when it's important to respond, reply, and speak up. In certain situations, we have to say something. But that may not be so easy. To speak up without engaging our stories or our physical flare of temper can seem almost impossible. But it is possible if we can be utterly awake and present at the moment we speak—awake in that we are not lost in a story or a cascade of physical sensation but are aware of all of this and are still able to speak forthrightly. This is a skill we develop in our meditation practice, the skill of being alert to our own mind, exactly where we are in that moment. That is intimacy in action.

When we first begin practicing and really being aware of our thoughts and feelings, we might be surprised at how often we are overwhelmed by a flood of anger and how quickly we are engulfed in it. After some practice, though, we begin to recognize the feeling as it builds in us. We may still get carried away, but we have a kind of awareness that makes it different. Through time, we recognize our anger when it arises, we feel it in our body, yet we are not its victims, and we are able to respond appropriately. We are neither advancing nor retreating; instead, we are acting appropriately to the situation. We are intimate with our feelings and the situation. There's an anonymous Chinese poem that is evocative of this:

When the wind blows through the bamboo grove,
The trunks clatter against one another.
When it has passed, the grove is quiet once more.

That's how anger can be an authentic part of our lives. It doesn't have to be an abiding thing. It is a signal that something is amiss. How can we respond to it? As long as we're not anchored in our hatred or aversion, these things can blow through.

Over time, by our mindfulness and awareness of the arising of this energy, we become stronger and less likely to be snagged; we are less likely to become attached to the anger. But if we hold the anger in, it gets so attached that moss grows over it, and it becomes hidden. Then unknowingly, in a subtle way, we give it out to everyone we meet. And when they throw it back at us, we think, "Why me? I feel no anger. I'm not an angry person."

From my personal experience, these insights and transformations don't necessarily happen when you're practicing seated meditation.

What happens is you do the work while meditating and learn how to be with anger. Then later you're walking down the street, at work, or washing dishes, and suddenly everything shifts, and it's a different way of perceiving yourself, the anger, everything.

PART TWO

Practicing with Anger

Uprooting the Seeds of Anger

Jules Shuzen Harris

There may be something that sets us off time and again as reliably as an alarm clock. This, says Jules Shuzen Harris, is a habitual flash point that can offer us an opportunity to see ourselves more deeply and with greater compassion. All we need is the space between trigger and reaction to mindfully look within. Meditation practice provides that space.

We operate under a common illusion that the things that make us angry lie outside ourselves, that they are external to us. Something out there is in opposition to our need for safety and security; it threatens our comfort or position. We feel a need to defend our vulnerable selves. Anger limits us. But if we have the courage to look at our anger and its causes and to learn from it, we can develop an open heart—a heart of genuine compassion.

My own journey in dealing with anger has included work with several systems of martial arts. Initially I studied the martial arts to learn how to defend against the enemy outside myself, which I thought was the reason for my anger. After some time, I was drawn to iaido, the art of drawing, cutting with, and sheathing a samurai sword. Loosely translated, the term *iaido* means being able to fit into any situation har-moniously. Unlike many other martial art forms, iaido is noncombative, which was key: to create a harmonious relationship with myself, I had to confront the enemy within—and the enemy was my own anger.

I have often observed that while we each experience anger in our own way, a more general sense of anger pervades our society. That is, as a culture, we are angry. Our sense of humor is very sarcastic. A lot of what we find entertaining involves putting someone down. We have slapstick comedy: people running around doing mean, spiteful things that we are supposed to find funny. Whether it is a television show or a new viral Internet video, we find humor in words that mock or put oth-ers down, or insults that allow us to watch from the outside as someone else is subjected to some form of humiliation. We might ask ourselves, "What's funny about that?" Not much. Laughing at others' misfortune is a kind of expression of our own anger.

Have we ever said to someone, "You're lazy" or "You're a bitch" or "You're an insufferable bastard"? Of course. We've all done that in one way or another. Or maybe we have said, "If it weren't for you, I would be better off" or "It's because of you that I am suffering." It is as if we be-lieve that by putting others down, by placing the blame or responsibility for our unhappiness on others, we can make ourselves better or relieve our own feelings of inadequacy. But anger doesn't make us feel better. As Chögyam Trungpa Rinpoche said, "You cannot really eliminate pain through aggression. The more you kill, the more you strengthen the killer, who will create new things to be killed. The aggression grows until finally there is no space; the whole environment has been solidified."

Among the Three Poisons we find the Pali term *dosa,* "anger." The Three Poisons of anger, greed, and delusion keep us in bondage and control us—they overwhelm our best intentions and cause us to do harm to others. We may even cause the greatest hurt to the people we most care about. We don't want to hurt them, or ourselves, but we are driven by our anger. Many times we find that a feeling that arises in us is the outward manifestation of a deeper underlying emotion or experi-ence. We might explore this possibility by asking ourselves about where our anger really comes from. What is the other side of anger? Fear. We can't free ourselves until we work through both our anger and our fear. And what is the cause of fear? Ultimately, it is the fear of nonexistence, death, the fear of losing ourselves and being forgotten. But a fear of death translates into a fear of living, because impermanence is itself a fundamental condition of our lives. In this fear lie the seeds of anger.

How do we break the cycle of anger? We all know anger from experience, but when we are asked to pause and consider "What is this anger?" it's not always so easy to see what it is. Yet when we approach our feelings of anger with awareness, with mindfulness, it becomes a productive part of our practice. We find, after all, that anger has something to teach us.

Anger is what Thich Nhat Hanh calls "habit energy." Like most habits, it takes just one particular event or word or incident to trigger us, as quick as a snap of the fingers. Just because we have a *kensho* experience and see into our true nature and maybe for a second or two experience some sense of bliss, that doesn't mean that we won't return to habit energy five minutes or an hour later. If someone does something that irritates you, ask yourself the question "Who is it that is ticked off? Who is it that's angry?" We'll find that there is no self to get angry or to defend.

And yet there may be something that sets us off again and again, as reliably as an alarm clock. Maybe we know what some of those things are. Often other people can tell us what brings out our flashes of anger even if we are not ourselves aware of them. But these habitual flash points offer us an opportunity to see ourselves more deeply, with a fuller understanding and with greater compassion; to look at what incited our angry reaction; and to follow the thread within ourselves. All we need is the space between trigger and reaction to mindfully look within.

So where do we find this space to separate ourselves from our anger? Many Buddhist traditions teach that all things are insubstantial. When we see this, we see that the support for anger and hate is eroded and eventually destroyed. This speaks to one of the three marks of existence—impermanence. We have all found ourselves in situations that illustrate the transitory nature of events. Something happens to us that makes us angry; perhaps we get into an argument at home with a partner at the very start of the day. A couple of hours later, we're at work and we're still thinking about the incident. More time goes by, and we continue to stew over it at lunchtime, and by the time we get home, we're still holding on to it. But where is it? Where is the incident? It's like last night's supper—it doesn't exist.

Over and over again, I tell students dealing with anger, "This practice is about being mindful." While that may sound simple, it is in fact a very, very difficult practice because it goes against a lot of what we hold sacred. Many of us have a particular group of gods that we worship. It's not God, Jesus, or Buddha. We worship pleasure, comfort, and security. Despite knowing that everything is impermanent, we still hold on to objects that we think will bring us security. We cling to what we believe will spare us from discomfort, and when these things slip out of our grasp, fear and anger arise. Part of mindfulness is looking at our reactions and perceptions—if we are all truly one body, why are we cutting off the relationship with our partner, our coworker, or our friend? If my hand is in pain, do I cut it off? Of course not. I take care of it. I take some Tylenol. I look more carefully into what might be causing the pain— maybe it's an injury, or it could be that I'm developing arthritis and need to think of some therapies. But when it comes to anger, we cut ourselves off because we have an investment in maintaining who we think we are. Anger limits our expression of seeing our whole self. As a divisive force, it prevents us from living a fully rich life of connectedness. Instead of experiencing the one body that pervades everywhere, anger isolates us and reinforces the sense of a separate self, preventing us from identifying with and feeling compassion for others.

Mindfulness is cultivated through meditation practice. That is one of the reasons I like the focused practice period of *sesshin,* several days of intensive sitting. It is amazing how much stuff surfaces in sesshin. In my first few years practicing Zen, I thought of myself as a pretty laid-back, easygoing guy. But then during these intensive meditation periods, I couldn't believe the amount of anger and rage that came up. I was ready to kill the teacher, kill the monks, and burn down the monastery! It stood in stark contrast to my ideas of who I thought I was. My anger was exacerbated by having the duty of scrubbing the toilets with a toothbrush. But all along the way, I continued meditating. And at some point, scrubbing the toilet with a toothbrush became a practice of mindfulness for me.

When we work with anger in Buddhist practice, we work with it a little differently than you would in psychotherapy. We don't ask you to beat a pillow, open the window, and scream. When I was a psychotherapist, I had a Bozo the Clown bop bag in my office; you could hit it and it would just bounce back. And I would say, "Just keep pounding it, get it all out!" But that's not our approach. In Buddhism, we work to illuminate the fundamental truth of our self-nature. When anger arises, it is pointing to something. Our anger is a clue to our underlying beliefs about ourselves. It can help to reveal our constructed sense of self-identity.

Today many psychotherapists embrace Buddhist practice as a way of looking at ourselves in relationship to others. The Identity System developed by Stanley Block, MD, involves two processes called "mind-body mapping" and "bridging." Mind-body mapping as a part of Buddhist practice requires an openness to adapting the dharma for a particular time, place, and person—in this case for the Western psyche. You begin mind-body mapping by paying attention to a particular thought that is on your mind, perhaps one that is connected to strong feelings. Then, using this first thought as a focal point, you trace the paths of further thoughts and ideas that are generated out of the initial thought. At the same time, we give attention to how our thoughts feel in relationship to the body. We all have personal requirements, thoughts, or rules about how we—and the world—should be. While they may remain hidden from our conscious awareness, we can recognize them by our anger, which arises when our requirements are broken. By deepening our ability to be fully present, we have a better chance of seeing our requirements and letting them go, uprooting the seeds that sprout into anger.

This exploration, together with an approach called "bridging," has proven to be a valuable tool. Bridging is akin to mindfulness. When you are washing the dishes, you are focused on touch, the place, the water on your hands, the feel of the sponge; or when you are driving your car, you listen to the hum of the engine, the vibration of your hands on the steering wheel. Bridging and mind-body mapping help us deal with the shadow beliefs we carry with us—"I'm not good enough," "I'm undeserving"—which create negative story lines. Our anger can be seen as a defense against these vulnerable feelings and negative self-beliefs. The deep-seated fear and anger we harbor has to do with our feelings of a damaged self. Mind-body mapping and bridging enable practitioners to see how they create their suffering in relationship to the body rather than a situation outside themselves. From a Buddhist perspective, we are trying to reach the place where there is no separation, no subject, no object. Bringing our mind back again and again to a place of present-moment awareness, we create a space where we let go of our habitual reaction patterns and our recurring negative feelings. We then open the opportunity to view ourselves—and others—with real compassion.

Our meditation practice is also a place where we can work directly with our experience of anger by becoming the anger. To "become the anger" does not mean to act it out. It means we stop separating ourselves from it; we experience it fully so that we can understand what's behind it. In sitting zazen, we can encourage the anger to come up. We become intimate with anger, and in doing so, we watch it dissipate.

We have to look deeply into the cause of our suffering. Our anger not only creates suffering for others, but it also creates more suffering for us. We might take a mind-body perspective that what we think affects every cell in our body. Neuroscientists suggest that our neurons are affected by our immediate environment. If we are in a hostile, argumentative, negative environment, then that affects our neural networks and neurochemistry, and our nervous system becomes conditioned to react every time we go into that environment. So we could say that very environment becomes toxic. We've all had the experience of walking into a certain space and feeling at home, and going into a different space and becoming very agitated or depressed because of the subtle energy or our unconscious relationship to the place.

We must remember that we create our own anger. No one makes it for us. If we move from a particular event directly to our reaction, we are skipping a crucial awareness, a higher perspective on our own reactivity. What is that middle step, that deeper awareness? It is mindfulness about our own beliefs, our attitude, our understanding or lack of understanding about what has really happened. We notice that a given situation reliably provokes our anger, and yet somebody else can be exposed to the very same situation and not react angrily. Why is that? No one can tell us: we each have to find the answer ourselves, and to do that, we need to give ourselves the space to reflect mindfully.

We're going to keep getting angry. It's going to come up. It has come up in our lives before, and it will come up again. This practice is about becoming more mindful, becoming aware of how we are getting stuck. With care and work, we find ways to get unstuck. But we also know that the moment we get unstuck, we're going to get stuck again. That's why it is called a practice—we never arrive. So when you find yourself upset or angry, use the moment as a part of your practice, as an opportunity to notice and uproot the seeds of anger and move into the heart of genuine compassion.

Another Black Mark

Karen Connelly

"No, Mama, no! I going draw on the couch!" When Burmese Lessons *author Karen Connelly loses her cool in a battle of wills with her three-year-old, she learns valuable lessons about mindful parenting.*

Timo, will you please give that to me?"

"No."

"That isn't your toy, Timo. That belongs to Mama. It's not a good idea to make a mess, okay?" I purse my lips and shudder, wondering why on earth I would say that it isn't a good idea to make a mess. That's just fanning the fire.

Timo, a three-year-old master of the universe, stands on the other side of the sofa, an open challenge animating his small face. His dark eyes sparkle with pleasure. From his point of view this is a game we've played many times before, chasing each other around the sofa. Naturally, he knows that he has something he's not supposed to have, something that I want, but that only adds to the excitement. Like many parents, I'm often distracted as I engage with my child; the phone needs to be answered, the rice on the floor needs to be cleaned up, this one newspaper article has grabbed my attention—just this one, please, just a minute, just a minute!—as he stands beside me at the table or crawls on my lap or shouts for me to come now and I pretend to engage with him while simultaneously ignoring him. He always knows when I am ignoring him.

Ha! Now he knows I am genuinely involved. No wonder he's thrilled.

I've followed him from the kitchen to the living room, a distance of twenty feet. We are just steps apart now, but I don't want to make another wrong move. His left hand is outstretched, like a runner about to sprint; his right hand clutches an extra-thick permanent black marker, which is poised above the tawny back of the sofa.

This is a moment for practical as well as philosophical parenting concerns. Why is that leather sofa dark yellow? What were we thinking when we bought it? Why was that permanent marker left in the kitchen drawer, among the washable kiddie felts and crayons? Why must I care so much?

Because Timo has wrecked the CD player, dug up the houseplants with his bulldozer, and ruined every lipstick I own. He searches out the lipsticks, crawls up bathroom shelves, hunts for them in my overnight bag, ferrets them out no matter where he goes. After drawing all over his face, the walls, the stairs, or, most recently, the bedspread, he smushes them to a pulp.

"Timo!" Unconsciously, I have raised and sharpened my voice. The effect of my harsh tone is instantaneous. The game look on my son's face hardens into anger. It's always like this. He gives me back the emotion I have just sent out to him. My reactions set the tone of the conflict that is to come; I am the adult, after all. Drive all blames into oneself, says one version of the *lojong* slogan for mind training, which isn't a recipe for more mother guilt but an admonishment to examine the nature of power and responsibility. I have power over my child. Yet I so easily misuse it. I do the precise opposite of that other Buddhist meditation practice, *tonglen.* Instead of sending out calm breath, I shoot a javelin from my mouth. We love each other, this boy and I, out of necessity, so that javelin always finds its mark.

He responds, equally sharply, "No, Mama, no! I going draw on the couch!"

"Please don't do that Timo, or Mama will be very . . . " What will I be? I want to say angry, a word he knows well. And I will be angry. But beneath the anger is usually a feeling of disappointment, even defeat, especially when the disagreement turns into a protracted battle. The threats may turn into reality—he will be hauled up to his room, have his toy taken away, or not go for the walk at all—but the tears come and the mood is unhappy for both of us. Don't bring things to a painful point, suggests another lojong slogan. I am increasingly conscious of the times when I could have done it differently and arrived at a happier outcome.

It's true that day-to-day parenting is full of snap decisions; sometimes we're in a hurry. Modern life requires an adherence to schedules, a tremendous degree of organization. Because my husband and I are self-employed, we are much freer with our time than many others, but we still need to manage busy timetables and juggle responsibilities. Children have to learn about that, with parents who encourage their participation but also train them in the difficult quality of patience. The big choices rarely involve children at all, at least not while they are small; the parents decide where to live, what to eat, what school the child will attend, when to go to the doctor, what morality to instill. What example to set.

All of our lives, we learn about being human by watching what other people do, but during childhood, it is our first and deepest form of education. Children want to do what their caregivers do; they want to be like us. Very little escapes their sensibilities. Our actions pass through them like electrical impulses, subtly or overtly influencing their behavior, flavoring their essence. In everyday conflicts with my child, I know that slowing down will add lightness to the air, a moment of breath for both of us. This black-haired boy resembles me in so many ways; he has the same quick temper, the same readiness to laugh. When I remember to play more, even through my anger, he responds in kind. But I often forget to play. I tighten up, clamp down. I want my will to be done; like the old Christian God, I, too, want to be a master of the universe, and of my child. But I am not. And he knows it.

We all know it. None of us can rightly cling to the arrogant notion of our dominion over the earth, not with the plethora of intractable wars, abusive governments, environmental and economic crises, injustices committed with impunity even in democratic countries. The only hope for our complex, fragile world is human consensus and negotiation, forms of dialogue that continue to be unpopular because they are unwieldy, time-consuming, and often dull. I know, because I try to employ them on a regular basis with my kid, and often we don't get to the end of the conversation. I just pull a dictatorship on him, throw him over my shoulder, and let him scream.

But he's getting too big and too smart for me to do that anymore, and I am too aware of how my tyrannical methods are doomed to failure because they poison our little society with bad feelings. When arguments escalate, especially around dinnertime, Timo will refuse to sit or eat; then my husband and I will fight over the right way to socialize a three-year-old while the meal gets cold and we lose our appetites.

Viewed from a distance, these moments can be funny and instructive, but when I'm in the moment, anger holds me in a vise grip. Other negative emotions are there, too, but anger is the heaviest. It keeps me from moving freely; it keeps my mind from loosening up enough to understand that the boy likes it when we are utterly focused on him. It's what he craves. We've usually been away from him all day; dinnertime is a perfect opportunity for him to arrange his starring role in a big drama. If we take fifteen minutes to play and chat with him before one of us disappears into dinner-making mode, he is usually ready to come and sit down with us again by the time the food is ready to eat.

Even though I understand this mechanism, I forget it. My anger fills the space quickly, like a brush fire, igniting whatever it touches. Anger is an important emotion; it can be the flame that wakes us to injustice and the need to speak out, inspiring us to be brave. But when I'm angry at my young child, I am usually stuck in old patterns of reaction, which is a form of laziness. In Thailand, where I've lived and meditated in the Theravada Buddhist tradition, the expression for quick-tempered anger is *jai-raan* (hot heart). Likewise, when someone tells you to calm down, they say, "Jai yen-yen" (cool your heart).

Jai yen-yen, like most wise advice, is hard to implement in the heat of the moment. "Angry! I will be really mad, Timo, if you draw on the couch! So give me the marker!" With that, I lunge over the cushions and try to grab the felt pen out of his hand. But with reflexes quicker than mine, he easily eludes me and hops into a run, clearing the corner of the sofa and dashing back into the dining room. Where there are white walls all around (albeit much fingerprinted).

He stands beside the antique-blue china cabinet, holding up the black marker like a knife. His face teeters between a frown and a laugh. "Come on, Timo. Please don't draw on the cabinet. Mama will be very sad. Let's get your markers out. We'll draw something together." With that, I turn my back on him and go into the kitchen, where I noisily rummage through the kiddie drawer, praying he will follow my lead.

Beside the kiddie drawer is a glassed-in shelf lined with bottles of liquor and wine. What will happen when my spectacularly willful and charming child is fifteen, curious about alcohol and drugs, surrounded by other teenagers who have never heard stories about the Dalai Lama and the importance of loving-kindness? It's just a black marker now, a stain on the furniture, a line on the wall, but who will he become when his own peers make him furious, or when a girl doesn't want to have sex with him?

I don't know who he will become. I only know who is he now. Pure in impulse, pure in power, perfectly honest in his response to the world and to me. I am still so much of his world. That will change swiftly—is already changing.

"Mama, are you sad?" He sidles around the edge of the fridge, with the marker flush against his chest. He's wearing his favorite Thomas the Tank Engine shirt; a black stain, already two inches wide, spreads like blood below his sternum.

Another lojong slogan: Abandon all hope of fruition. "I am a little sad."

"Why are you sad?" His voice is like a flute, high and silver, bright with concern.

"Because I don't like it when you don't listen to me. And because your shirt is all dirty now. Lift up the marker."

He holds it away from himself and awkwardly peers down at his chest. I expect him to burst into tears, but he smiles. "Look, Mama! What a mess!" He does a spontaneous little jig of delight and offers me the marker, which I take quickly, lest he change his mind. "Thank you, Timo." He pulls the shirt away from his skin so he can see the damage better, and laughs.

Acupressure Point of the Heart

Norman Fischer

Anger is a sore point. Yet if we know how to be patient with the pain, how to gently and skillfully massage it, we can be healed—by the anger itself. In this teaching, Norman Fischer offers a Zen-inflected method of working with the Vajrayana Buddhist practice called lojong, *or mind training. In the classic lojong text* The Root Text of the Seven Points of Training the Mind, *there are fifty-nine slogans, or aphorisms. Here Fischer delves into five that can help us heal our anger.*

Anger is impressive. When it flares, it takes over almost completely, controlling our emotions, our viewpoint, our words and deeds. The body tenses; the face reddens; the heart and mind race. We feel as if we were ready to explode. Anger is a very unpleasant emotion.

Yet some people enjoy anger. All that intensity can be intoxicating, even addictive. There's the adrenaline rush, the blasting thoughts, and the fact that anger makes you intimidating. People fear you, which can be flattering, and sometimes they can even be pushed to give you what you want.

For most people, full-blown anger isn't a daily occurrence. But milder forms of anger—which occur whenever we are slighted, disrespected, frustrated, or in any way thwarted in what we expect or desire in a given moment—do rise up every day. It seems anger isn't just one emotion among others; it's basic. Because we organize the world around our self-interest, naturally wanting things to go our way, and because, just as naturally, the world and other people usually don't cooperate with this understandable if unrealistic request, we are likely to be at least a little angry a lot of the time.

The closer you look at anger, the clearer it is that anger is deceptive. Anger, for instance, can be there when we don't experience it. We might sincerely say, "I'm not angry!" and yet we are angry, and others can see that we are by the way we speak, look, or act. It's odd that we could be angry without anger, yet it happens. And the converse can also be true: often we feel angry but the anger is actually a cover-up for some other powerful emotion that we don't want to face, usually fear, grief, or sorrow.

To practice with anger—rather than simply being a victim of it—is to make the effort to respect and understand it. This practice involves being willing to look more deeply at the complex of negative emotions, which naturally arise as part of our human condition. It requires that we take responsibility for these emotions so that we can begin to do something creative with them.

In classical Buddhist discussions, anger is viewed entirely negatively. The implication is that we ought not to be angry and that if we are, it's a failing of our spiritual practice. To be sure, anger is a problem—even if we think we like it. To be addicted to its rush is unhealthy, and to be an intimidating person is not as good as being a loved and respected one. So yes, anger is definitely a problem we need to deal with.

On the other hand, if we could channel and purify anger's strong emotional energy and not be pushed around by its irrationality and destructiveness, we might be able to use it as an ally to help us work for the good. But there's something else about anger that could be even more helpful than this.

Anger is information; it tells us something about who we are and what is on our mind and in our heart. Physical pain is negative, because it hurts, yet also positive, because it's the body's way of protecting itself by indicating that something is wrong and where it is wrong. Anger is a bit like this. It can show us something crucial about our emotional life that we may need to know in order to be healthy. Anger indicates that something needs attention; something needs investigation. If we are angry it's because we are thwarted and frustrated or afraid somehow and possibly we don't know it and we need to know it so that we can shift and grow. Almost always our various fears and frustrations signal times and opportunities for growth and change—if only we look them in the face. When we are willing to do that, we see things differently, more accurately. Instead of avoiding our fears and frustrations or beating our heads against them in anger as we lash out at ourselves, others, and the world, we are able to pass through them and become larger, more inclusive, and more compassionate people.

Torei Enji's poem "Bodhisattva's Vow" is a favorite Zen text of mine. In it there's a line that says, "Then in each moment's flash of thought / There will grow a lotus flower / And each lotus flower will reveal a Buddha." Once, on a retreat, I had a big insight about how absolutely and stunningly true these lines are. I realized that every thought and every emotion—even the most negative and painful—is actually a lotus flower once I get to the bottom of it, past my old habit of aversion and desire. That is, every thought and every emotion has a Buddha in it, something valuable, worthwhile, and even beautiful to show me. I just have to be willing to stay with the thought or emotion long enough—without reacting or spinning off.

And this is true of anger too. Anger is a lotus flower on which sits a Buddha awakening us. We can trust it and practice with it.

Buddhism is justly valued for its many effective and sensible ways of working with anger. All of these ways depend on basic mindfulness, the ability to create the inner space necessary to investigate and be fully present with an emotion. Strong emotions, especially negative ones like greed, anger, jealously, and so on, spin us around. Before we even know what we are feeling, we are already blaming and acting—generally unwisely. Mindfulness gives us a chance to be present with an emotion before we start spinning or even while we are spinning. To be mindful is to relax and allow our consciousness to open around an object. Mindfulness is a soft light illuminating what is there with honesty and sympathy. When we meditate, we are practicing mindfulness, whether it is mindfulness of the body, mindfulness of breathing, mindfulness of sounds, or mindfulness of thoughts and feelings arising and passing away. Mindfulness is subtle and radical. It's training ourselves in having a generous presence, a patient awareness of what is going on. Getting up from the meditation cushion, we can practice mindfulness throughout the day. Rather than being propelled and likely blinded by what we think we want, we pay attention, being present, willing, and interested to see more widely and openly what is actually happening. Such seeing changes what we experience, how we behave, and ultimately, the sorts of things that happen to us. Mindfulness is simply being with what happens in faith that our ability to do this will naturally change things.

But there are other, more intentional, active practices that support and are supported by mindfulness. In recent years I've been investigating the famous Tibetan *lojong* teachings. Lojong, which literally means "mind training" or "heart training," is a category of teachings on how to transform negative emotions like anger, greed, envy, and so on, into sympathy, love, and compassion. I have been practicing with the most famous of all the lojong texts, *The Root Text of the Seven Points of Training the Mind,* which is based on a list of fifty-nine practice slogans.

These slogans are memorable, often humorous aphorisms that point us in an advantageous spiritual direction. My Zen-inflected method of working with a slogan is to write it in a notebook, copying it again and again to fix it in my heart not as good advice but almost as a physical object. I repeat the slogan to myself silently during meditation. Breathing into it, I stay with the slogan until all of my ideas about it become boring and there is only the slogan itself, like a good, wise friend urging me on. When you practice like this, the slogan will spontaneously appear many times during the day. It will pop into your mind unbidden, a substitute for the many other mindless thoughts that would otherwise be popping up. And every time it does, it reminds you of your practice and of the necessity of working with your emotions not just when you are meditating and feeling spiritual, but all the time, especially in midst of life's various issues and problems. *Pop!* Here's the slogan again, little by little working its way into your thinking and conduct.

As I see it, these are the seven points of mind training:

- One, resolving to begin, which involves exploring your deepest motivation.

- Two, training in empathy and compassion with meditations to cultivate absolute and ordinary compassion and caring.

- Three, transforming bad circumstances into the path; in other words, learning how to make use of life's large and small misfortunes to increase your faith and understanding rather than letting them throw you off the path.

- Four, making practice your whole life, that is, no longer seeing "spiritual practice" as an optional activity distinguished from your life.

- Five, assessing and extending, meaning monitoring your practice efforts so you can keep on track.

- Six, understanding the discipline of relationship, since relationships are a principal site for spiritual practice.

- Seven, living with ease in a crazy world, which encompasses miscellaneous slogans to help you cope.

Here I'd like to discuss five slogans under point six, the discipline of relationship, that could be helpful in working with anger:

- Don't figure others out
- Work with your biggest problems first
- Abandon hope
- Don't poison yourself
- Don't be so predictable

DON'T FIGURE OTHERS OUT

Think of how much we all talk about our friends and relatives, analyzing their words and deeds, sizing them up as if we actually knew what made them tick. But just as you don't appreciate being reduced to this or that cartoonish, likely uncomplimentary, version of yourself, neither do they. And the fact is, any version of who you, they, or anyone else is, is incorrect. Sitting on your meditation cushion for a half hour is long enough to show you quite directly that you are full of contradictions, unacknowledged issues, and unfinished business. There are so many good and bad sides to you that it would be hard to define your character precisely. And others are just like you, which means no one has the capacity to figure others out. And yet we do figure them out—or think we do. And then, based on that mischaracterization, we react.

We do this especially with someone we are angry at. We know exactly who this person is, why he or she is unworthy of our regard and richly worthy of our anger. Why would we give this terrible person the benefit of the doubt? Never!

And yet the truth is we have no idea what is going on inside this person. We have no idea what really makes him or her tick. We are angry at a phantom, a figment of our own imagination. Don't figure others out.

WORK WITH YOUR BIGGEST PROBLEMS FIRST

Working with our biggest problems first is the opposite of what we want to do. Usually we prefer to take on something easy and work our way up to the tough things, but operating like this, we never seem to get to that tough stuff.

This slogan says, no, turn first toward what is really difficult. Screw up your courage and go there right away. This will take all the mindfulness you have been able to cultivate from your time on the meditation cushion—and more. It will also take forbearance, one of the most powerful and least appreciated of all spiritual practices. Forbearance is the capacity to patiently stay with something unpleasant or difficult, to face it rather than to do what comes naturally, that is, to turn away. Forbearance requires that we develop the capacity—in our body, in our breath, in our heart—to stand firm and aware without acting, at least for the moment.

When we are angry, we typically blame and lash out. Most of us are not courageous enough to lash out at the people we are actually angry at, so instead we lash out at someone else who is safer, take potshots, gossip, or just grouse and feel indignant in the privacy of our own minds. Yet these activities probably don't hurt the target of our anger at all. They do, though, hurt us and other people plenty. Working with the biggest problems first means that when we are angry, we turn toward the anger. Instead of leaping to blame, recrimination, or distraction, we feel the anger in our body, in our breathing, in our racing thoughts. When we practice like this, we will calm down, see more of what is actually going on, and, eventually, be able to act wisely.

ABANDON HOPE

What! Don't we want to be hopeful? Don't we want to hope that tomorrow will be better than today? That our spiritual endeavors will pay off? That our anger will transform?

In a word, no, we don't. If you investigate hope, you'll see how counterproductive it can be. To hope usually means to reject the experience of this moment, and therefore hope can be a kind of cowardice. Rather than face what's going on right now, we focus our attention on later, when things will hopefully be much more pleasant than they are at the moment.

In the case of anger, maybe we have some hope that, internally, the anger will somehow dissolve or that, externally, the person we are angry at will see the error of their ways and finally apologize and make amends. Or maybe we are hoping that if we do our Buddhist practice, everything will somehow turn out all right. But wishing won't make anger go away, so such hope is actually an obstacle.

The truth is, anger is very hard to overcome, and the job of seeing through it takes a lot longer than you think. Even when you believe you are finally finished with anger, subsequent events will prove that you're not. Hope can breed laziness and even impatience. Yet patience, which requires an active courage, is what you need the most. So, internally, you really do need to have the commitment to go on working with your anger. You even need to take some delight in this work, because if you view anger as an entirely negative thing that a nice person like you shouldn't be feeling and you're hoping that your spiritual practice will swiftly purify it from your heart, then the shock and disappointment you'll feel when this turns out not to be the case will be a major impediment.

Working on your anger in the hope that this good work will somehow cause the other person to be different will also likely not pan out. Of course it does sometimes happen that when we soften, the other person does too. On the other hand, it is very probable that this other person has a life larger than simply their interactions with us and that the causes of this person's anger are deeper and more extensive than our interactions with him or her. So we have to abandon hope and simply be willing to go on working with our anger, without expectation that others will become nicer to us if we do so. In fact, our efforts will probably pay off, but only when we stop hoping that they will.

Don't Poison Yourself

Poison in this case means self-centeredness. Although this is changing, it is taken as a virtue in our culture to look out exclusively for yourself and compete against the many others who are vying with you for a place in the sun. Of course each of us does have to be responsible for ourself and not expect others to take care of us. But at the same time, it is clear that excessive self-concern is counterproductive. It leads to paranoia, greed, and negative personal and social consequences.

The antidote to this poison is a wise concern for others that will balance self-concern. This balance is not a mathematical equation or a tortured compromise but, rather, a naturally wise way of being. Take, for instance, a parent who is primarily concerned for his or her child's welfare. Without some healthy self-concern, the parent's concern for the child can't be sustained. If the parent doesn't take care of his health and psychological well being, which requires a modicum of happiness, how is he going to do a good job caring for his child? If he is grumpy, ill, and depressed, how well will he care for his child? So self-concern is not bad—it is required. But when self-concern is practiced as an end in itself and not for the sake of others, it easily becomes poisonous. We can literally become poisoned with self-obsession.

To practice this slogan is to notice that when we become defensive and aggressive, it's usually because of the poison of self-concern. Imagine how your experience of anger would be different if in a moment of anger you remembered the slogan "Don't poison yourself" and immediately turned your attention to others—maybe even to the person you are angry at. How is it from his or her point of view?

Don't Be So Predictable

This slogan is the complement of "Don't figure others out." It means don't be so sure you have yourself figured out. To do spiritual practice seriously is to cultivate a sense of openness and possibility—in relation to others and especially in relation to yourself. Remember, in each moment's flash of thought there is a lotus flower that will reveal a Buddha.

Most of us have plenty of evidence, over a lifetime of experience, that we are this way or that way. We are an angry person. A compassionate person. We are cheerful, phlegmatic, depressed, repressed, expressive, extroverted, introverted. All of this is fair enough. We have genetic predispositions, and we have been formed by culture, family, and habit. That conditioning doesn't just dissolve because we want it to. But we are also living creatures with the capacity to respond creatively to what happens to us in any given moment. We all know this. None of us believes that we are 100 per cent of the time doomed to have the same reaction to things we have had before. Life is various. We have free will. The whole idea of spiritual cultivation—or education in general for that matter—is that we can change.

But most of us have a commitment to proving the opposite. We take pride in being the way we say and think we are. Even when we say we want to change, a deeper look shows us that while, yes, we do want to change, we are also so committed to, and comfortable with, the way we have defined ourselves that we sneakily work against the changes we so fervently want to make in our lives.

The slogan "Don't be so predictable" asks us to examine this sneaky phenomenon. And to be honest about it. To notice, let's say, in the case of anger, our generic response, whatever it is, and pay close attention to it—not simply mindlessly repeat it time after time. Let's say that when we get angry we clam up. We observe ourselves doing this. We investigate: Is this just an old habit that we have in fact outgrown? Where does it come from? Do we like it or dislike it? Do we find comfort in it? How does it feel in the body, in the breath? Is something else—in this moment—possible? Could we be a little more creative, a little less lazy, in the way we respond?

Challenging ourselves in this open-ended and curious way, without expectations or mandates that it be this way or that way, is practicing this slogan.

Insofar as anger always presents us forcefully with the possibility that we could challenge our usual way of doing business, it can be a very helpful reminder of who we are now and who we might become. Anger is an acupressure point in the heart. It might feel sore and raw when it is bumped, but that's good. If we know how to be patient with the pain, how to gently and skillfully massage it, we can be healed—by anger itself.

Beginning Anew

Sister Chan Khong

If you want to maintain relationships that are happy and healthy and heal relationships that have been damaged by anger and resentment, the key is honest and loving communication. Sister Chan Khong offers a four-part practice for effectively sharing thoughts and feelings with friends, family, and colleagues.

Anger is not a stranger who shows up unexpectedly; it doesn't come all at once. Usually, we have a lot of little hurts or annoyances and we don't express them until they become so big that we explode.

Often a couple that has been together for many years will come to me for advice because hurts have accumulated over time and their relationship has come to the breaking point. One woman told me that she had been hurt by something her husband said on their first day of marriage, over thirty years before. But because it was the beginning, she hadn't wanted to start a fight, so she didn't mention it. "That's okay," she said to herself. "It's not a big issue." But the hurt remained in her for thirty years, and as more hurts accumulated she couldn't bear it anymore, and she decided to leave him. Hurt, accumulated over time, is called an internal knot because it's so hard to untangle. If you have an internal knot, don't wait until it becomes so tight it can't be undone.

I've spent many years teaching a practice called Beginning Anew. The practice consists of four steps that can transform our relationships, even when there is a big wall of anger between us and the other party. But the most transformational part happens before we even begin those four steps. First, before anything else, we need to take care of ourselves and our anger. Often when we're angry, the feeling is so strong that it tricks us into thinking we need to communicate it right away. We want to fix the other person or prove that they're wrong. But when you're drowning, you can't save someone else. You need to take care of yourself first.

When you're angry and you shout at someone, he won't listen. He'll be afraid of your anger and try to escape, deny culpability, or fight back. Even if you don't shout or say something harsh, any anger you feel will show on your face, and people around you will be able to tell that something isn't right. Don't swallow your anger and try not to show it. Swallowing your anger means it gets lodged deep inside you, which can make you sick and unhappy. Being calm doesn't mean hiding your anger; it means taking the time to sit with it so that you're not controlled by it and you have a chance to restore harmony in your relationships.

The first thing to do is to notice your anger and name it. This is a good time not to talk and instead to come back to yourself and pay attention to your in breath and out breath. Deliberately take your focus away from the situation or the person who angered you and dwell on the air entering your nostrils, going into the bronchia, and spreading through your lungs. Breathing out, focus completely on the air going out of your body. Somebody may have done something terrible, but at least you have the time to breathe in and out.

In the moment when you're full of anger, it can be very difficult to remember your breathing. If you have access to a bell or the sound of a bell on your phone or computer, you can use that sound as a reminder to return to your breathing. It can also be helpful to remove yourself from the person who is the target of your anger. Go for a walk and feel the earth under your feet. Walk and breathe and take your time. There is nothing to lose and a lot to gain by taking a few moments for yourself.

In our monastic community, we have one sister who is wonderful but very quick to anger. She knows this. In meetings she often gets upset by something another sister says. Whenever this happens, she gets up very quickly, like an arrow, and leaves to go for a walk. When she comes back, she is smiling and can sit down peacefully again. Having refreshed herself, she is able to listen.

It's very hard to listen when we're angry. Our anger changes our perceptions. When we're angry, we feel we have a right to be angry because things didn't happen in the way we wanted or expected them to. Anger is natural and is part of us. But remember that when we're angry, we may not be seeing things clearly. When we focus our attention on our breath, we calm our mind. When our mind is calm, we can see more clearly. Our mind is like the surface of a lake. When the lake is calm, it clearly reflects everything in the scene above. When the lake is agitated by a strong wind, we see only broken-up pieces of color. If there's a full moon, we'll just see scattered bits of gold here and there; we won't see the whole full moon. When we're angry, we perceive only one part of the reality. So it's better not to act right away, when our perception is not clear.

Our perception is always at least a little wrong. As long as we're not enlightened, we can't see the whole reality of a person, a group, or a situation. The Buddha said we are like a blind person who touches an elephant's tail and thinks it is a broom because he can't see the whole animal.

The awareness that our perception is always partial helps us to be humble. When you see something a certain way, question your certainty. You could be wrong or you could be seeing just one part of the person or situation. In order to see deeply, we need to practice stopping, *samatha*. We need to stop all thinking, release our mind from the object of our anger, and allow our mind to become calm so that we can see more clearly. Any time we are filled with a strong emotion, such as anger or infatuation, our perceptions are particularly blind. When we are so enthusiastic in our anger or our love, we are full of that emotion and have a strong urge to act on that feeling right away. But in such situations, we are seeing only a small part of the reality, and so we can easily make rash decisions and act in ways that end up being hurtful to ourselves and others. To mistake an elephant for a broom is not a serious problem. But if we hastily choose a life partner or hurt a person in anger, we might suffer the consequences for a long time.

The practice of Beginning Anew can help people resolve difficulties and communicate when they are hurt, but it isn't a practice to do in the heat of anger.

You can start Beginning Anew at any time, but it has the strongest effect if you start practicing *before* anger has taken root between you and the other person. If you set aside time to communicate in this way each week, then when there is hurt or anger, you can resolve it much more quickly and easily. To Begin Anew, set aside a regular agreed-upon thirty minutes and choose a space where you will both be comfortable, not rushed, and feel able to speak freely. The practice has four parts, but if you don't have time for all four each week, even doing the first part for ten or fifteen minutes will transform the communication in your relationship. The four parts of the practice are flower watering, expressing regret, expressing hurt or disagreement, and asking for more information.

STEP ONE: FLOWER WATERING

The first step is to show appreciation for the other person. This is called flower watering. While one person speaks, the other person just listens as he or she is appreciated. When you aren't having a problem with someone, it's easy to remember his or her wonderful qualities. So it might help to keep a notebook or a file folder on your computer where you list all the things about your loved one that bring you happiness. Sometimes, a loved one does something thoughtful for us, or does something that expresses a talent or quality that we appreciate, but we are too busy to thank them. You can take notes to help you remember.

Flower watering can also be done at work. Sometimes in the office a colleague does good work but we take her for granted. When she makes a mistake, however, we might say right away, "Why did you do that?" In the work environment, you can make time for people to appreciate each other on a regular basis. With flower watering, you begin to create a culture of appreciation in which people are able to listen and feel supported by each other. Then, if you want to let someone know that something they're doing isn't working, they'll more likely be able to hear it. Sometimes we really appreciate someone, but we keep it inside. Then when we disagree about something and speak out, that person thinks that we don't appreciate them.

In the family, it works well to choose one day a week to practice Beginning Anew. Choose a time when all the members of the family can be together. Sit together silently for a few moments so everybody can follow their breath and calm their body and mind. Then one person speaks at a time while the others listen and continue to breathe. Everyone gets a turn. Be sure to share appreciation even when there is no hurt or anger that you want to address. One man said to me, "For many months my wife doesn't say anything. When she starts to appreciate me, I know it's because she's about to complain." Also note that sometimes people begin to express appreciation automatically, mechanically. Make sure there is something genuine that you truly appreciate about each person, something specific. Genuine flower watering will keep your relationships healthier and happier and more resilient when there is a difficulty to express.

Step Two: Expressing Regret

The second step is expressing regret or apologizing for anything you would like to have done differently or better. If you see you've made a mistake, you need to have the courage to apologize before it becomes a knot in your colleague, partner, friend, or loved one.

When you truly apologize for something you regret, any hurt the person felt may be completely dissipated by your apology. Expressing regret on your own initiative, before the other person has even let you know that he or she is hurt, is a way to refresh your relationship. Even if you are apologizing for only part of a situation, if your regret is genuine, the other person will hear it and feel some release.

Step Three: Expressing Hurt or Disagreement

Because each of us has perceptions that get in the way of truly seeing, we need to let other people know when we are hurt. Perhaps we think they should already know how we feel or perhaps we believe that they hurt us intentionally, but often their perceptions are clouded—as ours are—and they don't know how they have hurt us. The difficulty we perceive may not be as big a difficulty as we perceive it to be. We may just see things differently from the other person. If we live with someone or see them at work every day and we don't express our hurt or disagreement, then we stop being present around them; we retreat. That's why it is so important to express your hurt or disagreement. You may be scared to speak, but if you speak from a place of calm and love, you will be speaking in a way that is easier for the other person to hear.

There are two ways to behave when you are angry. You can speak as if you were throwing your words out like darts, and the other person will shut their heart and be like a wall. Or you can speak in a humble way, and the other person will open to what you are saying. If you speak with openness and acknowledge the limits of your own perception, the other person has a chance to explain their point of view.

I know a woman whose teenage daughter told her she was moving out, and that very day she packed her bags and went to a friend's house. The mother was angry. She'd worked hard and sacrificed many things for her daughter, so at first she wanted to yell at her and ask, "How could you?" Luckily, her daughter was not there for her to shout at, and instead, she focused on her breathing until she was calm. Then she phoned her daughter and explained how much she appreciated her, missed her, and wanted her to come home. She also apologized for any hurt she had unknowingly caused. The daughter didn't move back right away, but they were slowly able to rebuild their relationship. Because the mother could express herself clearly and with love, the daughter could hear that her mother was not judging her. Eventually the mother and daughter lived together again, but much more peacefully. If you can explain things with humility, curiosity, and genuine regret for any hurt that you have caused, then there never has to be a war.

THE FOURTH STEP: ASKING FOR MORE INFORMATION

The last part of Beginning Anew is listening to the other person. You ask them to share their perceptions and feelings or any difficulty they might be going through. Perhaps something is bothering the other person that you aren't even aware of or that doesn't have anything to do with you. This is a chance for you to learn. You might ask, "Did I say or do something to make you embarrassed or annoyed?" You ask because maybe the other person is only a tiny bit bothered and doesn't want to say anything, but if you ask with genuine interest and a willingness to listen, then they can share their hurts and regrets and you can renew your relationship before the hurts have built up a wall. You might ask, "Did I hurt you, even a little bit? Please tell me." If you ask this question only when you are calm and clear and able to truly listen, then you can breathe and keep your heart open as the other person shares his or her suffering. What the other person says may only be partially true, as it is their own perspective. Yet this is not the time to correct or argue; this is the time to listen and understand.

When we are angry and we stuff that anger down, we build a wall inside us. These walls can get very tall, and soon we are not speaking to someone we've always loved or we begin to hate someone, even someone with whom we share a life and a family or a job and a purpose. Beginning Anew is a tool for helping dismantle the wall, brick by brick.

If there is a big wall between you and another person, it may be that you have to water the flowers in the other person for a very long time before you get to the second, third, and fourth steps. Sometimes people tell me that they write letters to a family member who is not speaking to them and they get no response back. It may be that you manage to slowly reestablish communication with that other person, or perhaps you just continue to share your appreciation for them and hope that they receive it. You know you're doing your best. Perhaps you start by Beginning Anew just with yourself, appreciating any good qualities you are cultivating, expressing regret for ways in which you have not treated yourself well or for ways you behaved that you didn't like. You can ask for more information from those around you so you can see yourself and the situation more clearly.

If you start this practice now, before there is a wall between you and the other person—when there are perhaps just one or two bricks in the way—then a wall will never be built. Instead, you and your loved one can enjoy the flower garden you have watered in yourselves and each other.

When the Tornado Touches Down

Shozan Jack Haubner

Buddhist practice stirs up a lot of energy and emotion, says Shozan Jack Haubner, and sometimes it can get downright ugly. He offers an intimate and humorous look at life inside the Zen monastery where he resides.

A lot of pissed-off people wind up at our monastery. This place has a tractor beam like the Death Star in *Star Wars* that pulls in anyone within a thousand-mile radius with a four-letter word on the tip of his or her tongue. Her marriage tanked, he's got an itch in his brain he just can't scratch, she's forty-five and smells of cabbage and lives in a small studio apartment and nobody ever calls her back. . . . They all wind up here, sold on the promise that Buddhism can alleviate suffering.

I said "they" all wind up here, but I guess I mean "we." I had one of those moments recently where, upon the much-anticipated departure of an enemy that, as a Buddhist, I could never quite admit was an enemy, I found myself peering around the zendo and thinking, "Wow, there are no assholes living here anymore." Whereupon came a sinking feeling: "Wait a minute, there's always at least one. So if I'm looking around the zendo and I can't find him. . . . Guess who the asshole is!"

Zen practice is good for angry people. The form is tight. It squeezes that deep red heart pulp, pushing up emotions from way down inside you. A lot of "stuff" comes up when you do this practice. Zen gets your juices flowing. And with these juices come seeds—the seeds of your behavior, your character, your anger, all flushed out into the open for you to see.

In Zen we learn that human consciousness is an eminently natural operation. You plant a seed; it grows. Similarly, when something happens to you on the outside, in "the world," the seeds of this experience take root within you, becoming sensations, thoughts, memories—your inner life. Conversely, when something arises within you, some inner experience, a notion, emotion, or dream, then the seeds of this inner event are disseminated on the outside, in the world, through your words and actions. Buddhists call this codependent origination: all things arise together in a mutually interconnected and interpenetrating web of being. "To see the world in a grain of sand," William Blake wrote. Or as that great metaphysician Tom "Jerry Maguire" Cruise put it: "You complete me."

Sounds romantic. But what if the seeds at the root of your behavior are the seeds of hate and anger?

A year ago I was walking down a bustling city street with my mentor, whom I love. We got into a fight about something, and I smacked him. It came out of nowhere and was meant to be light. Only it clearly did not come out of nowhere, and it was not light. I can still hear the thwack of my open palm against his belly. There was a long stretch of silence, wherein I should have begged for his forgiveness. But I couldn't admit to the violence that had just erupted from within me. I couldn't tell whether I meant it, whether it was real, where it came from, or how it got there.

I have violence in me, unfortunately. The seeds were planted long ago by my father, the poor man. How about all the times he didn't whack me? The time he sighed and let it go when I stole one of his antique firearms and ran around the house with it or sat on a sibling and released a cloud of flatulence? No, I remember only the three or four moments when his anger broke through.

All it takes is one seed. I've apologized, and even sent a cute homemade card with two stick figures sitting zazen side by side. But my blow planted a hate seed in my mentor, and something irreconcilable has grown between us. I can't seem to reclaim the friendship. I feel like I'm losing him.

Zen practice can be a tricky thing, because done right, sooner or later all the issues and energies you've been repressing your whole life will ooze, trickle, and burst to the surface through your tight little smile. And I'm afraid that the practice itself doesn't necessarily equip you to deal skillfully with these issues and energies. This is one of the big misconceptions about spiritual work: that, if applied correctly, it will make us "better people" (whatever that means). Zen is not a psychiatric or therapeutic discipline; it's a spiritual one. It's supposed to get energy moving on a deep, fundamental, life-changing level. Its purpose is to orient you toward the truth, toward reality, whatever this takes. It's not supposed to boss you around with behavioral or self-help dictates or to shoehorn you into the slipper of well-adjusted citizenhood.

In other words, spiritual work isn't always just "instructive"—it's also transformative, and this kind of transformation can get messy. The Sanskrit term for this is *clusterfuck*.

Some people, for example, seem to be born angry. Not me. I was born a coward. So when the energy gets moving through Zen practice and I suddenly become angry rather than a quivering eunuch, this can feel like an improvement—or at least a new way to be screwed up rather than the same old patterns of screwed-up-ness. A sharp word suddenly tastes good in my mouth. Anger takes on the illusion of upward spiritual mobility in comparison with my habitual cravenness. In reality, however, it's a lateral move—to an adjacent room in the same hell.

None of this happens in a vacuum. Zen is a group practice, but the thing about groups is that they're made up of people, and we all know what people are like. So not only does Zen practice flush your issues out into the open, it does so within a certain context; it flushes them into the "container" of your relationships with fellow monks and nuns. Energies and issues that had no discernible dimension within you are externalized and embodied with the "help" of your peers, one of whom, say, unwittingly takes the form of your stepmother, who once bullied and humiliated you. Meanwhile, to this peer you represent the weakness and stupidity within himself that for more than thirty years he has felt the compulsive need to stamp out, as his father once tried to stamp it out of him. (In beating ourselves up, we usually pick up where our parents left off.) Only neither of you realizes (at least initially) that the other represents something within yourself that needs to be dealt with, for it is only in the dramatic playing out of your interactions that these powerful patterns and deep psychological dysfunctions are brought to light.

I defer to Carl Jung, who spent a lot of time either in a nuthouse or in a monastery. "The psychological rule says that when an inner situation is not made conscious, it happens outside, as fate," Jung said. "That is to say, when the individual remains undivided and does not become conscious of his inner contradictions, the world must perforce act out the conflict and be torn in two opposite halves."

It's amazing to watch sometimes. These monastery battles royal can be downright epic. Forget about what happens when an immovable object meets an irresistible force. What happens when a weenie who's sworn off his cowardice meets a monster who can't help himself from bullying?

"First law of thermodynamics: Energy can neither be created nor destroyed. It simply changes forms!" So went the mantra of an erstwhile Zen peer, one of those quasi-scientific mystic types forever trying to link quantum physics with whacked-out spiritual mumbo jumbo. If you ever disagreed with him, he trembled, his jowls purpling: "That's . . . just . . . your . . . ego!" A regular fury farmer, this sower of hate seeds was one of those unfortunate American Zen sangha fixtures whose respect and admiration for the teacher is in inverse proportion to his resentment and suspicion of his peers. Once, a fed-up nun, ornery and pugnacious in her own right, shot back: "Listen you! In a universe that wastes nothing, where does the butthead energy go when you lose your temper? What form does it change into?"

In about a week she got her answer. One morning, this troubled monk we'll call "Tirade-san"—towering over six feet, girthy, garbed in his turquoise stretch pants and a T-shirt with a picture of the cosmos and an arrow indicating YOU ARE HERE—exploded at the *densu* (the monastery greeter) when she forgot to fetch a student from the airport. She in turn barfed a curdled remark on the *tenzo* (cook), after he misplaced her laminated chant sheets. The tenzo then went Vesuvius on the *shoji* (the zendo mother) when she innocently swung through the kitchen door to brew some green tea.

"Knock before entering!" the normally mild-mannered Pisces roared.

"Have a fucking cow!" the grandmother of three and part-time care-giver blasted back.

As *shika* (head monk), I felt like Bill Paxton in *Twister,* chasing the tornado of devastating emotion as it touched down from one end of camp to the other.

Later, when I pushed through the sutra hall's great double doors for the monks' nightly meeting, I could feel T-san's glare frying the hairs on the back of my neck. Turns out I had forgotten to give the densu the flight details in the first place, which oversight set off the whole Great Hissy Fit chain reaction that day. T-san bent his body language my way, trying to get my eye, like a boxer intimidating an opponent before the opening bell. Unable to meet his gaze, I studied my toenails—which, to top off the shameful matter, were badly in need of trimming.

Per meeting protocol, we circled up, bowed, and took turns voicing the various petty and passive-aggressive concerns that arise when a group of people with anger issues decide to engage in a practice that deprives them of sleep, comfort, personal space, protein, and even their hair. I nodded with great interest and jotted these concerns in my head-monk notebook, where they languish unaddressed to this day. Meanwhile, Evil Monk would soon have the floor, and I imagined him with a little toothbrush mustache, howling in German. I would get a chance to rebut him because the head monk speaks last, and believe me, I had every word—every last syllable—planned. *You can only take so much shit for so long!* I trembled inside, my sphincter clenched about as tight as the hydraulics in those machines that make artificial diamonds.

Finally, it was the man-ape's turn to speak. I turned and bowed to him, and for the first time that day I looked him dead in the eyes—half expecting to see two hollow black holes brimming with the souls of dead children. And wouldn't you know it, he was smiling. He laughed lightly and bowed that mammoth wrecking ball atop his shoulders, indicating that he had nothing to say.

In that moment the hate seed fell out of me, dead like a stone—petrified in its own uselessness like an insect fossilized in amber. He put his great meaty hand on my back on the way out of the room. That's all it took for me to break down sobbing in my cabin about twenty minutes later, alone but warmhearted. Desperate, gushing, cleansing sobs. It was the kind of moment that buys you another five years of patience with, and passion for, monastic life. It's one of those breakthroughs of the heart.

People ask what is the hardest thing about living at a monastery. Is it no sex, cardboardy food, zero sleep, sandals gone rancid from perpetual socklessness, the measly fifty bucks a month "monk's allowance"? Is it the isolation from society, the heinous robes, those bone-crushing nineteen-hour days spent in the zendo or in the blistering sun or piercing cold? The hardest thing about living at a monastery, I tell them, is working with people with whom you have nothing in common save spiritual desperation. We monks shave our heads, I continue, because if we didn't we would surely tear out all of our hair in despair from having to live and work with one another. Anyone who's ever been married or had kids, or coworkers for that matter (work and family—those *other* group practices), probably knows what I'm talking about. It gets real when the illusions drop away, doesn't it?

Yet nine times out of ten, the reason we get so irritated with the people who are closest to us is because ~~they~~ show us that we do not in fact correspond with the ideas we have of ourselves. We are meaner, weaker, dumber, and less interesting, tolerant, and sexy. In short, we are human, which typically comes as extremely disappointing news. You just cannot keep telling yourself how spiritually with-it you are when every time you sit down to read that Eckhart Tolle book the monastery cat jumps on your shoulders and claws your bald head and you fling it halfway across the room and scream, "Goddamnit, I'm trying to read about patience and equanimity here. Can you at least wait till I've gotten past the 'Pain Body' chapter?!" Not that I, of course, have ever done that.

I used to imagine that spiritual work was undertaken alone in a cave somewhere with prayer beads and a leather-bound religious tome. Nowadays, that sounds to me more like a vacation from spiritual work. Group monastic living has taught me that the people in your life don't get in the way of your spiritual practice; these people *are* your spiritual practice.

Through each other we discover that if we have the heart—the willingness, strength, courage—and then we have the capacity to plant seeds of kindness, compassion, forgiveness, and humor. But your heart must be quicker than your mind. Trust me, that organ between your ears is *always* spoiling for a fight. Its job is to divide and conquer. But the real fight is taking place inside you, within the "dharma organ," the heart, where the challenge is to unify and understand; where the seeds of love and compassion are struggling to lay roots, to gain ground.

Lend this struggle an ear. Just pause for three seconds. One banana . . . two banana . . . three banana. . . . Pause and listen. Pause and breathe. Pause and gather your scattered, wild energies, your shattered soul . . . before you fling that seed of hate into the wind.

Mark my words, times are tough and the ground is fertile. That seed *will* grow.

Anger as a Sacred Practice

Joan Sutherland

The practice of anger is not a practice in response to anger, intended to manage or fix it, but a practice of anger itself, based on an understanding of anger as something sacred to be handled with care. Zen teacher Joan Sutherland teaches on practicing with anger using the tools of inquiry, discernment, and remorse.

Of the emotions we tend to think of as afflictive, anger seems to be in a category by itself. When a group prepares to take the bodhisattva vows together, no one ever tries to make a case for lying or stinginess, but someone always does for anger. "There are some things it's wrong to tolerate," they say. "Anger can be righteous. Anger is motivating." In contrast, pretty much everyone agrees that it's no treat to be on the receiving end of a blast of anger, however motivated and righteous.

The way the bodhisattva vows are formulated seems to reinforce anger's difference. We vow to take up the way of not indulging in anger rather than the way of not being angry; it's the only conduct we vow not to indulge in, as opposed to just not do. Does this imply that the problem is in the indulgence rather than the anger itself? Obviously there's a spectrum from chronic irritation to murderous rage that looks like anger indulgence, but isn't the repression or denial of anger just indulgence with a different face? Is there ever a time when getting angry isn't breaking a vow?

In most Buddhist traditions, anger is pretty unequivocally a problem. The mildest judgment is that it's a form of immaturity. More severely, anger is seen as the most deadly barrier to enlightenment. Shantideva summed it up by saying, "There is no sense in which someone prone to anger is well off." By contrast, in recent times the repression of anger has sometimes been blamed for physical illness, psychological distress, and even interpersonal conflict. Forces this ambiguous, about which we're this ambivalent, have sometimes been called sacred, meaning entitled to a particularly strong form of respect, or taboo, and treated with extreme care because of their potential for danger.

If we look at anger as something sacred-taboo, we explore how anger usually works against the wholeness of things and how, instead, it might potentially serve that wholeness—within ourselves, in our relationships, and in the larger world. When the whole self is present and we are aware of the whole world in all of its complexity, we understand that we carry within us a fire called anger, capable of harming ourselves and others, yet also sometimes capable of illuminating or transforming things that would otherwise remain hidden and stuck. We are guardians of that fire, and there's a dignity in that, and a responsibility.

When we take on that responsibility, we open up the possibility of being tempered by the fire. The traditional image is of a lotus in the fire, a flower not consumed but refined by the flames. Let's call this a practice of anger. Not a practice in response to anger, intended to manage or fix it, but a practice of anger, based on an understanding of anger as sacred-taboo, to be handled with care and allowed to temper us. Most fundamentally and perhaps surprisingly, the experience of anger is transformed into a form of inquiry, compelling our attention toward things not being adequately attended to, within ourselves and in the world.

Strong feelings are inquiries the body makes of the mind. They ask: There's something happening we need to pay attention to. What's going on? And since their job is to get our attention, they do it in dramatic ways—the surge of adrenaline, the rush of blood, the clenched gut. Dramatic, but from an evolutionary perspective, probably helpful. Then things get a bit trickier, because the body's inquiry tends to be accompanied by a strong suggestion of how we should feel about what's happening, such as afraid, pained, angry. It's the voice of the organism, intent on survival, and while it's good at letting us know that something's up, it's not always so accurate at telling us what that something is.

We have a choice. We can simply accept both the warning and the suggested interpretation: If I'm feeling this way, there must be something to be angry about. Or we can make a differentiation. Without automatically assuming that the appropriate reaction is anger, we can accept that the body perceives a threat. We can stay with the sensations—hot, electric, vertiginous—without jumping to the story about why we're feeling this way and without immediately spreading those sensations into the world around us through our words and actions. We can allow in a little spaciousness, moving from "I'm so angry" to "Anger seems to have arrived."

Neither allowing ourselves to be possessed by anger nor trying to repress it—this is the first step of not indulging in anger. We've taken the role of host to the guest of anger, allowing it to have a seat on the sofa but not to light a fire in the middle of the living room carpet. We've created enough space and stability to begin a series of crucial discernments into the nature of our anger.

The first is whether we can be so certain about what we're feeling. When anger arises, we tend to assume it's justified. We think, if I'm angry, there must be a good reason. (Notice that we don't necessarily make the same assumption about someone else's anger.) Often when we're angry, that becomes the most important thing going on. In fact, anger tends to see things through its section of the emotional bandwidth, which leaves out a lot. Because anger tends to obliterate nuance and complexity, we have to consciously bring them back in, even against anger's seductive desire for what G. K. Chesterton called the clean, well-lighted prison of the one idea. Anger looks for justification, backup, evidence to support itself, and it usually doesn't take kindly to being contradicted. Are we comfortable with betting the farm on anger's interpretation of events?

My community, Awakened Life, used to gather during some retreats for a complaint circle, which we made into a kind of ceremony. Everyone had five minutes to write down something they were really angry about, their pet of all peeves. Everyone also had some kind of percussion instrument—rattles and drums and pot lids—which we'd play with vigor while each person read out their complaint with as much feeling as they could muster. It didn't take long for the entire circle to collapse into laughter, as we experienced the surprising monotony of our cherished and surely unique complaints, and the emptiness of their drama. Afterward the mood was always lighter, more spacious, and kinder. We could see how, even when we weren't consciously gripped by anger, it maintained an invisible crust over our hearts.

Whether our anger is such that a complaint circle could transform it or whether it seems more serious, it's a vital signal that something has gotten out of balance and needs attending to. This shifts our focus from how we feel to what's been upset in the larger context. Instead of being possessed by anger, we receive it as a messenger, and the message can arrive from within ourselves, from someone else's words, or from the world in which we're standing. Even when the anger is very upsetting, we're still focused on decoding the message so that we can discern how we might respond rather than react. One of the differences between the two is that a response is capable of incorporating the new understanding of the state of things that anger has revealed, while reaction remains focused solely on how we feel.

The next discernment is about the source of the anger. Is it coming from a very personal place within us or is it a force of nature speaking through us? In Zen there's something called flavorless words, which is what is said when the vastness speaks through us without our putting any personal spin on it. When we're speaking flavorlessly, what gets said is called a complete presentation of the whole, a holographic moment in which the whole universe is present in the words we speak. When we're expressing anger, is it essentially as impersonal as an erupting volcano, or is it coming from some deeply personal and therefore flavored place in us, arising from the impulse to wound or discharge uncomfortable feelings at someone else's expense?

If we have gotten out of the way, and the anger is coming without any spin on our part, it can be like lightening on a dark night revealing what's been denied or hidden. And like a flash flood, it can reshape even very stuck things. But flavorless anger is a much rarer occurrence than we'd probably like to believe, which is why anger ought to remain sacred-taboo. Sometimes anger has both flavorless and flavorful—impersonal and personal—elements, and in this case what we're after is an honest understanding of the mixture. That's a good place from which to decide what to do next.

The next discernment is who or what is being spoken for. Who is being offended and defended? Is it someone or something needing our help, or is our outrage actually personal even when it seems to be about something else? It's not wrong to act on someone's behalf because we find a situation personally unbearable; it's just good to recognize that that's part of what's happening so we can be more confident that our actions address what the person actually needs as well as what we do.

We don't make these discernments in order to judge our feelings and motivations, dividing them into piles of good and bad. Although the practice of anger asks us to explore and come to know ourselves very well, it isn't essentially about us but about the larger context when anger arises. We make this exploration because we want to get as close as we can to what's actually happening. In order to act in the most free and helpful way possible, we want to move closer to what's troubling, with less of our own stuff distorting our view.

Even when faced with an injustice recognized by all, our anger cannot be the only or even the most important thing going on. As with any other intensely compelling feeling or thought, it's helpful if we can restore its true proportion in relation to the whole: our anger is one of many things rising and falling together in a given moment. Sometimes realizing this is all we need to break the spell and wholeheartedly shift our allegiance from our reactions to actually responding to the situation. This is a humbling practice because it's very challenging to work with anger from inside anger. It takes time and effort and the willingness to fail a lot, but it can't be beat as a small, local gesture of commitment toward the sacred work of mending what's broken in the world.

It's sometimes our own hearts that are broken. When confronted with the pains and injustices of the world, we can jump to anger rather than stay with the sorrow that is our deeper and more difficult response. I can't bear that the world is like this. I can't bear that you are like this. Say that with outrage, then say it with grief. When we feel helpless in the face of suffering, getting good and mad can be a relief. Part of the practice of anger is being willing to stay with the underlying sorrow rather than jumping to that release. Staying with it opens the possibility of transforming sorrow, a transformation that also pours a healing balm on anger.

Sorrow isn't directly transformed into happiness; what happens is that young sorrow is transformed into mature sorrow, which finds its own happiness. Young sorrow is what comes of not getting what we want, things not turning out the way we wish they would, or the world not being the way we think the world ought to be. It's usually made of disappointment, frustration, despair, and anger as well as sadness. With mature sorrow we come to see the world as not-yet-completed, as full of poignant persistence even in the face of struggle and pain. The sun rises again, leaves unfurl again, people try and try and try again. There's something ineffably tender about how all things go on trying in an imperfect world—and this is something that doesn't need fixing, because it is in the trying that the possibility of awakening persists. Mature sorrow denies nothing; it just takes a long, un-self-centered view, and in that view it sees reason to open its heart to the terrible beauty of life. Much of anger's raison d'être falls away as that deeper sorrow matures. In a sense, the practice of anger is really one face of the practice of sorrow.

Which brings us to the question of motivation. People often see anger as a powerful spur to action and are worried that without it they'd become passive observers. The difficulty is that anger isn't a good long-haul motivator, since, like fire, it consumes all of its fuel, which is hard on the angry person and everything in the immediate vicinity. To the extent that anger is motivated by a desire to change something in order to relieve a discomfort inside ourselves, we're prone to disappointment and eventually despair, since the world is an unpredictable partner in that kind of project. In contrast, mature sorrow does have legs as a motivator. Mature sorrow takes a long view and puts itself in service to the possibility of awakening. The process might sometimes seem agonizingly slow, but fortunately our sense of satisfaction is linked to something more sustaining than individual events and our reactions to them. It's linked to the poignant beauty of the undeniable persistence of things, no matter what.

The final aspect of the practice of anger is remorse, which plays a key role in some expressions of Buddhist morality. Anger is such a powerful force that it's almost transpersonal in its heedlessness of the ordinary conventions of communication. It spurs us to say and do things we never would in any other context, and its effects can last a lifetime. This is why it is important to notice what happens when anger erupts. Do we ever feel better after an angry outburst? If so, is it because we're using anger to discharge our own discomfort? What's the effect on the other person? What's it like to harbor chronic forms of anger like judgment, or to be the target of chronic anger? Most important, what would you hope never to do again? That's what remorse means: an unflinching exploration of the results of our actions, a willingness to take responsibility for them, and the changes we make as a result. We look at ourselves with mature sorrow and ask what we can change to better serve wholeness in ourselves and our world.

This is what it means to take the sacred-taboo nature of anger seriously: we contain something with great potential for destruction and a limited but powerful potential for good, and we treat it with the kind of respect we'd give a radioactive substance. Because we can get angry, we have the responsibility to be careful and to do the hard work of inquiry, discernment, and remorse. Anger asks a lot of us, and it gives us something precious in return—an intimate, daily way to participate in the awakening of the world.

PART THREE

Going Beyond Blame

No Blame

Sylvia Boorstein

There are no human enemies, says Sylvia Boorstein, only confused people needing help.

The instinctive, immediate response to our own fear is assigning blame to its presumed source. Blame is probably an adaptive response to situations of immediate physical jeopardy in which there is no time for reflection. Even in situations where there is no immediate peril, directing anger at whoever (or whatever) frightens us is more acceptable to the ego than helplessness and despair. Terrible things happen in this world, and people do them: aren't there culprits, villains who can be blamed?

A story: I took a mandatory course for therapists in California called "Recognizing Signs of Child Abuse." The first presenter began with descriptions, accompanied by slides, of such frightful violence toward children that I could barely listen. I thought I could feel the people around me wincing, wishing, as I was, that the lecturer would move on to what could be done. Finally, she did.

"When it becomes clear," she said, "that the agency will need to take custody of the child in order to protect it, I say to the parent, 'I know that in your heart of hearts you want to be a good parent to your child. And I know it has been very hard for you to take care of her at this time in your life. We're going to help you. You'll need to leave her with us until you get strong enough to care for her yourself. Let's go down the hall together and I'll introduce you to the people who will make good arrangements for her. You carry the baby and we'll go together.' Mostly, the parent is relieved. I hold her hand or put my arm around her as we walk."

People exchanged glances that seemed to say, "This woman is a saint!" Then one person asked, "How can you stand seeing what these people have done? How can you not hate these parents?"

"It's not their fault," the presenter responded. "Almost all of them were abused themselves. Many of them have substance addictions. Their lives are not working. They see nothing but long, empty futures stretching out ahead of them, and then, on top of everything, a crying child. They can't do it another way. There is no point in blaming."

Can anyone ever do it another way? Is there ever anyone to blame?

Child abuse is extreme. What about the ordinary, inevitable ways that parents, bound by their own limitations, cause pain that is remembered and lamented by their adult children decades later? What about our parents? Can we recognize their mistakes and not blame them? And what about those of us who are parents? I remember, when I was a much younger parent, hearing the psychologist John Enright say, "You always chose right, given the resources you had." I thought, "Really? Even when I acted badly?" He meant it: no one to blame.

And how about at the level of world history, with designated friends and foes, allies and enemies? It is early March as I write this, and last week, people leaving Spirit Rock Meditation Center after a month-long meditation retreat said, "How is it out there? Tell us, so we won't be shocked when we hear the news." I said, "It's much the same as when you left it: greed, hatred, and delusion have not been uprooted, and people are quite frightened." I did not want to be political. I did want to prepare them, though, for the fact that although overt war had not yet broken out, it was about to. I also wanted to suggest that what the Buddha called the three torments of mind—greed, hatred, and delusion, themselves the results of ignorance—were the causes of conflict, not particular people or nations. I hoped it might protect them from the pain of enmity and the futility of blaming.

Shantideva, the sixth-century Buddhist commentator, gives this example in *A Guide to the Bodhisattva's Way of Life:* Suppose a person hits you with a stick. It does not make sense to be angry at the stick for hurting you, since the blows were inflicted by a person. Neither, he continues, does anger toward the person make sense, since the person is compelled by anger (or greed or delusion). Ignorance becomes the villain, overwhelming reason and creating suffering.

Is Shantideva still relevant in this twenty-first-century world? Certainly, decisions about war and peace are made by people, people we could name—and blame—as culprits. I wonder, though, if we are not best served by naming ignorance as the enemy to be defeated, even as we act firmly to oppose what we see as wrongdoing in the world, what we recognize as causing pain. This would leave us without human enemies, with only confused people needing help.

I am wondering what the world news will be by the time you read this. I am hoping that whatever it is, I will be able to refrain from blaming. That's difficult to imagine, since it is already seductive to assign fault. "If only that country, or that person, had done things differently last month, or last year, or five years ago. . . ." I stop myself, when I can, from this line of thinking. It churns up anger in me. And anyway, "if only" never happens. Something did happen, and whatever it was, here we are.

I often think of the familiar image of an infant left in a basket on a doorstep with a note pinned to its blanket: "Please take care of me." The natural impulse, for all of us, would be to pick the baby up, to care for it. I try to think about the world as an abandoned baby, left in dire straits by parents who could not care for it well. Could we be the benevolent agents who pick it up and, without blaming, take care of it?

Villains and Victims

Mitchell Ratner

At its core, blaming is about separation, about seeing ourselves as separate from those we are blaming. But we are not truly separate, says Mitchell Ratner. We are both wave and water, simultaneously separate and not separate, both individual and part of the greater whole.

In June 2003, I was in Israel and the West Bank as part of an initiative exploring ways the practice of mindfulness might contribute to the lessening of conflicts there. In talking with people, I was struck by how often Israeli Jews and Palestinians used the same language of blame in explaining their view of the conflict:

- This is the suffering we have endured, and are enduring, because of the actions they have taken.

- They do not value our way of life.

- They are criminal, inhumane.

- If we are weak, they will take advantage of us.

- The only way our way of life will be safe is to eliminate them from this territory, which by rights is ours.

Within this framework, there was little room for a peaceful resolution of the conflict. Mostly people talked about their hope that their side would prevail.

Counterbalanced against the deadlock of mutual blaming was another approach we talked about during our retreats: that one should not blame anyone, ever; that man is not our enemy, ever. In *Peace Is Every Step*, Thich Nhat Hanh explains: "When you plant lettuce, if it does not grow well, you don't blame the lettuce. You look for reasons it is not doing well. It may need fertilizer or more water or less sun. You never blame the lettuce. Yet if we have problems with our friends or family, we blame the other person. But if we know how to take care of them, they will grow well, like the lettuce. Blaming has no positive effect at all, nor does trying to persuade using reason and argument. That is my experience. No blame, no reasoning, no argument, just understanding. If you understand, and you show that you understand, you can love, and the situation will change."

My time in Israel sensitized me not only to the blaming others were doing but also to the blaming I was doing, in terms of how I talked about social problems, such as the conflicts in the Middle East, and in terms of how I lived my daily life. I began to see, also, why blaming is so attractive and how hard it can be to let go of it.

WHAT IS BLAMING?

The word *blame* has two distinct usages in English. In one usage, blame is simply about attribution of responsibility. Something was the cause or source of something else. This led to that. A fire inspector might, for example, blame the house fire on the faulty wiring in the kitchen. In this sense, blaming is problematic only if it is not accurate or comprehensive enough.

A second usage of blame, however, identifies an individual or group as responsible for a condition that distresses us. This usage adds censure, reproach, disapproval, or anger to the attribution.

- It can be very emotional: "You are a real jerk. You only think about what you want. Because of that, we never get anywhere in this relationship."

- It can be analytic and pseudocompassionate: "The problem is that because of the pain that you suffered in your childhood, you are unable to form a mature loving relationship with me or anyone else."

- It can be very subtle: "You should know better than to talk to your sister like that."

- It can be vague, with many unstated implications: "It is all your fault."

- It can be directed at ourselves: "I am so terribly disorganized, I was not able to tell you I could not make our appointment.

- It can be directed at whole groups: "The reason the behavior of those people is so uncivilized is because of their upbringing" (or history, or genetics, or misinformed religion, or lack of discipline, and so on).

In this usage, on which I will now focus, to blame is not simply a consideration of actions and consequences but a psychological attack on an individual or group. Often it is an attempt to punish others, or to force others to change a behavior that is distressing us, by undermining their sense of themselves as whole, competent persons. As Thich Nhat Hanh points out in the paragraph above, when we blame like this, it almost never gives us the results we really want. Usually the individual or group reacts to the attack and responds defensively: "No, I'm not," or counterattacks: "It is really all your fault." Or there may be external submission, accompanied by hostility, "I'll do it, but I won't like it or you"; immobilizing self-blame, "I really am irresponsible"; or later acting out, "If I'm an irresponsible jerk, then to heck with it, I'll show you how irresponsible I can be."

WHY DO WE BLAME?

Even though it doesn't work, there are powerful forces in most of us leading us to blame others in a hostile way. One "benefit" in blaming this way is that it reduces complexity. A group conflict, or a conflict in a relationship, almost always has a long, complicated history of contexts and actions that condition other contexts and actions. In highlighting one cause and ignoring a multitude of contributing causes, we create a world of villains and heroes, or villains and victims.

Another "benefit" of blaming others is that it takes responsibility for the distressing condition away from us and makes others (or a shadow side of ourselves) responsible. Often, in our distress, we simply ignore the ways we have acted that have conditioned someone else's actions. In a relationship, we may have grown distant, pulling back from emotional engagement, but then, during a dispute over a miscommunication, blame it all on our partner for not bringing up the issue earlier. Group dynamics can be even more complex. We can decry individual acts of illegal behavior, or institutional violence (such as the brutal behavior of guards at checkpoints), without seeing how we are linked to the systematic deprivation or inciting actions that condition these responses.

At a more subtle level, often when we blame we implicitly make others totally responsible for our emotional response. It is what they did that caused us to be angry, frustrated, sad, fearful, or disappointed. We ignore or play down the power we have to create our own emotional reality, through the way we frame a situation, through the way we work with the hurts we have suffered in the past. I may come down hard on the assistant who is late with an assignment, criticizing his work habits, blaming him for bringing more stress into my life. Someone else may respond with compassion rather than anger, discussing with the assistant the difficulties encountered in this assignment and working out ways to resolve difficulties earlier.

Blaming others for that which distresses us allows us to create a self-satisfying narrative about our lives that preserves a morally superior self-image. Our shortcomings are explained away by the actions of others. Erica Jong writes in *How to Save Your Own Life:* "How wonderful to have someone to blame! How wonderful to live with one's nemesis! You may be miserable, but you feel forever in the right. You may be fragmented, but you feel absolved of all the blame for it. Take your life in your own hands, and what happens? A terrible thing: no one to blame."

Self-blame is another way of maintaining a self-satisfying narrative. When we blame ourselves, we split off the cause of our problems from an idealized self-image. We separate the "good me," the "real me," from the "bad me," the "not really me." We are able to maintain our image of the "good me" by explaining to ourselves and others that the outcomes that distress us are due to the actions and attitudes of the "bad me," who is not really me.

In perhaps its darkest aspect, blame is used to justify force, violence, and punishment. Once we have established that the situation that causes us distress is "their" fault, because of their evil actions or evil natures, if "they" don't agree with us and change their ways, then we feel justified in taking action. We may seek to forcibly prevent others from acting in certain ways, to hurt them as they have hurt us, to teach them to see it our way through punishment, or to destroy them.

Why do we use blame? Perhaps the simplest answer is that we blame because we are not able to envision a more productive way of dealing with situations that distress us. Many of us grew up in families in which we were taught to blame, by parents and adults who modeled blaming as a way of dealing with frustrations. Schooling, movies, and celebrities reinforced the lessons. Implicitly, we perceive blaming as a way of protecting ourselves and those we care about. If we did not blame others, we would feel passive, ineffective, and taken advantage of. There is something poignant and tragic about blaming others: We are aware of the symptoms, but we have misdiagnosed the disease, and we persist in using inappropriate treatments that are destructive rather than helpful.

Ending Our Blaming

Buddhist psychology teaches that deep in our consciousness are internal knots, caused by our misperceptions, that cause us to act in ways that bring suffering to ourselves and others. The practice of mindfulness allows us, at deeper and deeper levels, to become more aware of our actions and our mental processes. When we see an internal knot and know it for what it is, it begins to loosen. Over time, we are able to untie some of our knots, and life flows through us more freely.

If we understand blaming in this way, as an internal knot, then our blaming decreases as we are able to see it for what it is each time it arises in our lives. Not long ago, a friend in a workshop related the untying of our internal knots to the process of toilet training. There are, she noted, three stages a child goes through. The first is when he is aware that he has soiled his diaper. The child tells the parent, the parent commends the child, and the parent cleans up the mess. The next stage is when the child is aware that he is soiling his diaper. The child tells the parent, the parent commends the child, and the parent cleans up the mess. In the third stage, the child is aware that he is about to soil his diaper. The parent commends the child and introduces the potty.

So it can be with blaming. Sometimes we recognize the blaming only much later. Insofar as we can, we clean up the mess the blaming has caused. Over time, as we become more sensitive to it, we can catch ourselves in the act of blaming another (or ourselves). If any mess has been created, we clean it up and proceed with another way of addressing the condition that is distressing us. With more practice, we become aware of the urge to blame before we have said or done anything. We note the urge, look deeply into its roots, and use this insight to work out an appropriate and compassionate response.

Making it sound as if letting go of blaming were as simple and straightforward as cleaning up after a child, however, reminds me of a story about Shunryu Suzuki Roshi. A student asked: "You teach us to just sit when we sit, just eat when we eat. Could a Zen master be just angry in the same way?" Suzuki Roshi replied, "You mean to just get angry like a thunderstorm and be done when it passes? *Ahh,* I wish I could do that."

Letting go of blame is not easy, because it forces us to confront many of our misperceptions and develop a very different way of being in the world:

- We become more open-minded, recognizing that every frustration, every conflict, can be seen from multiple vantage points.

- We accept responsibility for the ways we may be directly or indirectly contributing to the conditions that distress us.

- We understand that our happiness, contentment, sadness, and ill ease always arise out of our response to the stimuli we receive.

- We recognize that everyone else exists, with hopes and fears, strengths and weaknesses, just like us.

- We understand that conflicts end and reconciliation begins when we can mutually recognize our hurts, fears, needs, and wishes.

At its core, blaming is about separation, about seeing ourselves as separate from those we are blaming. The Buddha taught that we are not as separate as we usually believe ourselves to be. Even though our tendency is to construct a separately existing self from the stream of sensations, feelings, emotions, and thoughts, life is more subtle than that, more mysterious, more wonderful. When we are truly present, we live closer to life, with less reliance on, less clinging to, the constructed self. We learn bit by bit, glimmer by glimmer, that we are both wave and water, simultaneously separate and not separate, both individual and part of the greater whole. Each time the energy of blame arises in us, it is a reminder that in some way we are still holding on to our separate selves, still looking for security by separating ourselves from life.

Blame Everything on One Thing

B. Alan Wallace

*"Blame everything on one thing" is a traditional Vajrayana Buddhist slogan
or maxim that is part of what is called lojong, or mind training practice.
This slogan means that when something goes wrong and we want to blame
something or someone else, we should instead identify the true culprit:
self-centeredness. In working with this slogan, says B. Alan Wallace,
we will discover more happiness and harmony in our lives.*

The next verse instructs us to blame everything bad that happens to us,
from tragedy to ingrown toenails, on one thing alone: self-centeredness.
This is a very powerful antidote to a very natural tendency. When we
experience misfortune, we almost invariably look outward and say,
"Who did this to me?" If we identify a perpetrator, myriad mental distortions arise in response. Another person may well have acted as a cooperative condition contributing to our unhappiness, but that person is
not the real cause.

On the deepest level, taking karma into account, we are ultimately
responsible for our present circumstances and for the future we are creating right now with each action of body, speech, and mind. But we are

responsible on another level also, which can be helpful to consider. Imagine, for example, that someone drives into my car and puts a dent in it. In this particular instance I am blameless; my car was stationary. I can target the person who did it, and that person seems truly to blame for my suffering—the dent in my nice new car. But I have isolated this person. It's a sure bet that I am looking at the person who dented my car as an intrinsic, autonomous entity, and in this way I feed the fires of my indignation and self-righteousness.

What is the real issue here? Was I at fault in this particular context? Both the law and my insurance company would say that I was not. Someone has damaged a possession of mine and I have no freedom to choose whether or not I experience this particular circumstance. On a deep level I have stacked the cards to experience this through my own previous actions. But here lies the freedom: How do I respond? The dent in the car has no power to cause me any suffering unless I yield to it. The dent is only an external catalyst, a contributing circumstance, but by itself it is not sufficient to cause me suffering.

What are the added ingredients that cause me suffering? First of all, I had to possess the car. Watching someone drive into another person's car does not have the same impact on me as watching someone drive into mine. At a minimum, the suffering requires a person to drive into the car, the car that was driven into, and my possession of the car. But all this is still insufficient for suffering to arise in my mind. We have the ingredients for a cake but no oven. The suffering actually arises from the stuff of my own mind. If I were mindless there would be no suffering, but that is not an option. I cannot decide to reject my mind. Instead I must apply my intelligence: What element of my mind was responsible for my suffering?

The real source of my suffering is self-centeredness: *my* car, *my* possession, *my* well-being. Without the self-centeredness, the suffering would not arise. What would happen instead? It is important to imagine this fully and to focus on examples of your own. Think of some misfortune that makes you want to lash out, that gives rise to anger or misery. Then imagine how you might respond without suffering. Recognize that we need not experience the misery, let alone the anger, resentment, and hostility. The choice is ours.

Let's continue with the previous example. You see that there is a dent in the car. What needs to be done? Get the other driver's license number, notify the police, contact the insurance agency, deal with all the details. Simply do it and accept it. Accept it gladly as a way to strengthen your mind further, to develop patience and the armor of forbearance. There is no way to become a Buddha and remain a vulnerable wimp. Patience does not suddenly appear as a bonus after full enlightenment. Part of the whole process of awakening is to develop greater forbearance and equanimity in adversity. Shantideva, in the sixth chapter of his *Guide to the Bodhisattva's Way of Life*, eloquently points out that there is no way to develop patience without encountering adversity, and patience is indispensable for our own growth on the path to awakening.

So think of your own example. Recognize that anger or resentment is superfluous mental garbage, and that clutter and distortion serve no useful purpose in our minds. Suffering is not even necessary. Geshe Ngawang Dhargyey once made the comment that, once bodhichitta has been developed to the point of arising spontaneously, one becomes a bodhisattva and no longer experiences the common sorts of mental suffering. Although a bodhisattva may experience suffering in sympathy for others, the kind of self-oriented suffering we normally experience simply does not happen, because a bodhisattva is free of self-centeredness.

Blame everything on one thing. It simplifies life incredibly, and yet it truly is not simplistic. If we believe from our hearts that all of our misfortunes can be attributed to self-centeredness, this must radically transform our lives.

Do we have reservations? Isn't there some part of the mind that says, "Self-centeredness is not such a bad idea. It got me my job, a good salary, my house and car. How can this be my enemy?" On the surface, self-centeredness may seem like an aide who looks after our interests. There is one powerful answer to this: Insofar as self-centeredness dominates our lives, it brings us into conflict with virtually everyone else. Because most people are dominated by self-centeredness, their interests are at odds with our own. There is bound to be conflict, and conflict gives rise to suffering.

Imagine what life would be like without self-centeredness. Would we give away all our possessions, waste away from malnutrition, and die prematurely of disease? No. This would be a partial lack of self-centeredness combined with a large part of stupidity. If we are to serve others effectively, we must take care of ourselves. A bodhisattva has no self-centeredness, but there have been people in all stations of life, including kings, who are bodhisattvas. If we free ourselves of self-centeredness and really concern ourselves with the cherishing of others, then our own welfare comes as a kind of echo.

There are an infinite number of ways to serve the well-being of others. The motivation of cherishing others can engage the energies of a doctor, a teacher, a carpenter, or an auto mechanic; or it can move us to withdraw from active service to train for helping others. Any attention to our own welfare comes as a repercussion of this concern for others.

Well-being, contentment, and good cheer come also as side effects, for reasons that are easy to understand. If we devote our lives to the welfare of others, we immediately are in harmony with virtually everyone around us. They are looking after their own welfare and we suddenly appear as an unknown friend, in Shantideva's words. I look down right now on the town of Lone Pine in the valley below, population two thousand. They may not know it, but they have a friend. To the extent that I develop this cherishing of others, I become an unknown friend for two thousand people down there, for the animals living round about, for all sentient beings. My actions harmonize with the reality that I exist in fundamental interdependence with the rest of life.

Our lives up to this point may well have been dominated by self-centeredness, pursuing our own good to the detriment of others around us. The same attitude may well have dominated our previous lives. Our present state is the fruit of the years we have lived in this lifetime as well as the end product of countless past lives; lifetimes that encompass a bounty of self-centeredness. If we are not particularly satisfied with how we are doing right now, we may hold self-centeredness responsible. There are, however, beings who have taken a different course, bodhisattvas and Buddhas who from lifetime to lifetime have cherished others above themselves. As Shantideva says in a wonderfully potent verse:

> What need is there to elaborate?
> Fools apply themselves to their own welfare,
> While sages act for the welfare of others.
> Just look at the difference between them.

We work so hard at our own well-being, striving to the point of exhaustion. The Tibetan Buddhist teachers under whom I studied have frequently commented that if we gave nearly as much intelligent effort to authentic spiritual practice as we give to simply making a living, we probably would be highly advanced bodhisattvas by now, if not Buddhas.

We have allowed self-centeredness to exhaust us in the past, and in return have received very little good and a lot of anxiety. Anxiety is built into self-centeredness by necessity. As soon as we fix on *my* possessions, *my* this, *my* that, we must then be on guard to protect our turf against all other sentient beings, many of whom are also dominated by self-centeredness. Insofar as self-centeredness decreases, the anxiety and suffering will inevitably ease off.

Sechibuwa elaborates on this, and to a large extent we can confirm his findings experientially for ourselves. All mental distortions, he says—attachment, arrogance, hostility, resentment, jealousy—come from the root of self-grasping, and self-centeredness lies at the very core of this reification of our own existence. He makes the analogy that being subject to this self-centeredness is like wandering naked with a bundle of thorns on our backs. No matter where we go, no matter what we do, it gives us suffering. Whether we engage in spiritual practice or mundane activities, it is always there.

Sechibuwa advises us even to address our own self-centeredness in the following way: "Self-centeredness, I have identified you at last! You have dominated my life in the past, pretending to be my friend. You claimed to be my ally and promised me all good things, but in fact you worked to my detriment. Now that I see you I will not rest until you are completely vanquished, because you have tricked me, nestling in my mind as if to help me, while in fact you were a traitor. You promised me happiness, but you gave me grief and anxiety and suffering, and I have had enough."

Keep in mind that we are not speaking to ourselves. Self-centeredness is not the self but rather an obscuration, or affliction, of the mind. Look for it not only in the quiet of meditation but in daily life. Use the occasions in life that cause you unhappiness to identify self-centeredness. When misfortune arises, unhappiness occurs as a response. See if you can note the role of self-centeredness in the episode and see how self-centeredness is in fact the source of the suffering. In the absence of self-centeredness, an external stimulus can put a dent in your car, it can give you illness or physical pain, but it cannot give you grief or anxiety.

Sechibuwa makes another very important point. All of the Buddha's teachings, he says, and all the thousands of volumes of Indian and

Tibetan commentaries are designed for one purpose only: attenuating and dispelling mental afflictions. However these afflictions are categorized, they all boil down to self-centeredness. All of Buddhadharma is about vanquishing these maladies of the mind because they lie at the root of all suffering. The Buddhas have only one task and one motivation—to lead each of us from suffering.

If we take this seriously and even consider the possibility of loosening the bonds of self-centeredness, of looking outward and offering our lives to the world, it is frightening. And this fear expresses itself so articulately in the very terms of self-centeredness, "What will become of me?" No less than climbing a high mountain or exploring uncharted regions of the ocean, setting out on this great venture takes courage and faith. But we need not go head over heels. Faith is not a drastic thing; we can take it gradually. We can put one toe in first and begin to identify for ourselves the effects of self-centeredness.

It is worth investigating for ourselves how self-centeredness has brought us harm under the guise of protecting us. We can infer that it has similarly brought us harm in the preceding lifetime and the one before that. Now expand the mind to life before life before life, each one spanning various experiences, a certain sense of personal identity, a certain way of dying. In each lifetime we have had aspirations, yearning for happiness and striving to achieve it. But as long as we fail to recognize the true enemy, then our aspirations for well-being are severely hampered. We come to this present life as the culmination of everything we have lived for in all of our lives up to this point. Unless we employ skillful means as a remedy for self-centeredness, it will keep on perpetuating itself throughout the rest of this lifetime, through the coming *bardo,* or intermediate period, into the next lifetime, and so on without end.

Self-centeredness does not vanish by itself. As we begin to make an effort, we may quickly become discouraged and feel that it is not really possible to counteract self-centeredness. We may wilt at the thought, "My neural circuits are so conditioned to self-centeredness that I just cannot escape the pattern." It feels like self-centeredness has us well in its clutches and is firmly in control. After all, it has had a very long time to embed itself in our psyches. The results will be gradual as we counteract the conditioning of our mental, verbal, and physical behavior. At the same time, the results of skillful efforts are manifest, and we can experience them right in this lifetime.

If we take this seriously as a profoundly meaningful way to vanquish self-centeredness in our lives and to cultivate a loving concern for others, it becomes a central feature in our aspirations and our value system. It continues throughout this lifetime as an orientation—even if, at the end of this life, we still have a considerable amount of self-centeredness left. Nevertheless, a current is established that in all likelihood will continue building momentum. In the next lifetime it will be easier insofar as we have made effective efforts in this lifetime. How many lifetimes it takes depends upon the skill, the intelligence, and continuity of practice. If we dabble at it casually and intermittently, it will obviously take longer. But it is also possible to overcome self-centeredness in this very lifetime and become a Bodhisattva.

Blame everything on one thing. Gradually or swiftly, it is an effective means to counteract self-centeredness and end this source of misery, strife, and anxiety. Until we do, there is no question that it will continue endlessly.

Compassion for Those Who Cause Suffering

Christina Feldman

There are tragedies in the world that break your heart, acts of violence and oppression that seem too much to bear and impossible to comprehend. It's hard to release blame, says Christina Feldman, but it may be the only thing that allows you to move beyond despair. As hard as it is to release blame, it's a much greater hardship to hold on to it.

When I first encountered the Tibetan community in exile in India, I anticipated meeting a people crushed and broken by tragedy. They had endured unimaginable loss and pain—their families had been killed or imprisoned, many had been tortured and uprooted from their homes, and each of them had undertaken the long trek over the Himalayas, hunted, frozen, and starving, to find safety in India. I was stunned to meet a people whose hearts were amazingly intact. They grieved, cried, and expressed anger, yet bitterness and the desire for vengeance were markedly absent from their emotional landscape. Compassion and faith were evident everywhere. So too was the unshakable resolve to find freedom—not only the freedom of their homeland but, more significantly, freedom within their own hearts.

The classroom of compassion is situated in the midst of the deepest pain and suffering. Faced with the suffering of those you love, compassion and empathy arise naturally. Faced with people who inflict pain, you need to dive deeply within yourself to listen and understand. Compassion asks you to make the radical leap in your own consciousness to embrace the perpetrators of harm. It is hard practice, but genuine compassion embraces all suffering—the anguish of the blameless and the anguish born of hatred, ignorance, and fear. The mountain of suffering in the world can never be lessened by adding yet more bitterness and hatred to it. The spirals of fear and division are perpetuated by every gesture of rage and retaliation. You swallow the terror and rage, and you become it. Thich Nhat Hanh, a great Vietnamese Buddhist teacher and author of *Being Peace,* said: "Anger and hatred are the materials from which hell is made." To discover a heart without boundaries, you must discover compassion without boundaries.

Just as suffering can be the forerunner of bitterness and despair, it can equally be the forerunner of a deeper wakefulness and the first steps on a path of healing. You can flee from pain, ignore it, or place blame, or you can find the courage to turn toward it. The sorrow you believed yourself unable to endure can, in being embraced, become a profound turning point in your life. In the darkest moments, you can find a strengthening of your commitment to understand what compassion is. Facing the immensity of the suffering in the world, you come to see the pathways that are open to you. You can align yourself with hatred, bitterness, and division, joining the perpetrators of pain in their nightmare. Or you can learn to open, to commit yourself to healing. In the quiet whispers of your heart, you intuitively know the pathway you are called upon to travel.

At every turn, you face events and situations that test the limits of your compassion, tolerance, and understanding. There are tragedies in the world that break your heart, acts of violence and oppression that feel too much to bear and impossible to comprehend. You may find yourself adrift, wondering how you could possibly understand the heart of someone who inflicts pain upon the innocent. The possibilities of terror and danger live on the periphery of your consciousness. Your mechanisms of self-protection are endlessly provoked to the surface. In the face of threat, you find yourself striking out. Resistance and rage are assumed to be instinctive reactions to pain, but in truth they are impulses governed by fear. You contract, tempted to abandon the trembling of your heart. Separation and distance appear to promise safety, and you are tempted to build ever-higher walls to hide behind. Even numbness can seem attractive, offering a temporary sanctuary. Yet the attraction to numbness coexists with your deepest yearnings for intimacy and unity. You discover that there is no true safety behind the barriers you build; the terror and mistrust born of isolation flourish in that ground. The monster in the dark grows bigger and more solid in your refusal to meet it.

You can only hate from a distance; you can only love and understand through closeness. To find compassion in the midst of pain, you need to have a relationship to the pain. Vietnam veterans, like soldiers in wars through all of time, speak of the distance and disengagement they cultivated to enable them to fight. The psychology of hatred relies upon making your enemies less than human so you can find the permission and will to harm them. You do not always see the ways in which you make yourself less than human in the process, the damage you wreak upon your own heart. The psychology of compassion relies upon your seeing what is human—seeing yourself—in all of your enemies. The person you hate or feel the most bitter toward is, in the beginning and the end, someone who wakes in the morning wanting to be safe and free from pain, someone who is healed by a loving touch, who longs for tenderness and understanding. Only when you see yourself reflected in the eyes and heart of another can you understand that to harm another is to harm yourself. As Gandhi once said, "Where there is hate and fear, we lose the way of our spirit."

Compassion asks you to cross the borders that have been constructed in your own heart through fear, prejudice, and mistrust. You must ask yourself where you wish to make your home—in the endlessly fearful and fraught country of isolation and terror or in the country of understanding and compassion. A woman once told me of the years she spent hating a person who had abused her. Long after her abuser had physically departed from her life, he continued to govern her heart. In a very real way, he had dominion over her happiness and well-being. Bitterness and resentment filled her days, poisoning her relationships. Exhausted from the ongoing struggle, she spoke of the moment when she understood that the only way she could find an end to the suffering was to be intimate with it. To live a life pervaded by bitterness and hatred is like being locked in a burning house—and then to remember that you hold the key to the door in your own hand.

You should not be ashamed of anger; compassion is not a surrender of discriminating wisdom. Compassion has a ferocity born of the capacity to unflinchingly identify the causes of sorrow and pain. Compassion is vaster than a feeling; it finds its expression in wise action. The courage, balance, and resolve needed to end suffering are made manifest through the words and acts that are bridges to the world around you. A person without anger is probably a person who has not been deeply touched by the acts of violence, oppression, and prejudice that scar the lives of too many individuals and communities. The vast amount of suffering in the world is unnecessary. It is not intrinsic to life but intrinsic to fear, blindness, and hatred.

Anger awakens you; it can be a catalyst for furthering pain or for ending it. It can degenerate into bitterness and resentment, or it can be translated into the understanding and action that heal suffering. Your dedication to compassion is tested in the fires of anger. Anger can be the beginning of abandonment or the beginning of connection; this is the choice you are asked to make again and again in life. It is not difficult to see that the most cruel and violent people in this world are those who are most disconnected from others and most disassociated from their own hearts. The most compassionate people are not those who are immune to suffering but those who have refused to follow the pathways of disconnection. Genuine compassion begins the moment you withdraw your consent from abandonment. It doesn't mean that anger will suddenly stop, but anger will no longer end your connection with other people. A compassionate heart will feel anger and fear; wisdom teaches that you do not need to perpetuate them.

Rage and bitterness shatter us; they destroy the equilibrium of our own hearts and lives. This is a simple truth. Shantideva, a great Indian mystic, taught that the mind cannot find peace, nor appreciate delight or joy, nor find rest or courage, as long as the thorn of hatred dwells in the heart. There is nothing that can make an angry person happy. Unruly beings are like space; there is not enough time to overcome them all. Yet if we are able to uproot our thoughts, it is like defeating all of our enemies. You can be crushed by anger or awakened by it. To find a pathway through anger, you are asked to take the first step of releasing blame.

Blame binds you to the unending song of resentment; it can paralyze you. You replay the story in an endless loop, blaming those who misuse power, those who abuse the vulnerable. The continued retelling of the story can become a substitute for action.

It is hard to release blame, but it may be the only thing that allows you to move beyond despair. You may also begin to understand that, as hard as it is to release blame, it is a much greater hardship to hold on to it. You are locked in an unwelcome marriage with those you hate and condemn; you become a cause of your own suffering. Your life comes to resemble the lives of the Japanese soldiers found on a Pacific Island in the 1950s, still fighting a war that had ended long before. Tragedy, misfortune, and all the blame and mistrust born of them become the reference point in a life you cannot fully live.

In 1996, when the Truth and Reconciliation Commission met in postapartheid South Africa, the releasing of blame that took place was the beginning of healing. The commission was born of the realization that it would be impossible to punish every act of violence and harm that had occurred during the decades of apartheid. There were not enough prisons to hold all the perpetrators of violence.

In the commission sessions, torturers faced the people they had tortured, jailers faced the people they had beaten and imprisoned, killers faced the grieving families of those they had killed. The perpetrators took upon themselves the commitment to listen—and thus to overturn a legacy of division, mistrust, and hatred that had haunted their lives. Each person was given the space to be heard, to speak the truth of their pain and heartache, fears and hopes. Oceans of tears were shed in that room; there was no magic wand to erase the terrible acts that had happened. But in the listening, a possibility arose, a beginning of laying down the burden of pain, a possibility of a change of heart. Archbishop Desmond Tutu spoke of the alchemy of the commission, saying, "When we had listened to the testimony of people who had suffered grievously, and it all worked itself out to the point where they were ready to forgive and embrace the perpetrators, I would frequently say, I think we ought to keep quiet now. We are in the presence of something holy. We ought metaphorically to take off our shoes because we are standing on holy ground."

We are prone to idealize those who find nobility of heart in the midst of the greatest suffering. In reality, they are ordinary people, like any of us. To call them survivors would be to diminish their courage and commitment to healing. They have not transcended sorrow; their hearts still ache and grieve. Sometimes, in the midst of the greatest bitterness and resentment, you come to realize that you can never heal your own spirit as long as bitterness lives there. To rescue yourself, you must rescue those who have harmed you from the power of your own rage.

Releasing the burden of blame and hatred can, at times, only happen in the aloneness of your own heart. The people who have harmed you personally through their words or acts may feel no remorse, nor any willingness to listen to the consequences of their violence. The people you will never meet who have taken part in inflicting pain and terror may continue to uphold the righteousness of their acts. It is easier to forgive someone who truly wants to be forgiven. The challenge of compassion is to make no distinctions. Compassion asks you to see beneath events, to understand that acts of terror and harm are born of suffering and lead to suffering. Suffering is not just pain; it is also blindness and self-righteousness. If your anger is directed anywhere, it should be toward hatred, fear, and ignorance. If your commitment to compassion is to make a difference, it must be a commitment to ending the causes of suffering. Shantideva taught that if you become angry with those who harm you by their words or acts, you need to understand that the inflictor of pain is also harmed by their hatred and anger. Rather than being enraged with the wielder of the stick, you should be angry with the hatred.

Some years ago, a taxi stopped for me, and just as the driver picked up my suitcase, he was intercepted by another driver who wanted the fare. Within minutes the two drivers were wrestling over my suitcase, exchanging blows and verbal abuse. After a doorman successfully intervened and I was ensconced in the back of the first taxi, the driver began to tell me the story of his life. He spoke of the countless times life had been unfair, how he had been abused, how hard he had struggled to make a living, and how afraid he was of being taken advantage of. He spoke of the way that fear and resentment were part of his family culture, passed down through generations. The lineage of anger and suspicion goes back through time and generations, to a time before you were even born. If you could hear the unspoken, often hidden story of your enemies, you would find enough sorrow and despair in it to disarm all of your rage and hatred.

There is little that is noble in suffering, but there is something deeply noble in our willingness to open to suffering without fear. If suffering were brought into being by choice, no one would suffer. Suffering is born not of choice or wisdom but of ignorance. One of the primary manifestations of ignorance is the belief in the solidity of self and other. The territory of self is defined by all that I feel I possess—my body, mind, my opinions, beliefs, religion. "Other" is defined by all that I believe you possess—your views, religion, race, gender, and history. Fear is the offspring of separation—the fear of loss, of threat, of challenge, and of deprivation. When anything of "mine" is threatened or even disagreed with, I feel the core of my being threatened. Nowhere is the sense of self and other more pressing and solid than in the midst of fear and anger. There is no ease, peace, or freedom in ignorance and separation. To find the end of suffering, you are asked to be relentless in your questioning of separation. Compassion is not built on sentiment but on wisdom.

Authentic compassion is altruistic, but it is not unrealistic. Walking the path of compassion, you are not asked to save all beings, lay down your life for another, or find a solution for all the problems in the world. You are asked to explore how you can transform your heart and mind in the moment. You are invited to turn toward the places in yourself where resentment, rage, and hatred live. With honesty, you examine your mechanisms of self-protection and defense to understand whether they truly preserve anything at all, apart from terror and isolation. To cultivate compassion and openness of heart in the midst of fear and pain is to swim against the current of the reactions that have been built up through your life. You cannot make yourself feel compassionate; trying to be compassionate always feels contrived. You also do not need to think of compassion as a random occurrence that takes you by surprise. Moment by moment, you can train your heart to open where it has previously been closed, to be intimate where you have sought distance.

Compassion is built on the foundations of tolerance, patience, forgiveness, and understanding. Nurturing a firm base of equanimity within, you find an inner balance that enables you to stay steady in the midst of life's storms. These foundations are not distant goals to be realized in some future time but truths that you can find and cultivate in the very midst of intolerance and fear. You do not need to wait for random moments when the walls that separate you from others crumble; you can learn to deconstruct the beliefs and cherishing that keep those walls solid.

A young man who worked with the homeless population of London said that every night, when he went out on the streets to do what he could to get people into shelters, to ensure that they had enough food, or to persuade them to come off their drug or alcohol habits, he hated it. Every night, he said, he met his own aversion and often the aversion of those he was meant to help. He often felt insulted when people spurned his advice, felt resentful when people turned down his offers of aid, felt judgmental when people preferred to huddle in a doorway rather than take up his assistance. Going onto the streets at night was a journey into those corners of his heart he most wanted to avoid. Daily he would meet his own intolerance, impatience, and conditional generosity. Every night he met the division lodged in his heart between self and other. Every night was a journey of learning patience and receptivity that he had never thought he was capable of. Shantideva taught that it is our enemies that awaken our hearts.

Tolerance does not always come easily, but intolerance is no more than the habit of fear. You may be unconvinced that you can bear the loss and sorrow that life brings. The habit of protecting yourself against real or imagined danger and discomfort deepens. It is sometimes said that a quarter of the suffering in life is real and unavoidable, while the other three-quarters is born of trying to avoid the first quarter. None of us enjoys discomfort or difficulty, but the lengths we go to to avoid them are often greatly disproportionate to the reality of the experience. We become increasingly intolerant as our fear of pain grows. We believe that we cannot endure a harsh word, a moment of disappointment, a fleeting hunger pang, a moment of distress. We flinch in the face of another's disapproval, avoid situations that threaten to disturb our hard-won composure. We are intolerant of boredom, believing that life should offer us endlessly interesting experiences. We believe that we're fragile and so approach life with trepidation and anxiety. When we lose faith in our own strength and fortitude, the world seems to be filled with danger.

If you are to find the vastness of heart that can embrace even the most dire situations of pain and cruelty, you must begin by addressing your relationship to the unpleasant. Wisdom and compassion are not devices to fix your life, to ensure that you will be exposed to only pleasant people and events. We all have a certain measure of pain in this life.

You are not asked to like it, but you are asked to learn what it means to remain steadfast in the midst of the difficult and the challenging. In the confusion born of fear, you can begin to believe that you are somehow entitled to be undisturbed. Your tolerance levels can be remarkably low, your capacity for forbearance subdued.

The training ground of compassion begins not with the demand that you embrace your worst enemies or your deepest fears but with the willingness to be still amidst the small transgressions and irritations that are part of all of our lives. You have to wait in line at the supermarket while the person in front of you redeems a wallet full of coupons, someone speaks to you in a scathing tone, your moment of relaxation is disturbed by someone intent on selling you something you don't want, someone keeps you waiting—life continues to offer countless possibilities for resentment. Often we don't want to accept even the possibility of being disturbed. Our sense of balance at times seems remarkably fragile, able to be shattered by any hint of the unpleasant.

You can dismiss these moments as irrelevant, but they are in fact the moments when you learn about equanimity and forbearance. Tolerance cannot be built overnight; like raising a child, it asks for perseverance and dedication, even in the face of tantrums and outrage. The places where equanimity and tolerance die most easily are the very places where you are asked to embrace and learn what tolerance truly is. Shantideva taught that there is nothing whatsoever that is not made easier through acquaintance, that by becoming acquainted with small harms you can learn to embrace greater harms.

Meditation practice is a training in tolerance, patience, and equanimity. You learn to sit like a mountain, to be still and receptive in all circumstances—happy or sad, healthy or sick. Your knee twinges or your mind is uncooperative, and you can sense the flight response arise—you want to run and abandon the difficulty. Yet, in those moments, you learn to embrace that reaction too, without being governed by it. In cultivating compassion you will be expected to encounter your fear of pain. You learn to be steadfast and still, understanding that the first building block of compassion is your simple willingness to keep showing up for all of life. That willingness teaches you that you won't be destroyed by your exposure to the difficult or unpleasant. You discover a genuine inner balance and sensitivity that can receive the difficult without being overwhelmed.

Equanimity and tolerance ask you to meet your own demons of aversion, self-righteousness, and prejudice. They are the demons that give birth to the hell realms, which erode confidence. You begin to see that each time you follow the pathways of aversion, flight, and resistance, you undermine your faith and confidence in yourself. You are telling yourself that you cannot tolerate this, that it is just too much to bear. Each moment you bolt from the reality or even the anticipation of the painful, you are building yet another fence that makes your world just a little smaller. You are telling yourself that your demons and the demons you meet in others are mightier than the vastness of your heart. If you tell yourself this often enough, you come to believe it, and the habits of fear and resistance can take over your heart and your life.

I once found myself standing in a parking lot with a friend who had historically carried a low tolerance threshold. He was engaged in a well-worn litany of complaints about the idiocy of other drivers, the inconvenience of how the parking lot was mapped out, and the discourtesy of the people in the store we had been in. I found myself interrupting his tirade to ask him whether there was perhaps another way he could be responding to this mountain of perceived injustice. Looking bewildered, he said, "None of this should be happening." Sometimes we are so accustomed to living in the house of intolerance and blame that we no longer even question it. We believe that because we carry ancient traditions of resistance and impatience within ourselves, they will be with us until we die. The path of compassion asks us to overturn our habits, beliefs, opinions, and prejudices, to understand that our hearts can be transformed in every moment we are willing to be still, receptive, and aware.

You can take your meditation, your willingness to be still, into your life. You can learn to pause in the moments when you are prone to flee, to soften in the moments when you feel your heart hardening with resistance and blame. Cultivating tolerance is like opening the door to your heart. You might hope that only your friends come to visit, but you discover that your enemies too walk through that open door. Equanimity is a path you are learning to walk. Sometimes you open that door only slightly; that is all you can bear. Sometimes you stumble and slam the door, but your enemies and demons will wait for you. Just take your reflection upon tolerance into all the moments of your life and see how it is for you when your heart can open and when it closes. Begin to investigate where the greatest suffering and harm are and where the greatest freedom and compassion are. With patience and tolerance, you learn to cross the borders of prejudice, fear, and resistance that divide you from yourself and from others. I once saw a street sign on which someone had written, beneath "STOP," the words "being afraid."

The recipe for alienation is to support the opinions and prejudices that can deluge your heart. The recipe for compassion is the willingness to continue showing up for your life and all it brings to you. Compassion asks you to commit yourself to the end of suffering. You begin to discern not only what suffering is but what the cause of suffering is. Seeing the fears and resistance that attach themselves to the anxiety of "me," you see too that the healing of suffering rests upon your willingness to no longer abandon anything in this world or in yourself.

David spoke of his journey from pain to compassion after discovering that his father had been sexually abusing David's young daughter. David and his wife lived with a gnawing rage and anxiety for months after the discovery. Their children were given counseling, and the parents were told of their children's deep-seated trauma and fear. David needed to find a way toward healing without denying the atrocity. Attending his father's trial did little to calm his rage, as he heard his father confess to numerous other incidents of abuse. David's journey toward peace began with murderous rage. He realized that in the rage he was capable of killing his own father, and he also knew that he could not ever dismiss anyone who acted out of a fury like he was feeling. His first step toward healing was to find the courage to speak about what he found unspeakable to those who could listen without flinching. Deep grief followed, and then self-pity and pity for his daughters. He spoke of a meditation session in which he felt that the ocean of his tears was filled with everyone who had experienced loss through violence and abuse—Holocaust victims, street children, people in Rwanda, and all the rest. Somehow the raw pain began to subside, and he was able to be still in the grief. He acknowledged his need to begin to "inch toward forgiveness." He reflected on his father's life now, imprisoned, shunned and banished from everyone he had ever felt affection for. David was able to feel the tragedy of this life, too. He said he needed to think of forgiving as an ongoing process rather than a static state. Forgiving, he said, was not only for himself and his father but for his own children and even the next generations. He began to work in restorative justice, a voluntary process in which perpetrators meet with their victims, offenders meet those they have harmed. The truth of harm can be spoken and listened to. Forgiving can begin.

Tolerance lays the foundation for turning toward the unbearable and unendurable. Compassion is born of your commitment not to bar anyone from your heart. Compassion in the midst of violence and brutality relies upon equanimity and understanding. It is a way of breaking the cycle of violence and hatred, and it begins with your willingness to be still. The great and small tragedies in your life and world sometimes just ask you to stand before them with silence and humility. You do not always have an answer, but you can learn to be present—listening deeply, with a heart that trembles in response to pain. Sometimes that is all you can do and all that you are asked to do. Compassion does not always bring an end to pain, but it can dissolve the suffering we layer upon pain with resistance and fear.

Tolerance needs to be rooted in wisdom. Just as the near enemies of compassion are pity and condescension, the near enemy of tolerance is endurance. A woman who had lived many years in an abusive relationship told me that her meditation practice had helped her to learn to bear an unacceptable relationship filled with cruelty. We can misuse meditation practice to avoid addressing the causes of suffering and finding the wise action to end those causes. Mistaking passivity for compassion just allows abuse to continue. Tolerance does not condone the unacceptable; learning to open to so much of the unnecessary suffering that scars our world is not the path we are asked to travel. We learn to find equanimity and inner balance so we can stay present with the painful inwardly and outwardly.

There are times when you can do little to alter pain and can only be still in its presence. There are also moments when opening to the painful and difficult is just the beginning of a path that also asks for the courage and sometimes fierceness of compassion. Just as you would pull a small child away from danger without rage or blame, so too you commit yourself to ending the causes of suffering without rage or blame. Again and again in your life, you are invited to ask yourself what is needed to ease the suffering of this moment. Do you need to say no when it is easier to say yes? Do you need to risk losing the approval and affirmation of others in order to speak or act with integrity? Do you need to do what is required rather than what is easiest? Do you need to go to the places that scare you and be willing to meet the anger or condemnation of others? Compassion is not a search for popularity but a commitment to honesty.

The Buddha spoke of the wisdom of cultivating clear intention in our lives. Recognizing that your intentions are the forerunners of your thoughts and actions, you can learn to tend to them with care and mindfulness. The arising of suffering and also the end of suffering begin with the intentions you bring to each moment of your life. The intentions of loving-kindness and renunciation rescue you from their opposites— harshness and resistance. You can explore what difference it makes in your life to enter into each day and each moment with conscious intentionality. It means carefully attuning yourself to the rhythms of your heart and mind, moment to moment. Walk down the street and notice the places you open and the places you close. Notice what happens when a stranger smiles at you, and then what happens when you encounter a homeless person begging. Stay close to what happens in your mind when you meet someone who offends you.

Notice that in the absence of mindfulness you are driven by impulse and unconsciousness to close and defend. Compassion asks you to move from a life of reaction to a life in which you are mindful of your intentions. Be aware of the times you solidify resentment and bitterness by replaying your stories of what someone did to you. Explore the possibility of bringing loving-kindness and the willingness to let go to all of those moments. Ask yourself where you are choosing to make your home in each moment—in suffering or in the end of suffering. You can rescue yourself from division and alienation. The moments you do close down or become lost in outrage or blame are not moments of failure that warrant even more condemnation of yourself. You can compound suffering through self-blame or you can ask yourself what is truly needed to ease the contraction and fear. Through wise intention, you explore the possibilities of healing in the moment. You can only heal one moment of suffering and division at a time.

Compassion has no hierarchy of worthy and unworthy suffering; it makes no distinctions between the deserving and the undeserving. Wherever there is suffering, there is a need for compassion. Finding compassion for those who cause pain is an ongoing practice requiring remarkable patience and perseverance. It is a difficult journey, but the path of bitterness and division is far more painful. The path of compassion begins with your willingness to soften and stay present in all the moments when you are prone to recoil and flinch. You learn to open your eyes and heart in all the places you have been blinded by fear or rage. You begin to dismantle the boundaries that have too long divided you from others.

Fault Lines

Mark Epstein

If we were hurt in childhood, we often feel as if we are somehow to blame for whatever damage was done to us, or else we so demonize our perpetrators that we lose sight of their essential humanity and thereby never escape from our identification as a victim. There is, however, another way. Mark Epstein on moving beyond doer and done to.

I was driving in the car one morning after dropping my kids off at school, flipping impatiently through the stations programmed into the radio's memory, when I suddenly heard a familiar voice speaking in what seemed to be an unfamiliar context. It was a deep male voice that I recognized but could not place: a workingman's gruff but casual cadence tackling a subject that seemed so sensitive as to be almost obscene. He was talking about how hard it is to raise children when one's own childhood was less than perfect. "We take what is good from our parents and leave the rest. That's how we honor them," the voice was saying.

I quickly turned up the volume, trying to figure out who he was. Parenting is a common subject, but the speaker did not sound like the usual authority to be heard on public radio. He sounded more like a soldier talking about fallen comrades, and his subject was as much mourning as child rearing. It did not take much longer for me to identify the voice as that of Bruce Springsteen and to realize that he was giving the interview in anticipation of the release of an album. But the subject matter—having children in middle age and reflecting on how one's own difficulties growing up affected one's ability to raise children—was not the usual material of a star's publicity machine.

I was struck by the wisdom of Springsteen's comment that we honor our parents by taking what is good and leaving the rest. There was a Buddhist flavor to it, although I would be hard-pressed to identify what it was exactly that sounded Buddhist. In meditation, we are trained not to push away the unpleasant and not to cling to the pleasant—this was a little different. This was talking about not rejecting one's parents because they were imperfect, not trying to force them to acknowledge their shortcomings, not rejecting becoming a parent because of what was done to us, not dwelling on the scars one's parents created, not forcing oneself to pretend that one's parents were fine when they were not, but simply being able to take what was good while leaving behind what was not. There was no blame in Springsteen's words or in his tone—that was what caught my attention. After years of listening to Springsteen's music, with its claustrophobic evocation of growing up in a small mill town in New Jersey, I found his comments now to be all the more poignant. Here was a man who was able to honor his parents by refusing to replicate what they had messed up, a man who understood that in his very rejection of them was an appreciation of their efforts. In trying to do a better job, he was nevertheless able to keep his heart open to them, imperfections and all.

Where had this wisdom come from? There was little in the interview to indicate its source. When forgiveness is taught in most spiritual contexts, the emphasis is usually on sending loving feelings even to those who have hurt us most deeply. While many people find this approach helpful, it struck me that Springsteen was pointing to a different way. The forgiveness he was modeling continued to recognize the hurt that he felt. In taking what was good and leaving the rest, he was clearly implying that all had not gone well. Rather than cultivating a mind of compassion that could then forgive the most egregious abuse, he seemed to be finding forgiveness in the recognition of having simply survived. Emerging from his stark early years, undoubtedly aided by devotion to his music, he discovered that he was not destroyed. His own generative capacity, his own desire for a family, and his own ability to love were all reasonably intact. It seems to me that this recognition of his own intactness must have relieved him of the need to blame and permitted him to forgive in a natural rather than a contrived way.

The source of forgiveness, Springsteen seemed to imply, lies in the realization that we are not solely products of what was done to us, the realization that there is something essential within us that is not necessarily tarnished by calamitous experience. While this contradicts many of the assumptions that a hundred years of psychotherapy have helped create in our culture, it is a notion that finds much support in the spiritual traditions of the East. In Buddhist cultures, there is a more willing acceptance of a capacity for joy or love that is not dependent on external circumstances, not compromised by trauma or mistreatment, and capable of surviving destruction. While the classic Eastern route to accessing this inherent joy is meditation, Springsteen's comments suggest that, at least for him, the making of music may have been just as redemptive.

The discovery that one's capacity for joy is inherent and not dependent on external events is the antidote to the all too common predicament of the abused child who assumes too much responsibility for that which he or she had no control over. Springsteen's ability to leave behind what he did not respect of his parents' behavior flies in the face of how most people respond to such trauma. More commonly, those who are trespassed against in childhood have a terrible time seeing the truth clearly. They are much more likely, for instance, to feel as if they are somehow to blame for whatever damage was done to them. Or they may so demonize the perpetrators that they lose sight of the perpetrators' essential humanity. In one scenario, they cleave too tightly to the abuse; in the other, they reject the abuser totally but never escape from their identification as a victim. A vignette provided by one of my patients may shine some light on this.

Joe, a forty-year-old married man, remembered himself at age ten, answering the door when his estranged mother unexpectedly paid his family a visit. She had left when he was five, abandoning her husband and four children and precipitating an unrelenting depression in Joe's father. Upon seeing his mother in the doorway, Joe ran immediately to find his father, shouting, "Daddy, Daddy, this is what you've been waiting for!" Rousing him from his study and taking him by the hand back to the vestibule, Joe discovered that his mother had left as suddenly as she had arrived. "I felt so guilty," he told me, as if it had somehow been his fault that his mother had disappeared again.

Years later, Joe had a major revelation when he realized that his wife's drinking was her problem and not his fault. Until that revelation, he had been in the all too familiar habit of trying to get her to stop so that he would feel better. He had made his well-being completely dependent on how his wife behaved. Her drinking blighted their love, made it impossible for him to take refuge in the closeness and comfort of their relationship, and made him furious and unhappy. He took his wife's drinking personally, as if it were directed at him, as if it were a reflection of her lack of love for him or his own unworthiness. The same overresponsibility that led him to feel guilty over his mother's departure when he was ten also colored his relationship to his wife. Only after attending a series of Al-Anon meetings did he begin to accept that her drinking had little to do with him. This left him in a new predicament. Taking what was good and leaving the rest, not rushing to the assumption that it was all his fault, and separating his own capacity for well-being from the circumstances that surrounded him permitted Joe to begin a process of separation that extended back to his mother and into the present to his wife. Joe made new boundaries that eventually caused his wife to seek help. He found a capacity for forgiveness that was not a whitewash of how he had been, or was being, mistreated: it emerged when Joe could acknowledge the hurt he was subjected to while not entwining himself more than was necessary with the trauma.

Joe's example points to a new and unusual way of thinking, one that the psychoanalyst Jessica Benjamin has called "beyond doer and done to." To Benjamin, the most common reaction to the powerlessness of trauma or abuse is simply to reverse the scenario: to try to assume some power by becoming a perpetrator oneself, by blaming or hurting the other person or by blaming or hurting oneself. She has called this a seesaw mentality: one person is up while the other is down. The primary way out of trauma in this mentality is to seek vengeance or revenge, to lower the other while raising up oneself. In the mode of "beyond doer and done to," something shifts. People, even those who have hurt us, are no longer experienced one-dimensionally, as either all good or all bad. Self-esteem is no longer dependent on being the winner, or on being right. Up and down are no longer the only criteria by which life is measured. The seesaw gives way to a merry-go-round, known in Buddhist culture as the wheel of life. In this model, it is clear that we cycle through all the manifestations of what it means to be human. We move from state to state, sometimes causing each other pain and sometimes bring-ing each other joy. As the seesaw gives way to the merry-go-round, an appreciation is gained of the difficulties and complexities involved in being human. Not only are we all completely capable of hurting one another, but we are also capable of a profound empathy, even for those who have hurt us or for those we disdain.

In Springsteen's few short comments on the radio that morning, I heard a voice of wisdom calling out across the generations, one that seemed to be reaching for a new way of relating. A master of the adoles-cent love song, Springsteen has a catchy tune that I found myself hum-ming that day, one of those simple songs with an infectious hook that I often repeat like an unconscious mantra: "All I'm thinkin' about is you." As much as I love that song, his words that morning went even deeper. We honor our parents by taking what was good and leaving the rest, he said. I could feel that old seesaw implode.

Empty Graves
and Empty Boats

Rachel Neumann

At her grandfather's grave, Rachel Neumann's rage erupted, but who was there to yell at in those long-buried remains? There's no one to blame when an empty boat rams into you, and in the end we are all just empty boats bumping against each other.

There are as many different kinds of anger as there are waves in the ocean. When my older daughter gets angry, there is a deluge of tears. As I watch, she goes limp and sobs into the floor with the unfairness of it all. My younger daughter's anger is a tornado of hits, kicks, and screams. She can't be comforted, reasoned with, or carried out of the storm until it has run its course. My partner's anger is quiet and sullen, thick as the southern Mississippi air. Only a slam of the door or a fist on the table occasionally punctuates the silence. Me? I shake with a blaming, seething anger, full of my own righteousness and ready to enumerate the faults of everyone around me.

I've always been a blamer. Sometimes I blame World War II for this. Our family's survival was tenuous, the exception rather than the expectation. If almost all of our relatives hadn't been killed, then perhaps I wouldn't feel so alone in the world. Sometimes I blame Western culture, capitalism, sexism, and all of the institutions that keep us separated and thinking we have to go it alone. Sometimes I blame myself.

Growing up, I was pretty sure the world would fall apart if I didn't check that we had food, take care of my little sister, and make sure the front door was locked. Our whole family's survival felt like my responsibility and mine alone. Even after I left home, whenever I got overwhelmed in relationships or at work, my mind would return to this well-worn path: "Why do I, alone, have to do everything?"

When I was seven I went to visit extended family in La Jolla, California. Every morning we would walk to the beach, where the waves were small but restless. They would crash against the shore, retreat to gather force, and then crash again. The man I was staying with would let the waves beat against his ankles. Then, as they receded, he would say to them, "Are you mad?" drawing out the last word to make me laugh. Blaming is like those waves hitting the shore over and over again. It hits a contradicting reality, disintegrates, and then gathers force again.

There is a parable about blame first recorded by the Chinese mystic Huang Tzu more than three hundred years ago. Imagine you are in a rowboat on a lake. It is a beautiful calm day, and you are enjoying the peacefulness of the moment. But then you notice there is another boat heading straight toward you. You shout, "Look out!" and wave your arms, but the boat keeps coming. You try to steer out of the way, but it's too late. You keep shouting, but the boat keeps coming. It rams into you, knocking you into the water. You are cold, wet, and your beautiful day—your serenity—is ruined.

"What are you doing?" you yell at the driver of the other boat. "Why don't you watch where you're going?" Then you look into the other boat. It is empty.

This story helps remind me that the bumps aren't personal. We're all just empty boats bumping up against each other. But even knowing no one's inside, I usually find myself peering in, looking for a culprit. People should remember to tie up their empty rowboats or, if they are tied up, to tie tighter knots.

How do I undo a lifetime of blaming habit? I've found there are only two effective antidotes: gratitude and coresponsibility. But gratitude is a tricky emotion. As soon as I think I'm *supposed* to feel it, as soon as I catch a whiff of even the slightest hint of obligation, any gratitude I might have felt is replaced immediately with resentment. So I was taken off guard when, a couple of years ago, I came across the *Kataññu Sutta*, a Pali teaching on gratitude. It says: "Even if you were to carry your mother on one shoulder and your father on the other shoulder for a hundred years, and you were to look after them by anointing, massaging, bathing, and rubbing their limbs, and they were to defecate and urinate right there on your shoulders, you would not in that way pay or repay your parents."

This no-excuses, go-ahead-and-pee-on-my-shoulders type of gratitude is so counterintuitive to my well-worn and boring rut of blaming that I've made a conscious decision to move toward it. After all, what if it didn't matter who locked the door or made the dinner? I am here, alive, and healthy, and I could not have gotten here on my own.

Recently, when I was getting over the flu, my mother came over for dinner. In the morning, I'd set the table and prepped some food. After work, I picked up the kids, took them to an after-school class, and got groceries. When I arrived home, I tripped over my mother's shoes. She was sitting on the couch, checking her email. Bob Marley was blaring from our stereo. Her jacket and half-eaten snacks were on the floor, and there was a trail of dirty dishes in each room. I carried in the grocery bags and started toward the kitchen.

Putting the lettuce and cucumbers away, I thought, "How like my mother to make a mess and not help with dinner. Can't she see how tired I am?" It was an old thought and it sounded old in my head, coming out in a croaky whine. A few months earlier, my mother and her best friend had taken my older daughter for two whole weeks. My daughter had come back thrilled, full of stories, and without a scratch. I owe my mother a huge gaping shoulder-carrying debt of gratitude. And yet my critical mind kept rattling on.

Then I put down the vegetables and I stopped. My father had arrived, and he and my mother and my partner and children were all talking at once, interrupting each other to show off various new skills and the day's creations. If my mother weren't so good at taking care of herself, she wouldn't be able to be so generous or have the energy or physical ability to take my older daughter on a trip or hold my younger daughter upside down, as she was doing now. In that moment, I was flooded with gratitude. There was my loving partner and my healthy, happy children. There was the delicious dinner I was about to eat and the fact that my parents were both alive, basically well, and—though long divorced—able to easily join together for a meal. I was so thankful I could not speak.

I leaned against the kitchen counter. Then my mom waltzed in. "Anyone need help making a salad?" she asked.

Blaming is neither true nor not true. It doesn't take me even one tiny step closer to mine or anyone else's happiness or freedom. Lately, whenever someone is blaming or praising me, or when I'm blaming or praising myself, I practice this response from Zen teacher Thich Nhat Hanh: "You are partly right." "You are partly right" means that there is some truth to the story, but it's not the whole story. I love this because it acknowledges responsibility but also acknowledges that each story has more layers than one person can possibly see.

While "fault" isn't a particularly useful idea, "responsibility" is. We humans are intricately and necessarily connected to each other, not just for our happiness but also for our very existence. If this is the case, then it makes sense that we are responsible for what happens to each of us, both the good and the not so good.

What about the really bad things? Those are someone's fault, right? The person who hits his small child, the slave owner, the scientists who designed the gas chambers, the person who sees violence and does nothing, aren't they—aren't we—to blame? If we know who is at fault, maybe we can make sure that they don't do it again. But blame doesn't work that way. Assigning and taking responsibility provides an opportunity to change. It gives us choice and power. Blame negates responsibility. It ends the sentence, closing off possibility.

I just came back from my first trip to Germany. Soon after I arrived in Berlin, I visited the Holocaust memorial, a central city block of rectangular concrete slabs. A tour bus stopped and a gaggle of teenagers got out, jumping on the stones, laughing and taking pictures of each other with their phones.

Next, I visited the grave of the man I used to walk with on the beach in La Jolla. A week before leaving for Germany, I'd learned that this man was really my father's biological father, my biological grandfather. My father had lived with him for years, believing that this man was a family friend. This man never told him the truth and never acted like a father to him. He died without ever calling him "son."

I knew none of my other grandparents and would have liked to have known I had a grandfather, especially this man I used to walk with along the beach. I was sad, but I didn't get angry until I saw his grave.

He was buried in an old cemetery in the heart of West Berlin. The site was chosen long after his death, after his cremated ashes had been ignored in the storeroom of an East Coast funeral home for years. Even though he had been forced to leave Germany, he often went back after the war ended and still felt at home there. The graveyard was chosen in part because he had friends buried nearby.

It took me two buses, a walk, and some mangled German conversations with strangers for me to find the cemetery. It was late afternoon when I arrived, and in the fading light, I missed the posted map and couldn't find his grave. As I walked among the gray tombstones and dark shadows from the chestnut trees, I started to feel a creeping panic. What if I couldn't find it? What if I had to leave without ever seeing him again? If I couldn't find his grave, I'd be left in the woods. Alone. Lost.

I was getting ready to leave when some pale light on the flat top of one of the cement stones caught my eye. Up against a wall in the far corner of the cemetery, I saw the black scrawl of his name.

Anger, my familiar furious blaming anger filled me. We had so few relatives. How could this man have lived with my father and said nothing? How could he have left us there all alone? I wanted to yell at someone, to shake the tombstone until an answer fell out.

But I would have been yelling at an empty grave. My grandfather was not in there. Even the remains of his body, cremated and long buried, had been absorbed back into the earth. There was no one to yell at. There was no one there to blame, just an empty boat.

If my grandfather was anywhere at all, he was in me. We have the same nose, the same genetic material, the same tendency toward logical argument, and the same love of the ocean. I also inherited, from him as well as others, the same seeds of anxiety and fear. Letting go of blame doesn't mean I'm letting my grandfather "get away" with something. I'm responsible now for what secrets I continue to keep, what blame I pass on.

Someone had left fresh chestnuts on the top of the grave and, amid them, a dying red rose and some polished stones. I picked up one of the smooth brown nuts. Even in the last of the light, it was gleaming, full to bursting with the seed within. I rolled it between my fingers, then returned it to the top of the stone. Evening had fully arrived and the sky was dark, the air cold. I left the cemetery empty-handed and walked lightly, but not alone.

PART FOUR

Finding Forgiveness

What Dogs Do: When an Object No Longer Offends

Karen Maezen Miller

By making a home for her late father's dog, Karen Maezen Miller gives abode to her father as well: reconciling differences, settling transgressions, allowing things between them to be over and done.

The Lord is my shepherd;
    I shall not want.
He leadeth me beside the still waters:
    he maketh me to lie down in green pastures.
He leadeth me in the path of righteousness for his namesake:
    he restoreth my soul.

This is not quite how it goes. I know it is not quite how it goes. I don't remember how it goes, but I mumble it anyway. It is the least and the most I can do.

Thirty-five years before this day, I won the Bible Bee at a summer church camp in north Texas. I was fourteen, a champion of rote versology, and Jesus had just become a superstar. But a new language was overtaking the familiar King James version of my spiritual upbringing, and I was soon knocked from my cozy throne. I still knew the stories, I could recite the laws and lessons, but the test questions had changed. Was I saved? That's what Christians suddenly wanted to know, but I was no longer sure by whose standards I qualified. I was not born again that summer. And when you're not born again, pretty soon it's all history.

Now, standing by the bed in the ICU, the respirator inflating Father's chest like a pipe organ, I leave aside the Buddhist incantations that I've naturalized and whisper remnants of the old song. *I will dwell in the house of the Lord forever.*

I'm thinking that my dad would like it, should he still be able to do something as sentient as like, in this mechanical suspension before my sisters can arrive to make the last decision. By anyone's judgment, my father is a failed Christian and I am a forsaken Christian, except that in death, as in life, we are all one thing. Words matter in times like these, but not the words that once brought us to blows.

My father didn't love easily, and so he was not easy to love. For as long as I could remember, my mother ran interference for him. "Your daddy really loves you," she'd say. We all had reasons to doubt. As soon as I could steady myself on two feet, I kept my distance.

One time my two grown sisters and I reminisced about the good old days.

"What was your most traumatic childhood memory?"

"When Daddy kicked Karen down the hall." Both my sisters said it. I had no recollection, but I didn't need one to believe it was true. My father was the kicking kind. He kicked dogs and small things underfoot, a class of brute that surely doomed him to hell.

Life was plainly hell for him already. His was an unrelenting darkness without the grace of even one flicker of faith. After Mom died, my sisters and I would imagine his decline, certain that the burden would befall us to be kind to an unkind man and generous to a scrooge. We weren't at all sure we could do it.

In his loneliness, he had taken a dog, a rescue, although we hesitated to think Dad much of a hero. The dog was skittish and untrained. She wet the carpet many times a day.

And then things turned out differently. My dad began to do things differently.

He imagined a new life in a new place, far away. He set about, with the intention and resolve he had lacked in nearly every other year of his life, to accomplish something. He gave away or sold all the stuff we were so sure we would be saddled with. He sold his home, the albatross we'd already hung around our necks. He loaded up his dog and his truck and moved to a mountain town where, six months later, he could no longer breathe.

There, looking at his pallid agony, the cruel limits of a life lost to pain, I cried and I smiled, realizing that only I could supply what had been so sparing between us.

"I love you," I told him just before we turned everything off.

And then, to my sisters, "I'll take the dog."

That spring, my mother had come to me in a dream. Four years dead, she was standing on my front porch. I rushed up and hugged her. Her body was like ash in my arms, crumbling and decayed, but I was not afraid or repulsed. She took me up. We flew into space, into the vast darkness and pulsing light. I felt celestial wind in my face. It was exhilarating.

I asked her, "Is there a heaven?"

She said yes.

"What's it like?"

Like this, she said, like this.

It was an attribute of her deep faith and her final, modest confusion that my mother believed she was dying on Easter, and it was, for her. But for the rest of us it was in the small hours before Good Friday, the dark night after Maundy Thursday, the day commemorating the Last Supper, when Jesus gave his disciples a new commandment, to love one another as he had loved them.

Not too long ago I chanced upon a telling of what has become a bit of family lore, that my mother, a devoted Lutheran and good church-goer, had never known I was Buddhist. She would not have stood for that, the reasoning goes among my relatives, who had mistaken the strength of her faith for hardness. True faith is not hard at all. It is soft in its resilience, yielding in its certitude—the vehicle for absolute grace.

What is true for me, what I remember, is what my mother said when I told her of my first encounter with my Zen teacher and the peace I had found. What she said then was what I recognize today as the ultimate sanction a mother can give.

"Now I don't have to worry about you anymore."

In the dream, my mom brought me back to my own front door, and then she said something.

"There's only one thing I want you to do."

"What is it?" I would have done anything she said. I was filled with immense joy and thankfulness.

"Love Jesus," my mother said.

I will, I said. I will.

Only later, upon waking, did I wonder. And then I stopped wondering.

There are many names, many stories, but only one love, and only one place or time that I can love them all without exception.

I did not want a dog.

I am not a dog person. I am not a cat person. I am only intermittently a person person. In that regard, I have never been anyone but my father's daughter, unable to outrun his footsteps in the hall.

But I've learned that it takes a mother to heal a daughter, a daughter to heal a father, and a dog to heal us all. There is a shepherd's psalm to soothe in every wilderness, and this dog has brought me mine.

There were troubling signs from the start.

My husband flew to Denver, rented a minivan, and drove the dog, her blanket, her bowl, and her toys 833 miles to our doorstep. She catapulted from the car, darted through the front door, and peed on the Oriental. *No one should have to put up with this.*

And then, the hair. Clouds of fur drifted along the baseboards, coated the sofa, and clung to our clothes. Was it stress, allergy, vitamin deficiency, or climate change? Was it her food, water, flea treatment, or shampoo? We called the vet. *This can't go on.*

And then, the yard. Her pee killed delicate mounds of moss; her poop pocked the pristine footpaths. *What is that smell?*

And then, worst of all, the walks. I chafed at the bridle; I yanked at the leash. She bolted in front, chasing cats and squirrels, sprinting and vaulting, exposing my complete inadequacy as a handler. She loved it. I hated it. *I hate her.*

And then.

Little by little I shed my resistance. Like a lark, I've made a nest from never-ending dog hair. I quit pinching my nose and picked up a poop scooper instead. When my dog places her quivering muzzle on my lap telling me its time to go for a walk, I release my selfish grip on the day. So many walks around the block, and each time I come home to a very different place, all because of what dogs do. They save your life by making you leave it behind. Good dog, Molly.

Follow a dog, or a horse, or an elephant, for that matter, and with every step you're brought to new ground right under your feet. You're brought to that new ground whether you follow anything or nothing at all, but these animals can help you notice it. If you detect a residue, a stain, or a whiff of lingering stink, you know perfectly well that you'd better scrape it off.

Just now, mired in the familiar stench of an old story, my dog, Molly, has led us somewhere fresh and clear. Do you see?

I love my dog. And that means I'll take the dad.

We have a saying in Zen: "When an object can no longer offend, it ceases to exist in the old way." It doesn't mean we just think of it in a new way or assess it in a new and favorable light. In Zen, we always mean what we say, and then some. Eliminate your separate, self-reinforcing view, and an offending object ceases to exist in the old way. There is no one left to take offense. There is only love, the love that never leaves.

Life is all about love. I can't imagine what more there could be to it. We've all come here for love: to get it and to give it, there being no separation between the two sides of the transaction. Love is the reason we do everything, and love is the reward. Love is the spirit, and love is the form.

As sons and daughters, sisters and brothers, mothers and fathers, dog walkers and cat fanciers, we are all caregivers, and love is the care we give. Actually, that expresses love in a stingy way, as though it were rationed from one to another. Love is far more than that. Love is what we are when we drop all the things that stand in the way.

The last night in the ICU, I felt my father's life recede and I lost my footing. I could not stand. I could not walk. The nurses wondered if I had the flu and suggested that I go to the emergency room.

"No," I said, "it is my father dying." They assumed that mine was an emotional response. But it wasn't emotional. It was real. I clung to my chair like a raft against the undertow. And then I felt, as never before, that my father was *me,* that altogether we were but one life, interdependent and inseparable.

When all was said and done, we turned off the machine and death came. I spoke prayers, verses, and encouragement, and I found out how easily I could. The poet is not wrong. *Surely goodness and mercy follow us all the days of our lives.*

So it turns out the dog is not difficult. She is even-tempered and sweet, uncomplaining, an ordinary dog.

I love her, but I do not love her as if she were something else. She is not my baby or my bane. I do not pamper or perfume her. I love her as a dog, true love allowing each and all things to be just as they are.

"She was my father's dog," I am quick to explain to others on first meeting, and then I stretch the unspoken for a moment after, because what I really mean is "She is my father."

By making a home for her, I've given abode to my father as well: reconciling difference, settling transgressions, allowing things between us to be over and done. Should I enliven old wounds with resentment or rumination, I only kick myself.

I can answer my mother and the others now. I am saved, the rift restored. In that reunion, I do not fashion my father as better or worse, not into a midget or a monster, but leave him unencumbered, with his dog and his daughter, at peace, unleashed forever in a field of love and forgetting.

Forgiveness Is Our True Nature

Ezra Bayda

People often say that it's impossible to forgive others until we forgive ourselves. Yet, according to Ezra Bayda, that formula is a little too pat. The heart of the matter is that there is no solid self. There is no self forgiving another self. Waking from this illusion, we step into the universal heart: the essential fact of our basic connectedness. We discover that forgiveness is our true nature.

What does it mean to forgive? Is there someone you don't want to forgive?

Forgiveness is often tainted with the idea that there should be some form of magnanimous acceptance of others even though they did us wrong. This understanding of forgiveness is not what a forgiveness practice is about. Forgiveness is about practicing with and healing resentment, the resentment that blocks our desire to live from our true nature. Forgiveness is about loosening our hold on the one thing we most want to hold on to—the suffering of resentment.

In forgiveness practice, we work to see through our own emotional reactions. We practice noticing what stands in the way of real forgiveness. Genuine forgiveness entails experiencing our own pain and then the pain of the person to be forgiven. This experience can help dissolve the illusion of separation between ourselves and others.

Think of someone you feel anger, bitterness, or resentment toward: your mate, your parents (living or dead), one of your children, your teacher, your boss, a friend—anyone about whom there is active agitation in your heart. To make your understanding of forgiveness practice more experiential, keep this person in mind as you read this chapter.

When you bring this person to mind, how does it feel? Holding on to resentment often has the feeling of an unsettled account: "So-and-so has hurt me; therefore, they somehow owe me." As we cling to the hard, bitter feeling that someone owes us, we may also feel the need to pay this person back. As resentment festers, the attitude of "I'll show them!" takes over and hardens us. We shore up our hardened heart with the sense of false power and righteousness that arises with resentment.

If someone were to ask a spiritual teacher, "What should I do with all of this resentment I feel against my friend?" the teacher might respond, "It's not good to hold on to resentment. Why don't you just let it go?" But can we just let it go? Even when we know how much resentment hurts us, we often don't have that option. If we could just let it go, we wouldn't be stuck in the throes of resentment. Letting go is not a real practice. It's a fantasy practice based on an ideal of how we'd like things to be.

Genuine forgiveness has three stages. The first is simply acknowledging how unwilling we are to forgive the other. We let ourselves experience the degree to which we prefer to hold on to our resentment, anger, and bitterness, even when we see how it closes us to living a genuine life. We see how we resist our inherent openness by choosing to stay stuck in our hardness. By bringing nonjudgmental awareness to how we resist forgiveness, we see clearly, not in order to feel guilty—which would be the result if we were living from the ideal that we shouldn't be resentful—but to enable us to experience resistance for what it is. We have to experience in our body how our unwillingness to forgive feels. We have to see our self-centered judgments clearly as thoughts, rather than accepting them as objective truths. Staying with the physical experience of resistance allows a sense of spaciousness to gradually develop, within which the tight fist of our resentment can be loosened. We can't move on to the second stage of forgiveness until we've entered into and experienced—in both our bodies and minds—the depth of our unwillingness to forgive.

The second stage is bringing awareness to the emotional reactivity toward the person we resent: to experience it without judgment, to see it with an open mind. As we visualize the person we resent, we notice what emotional reactions arise. We ask, "What is this?" Is it anger, resentment, bitterness, fear, grief? Whatever arises, we just experience it within our body. If we get lost in thoughts, memories, or justifications, we keep coming back to what we feel in the body. Where is the tightness, the contraction? What's the texture of the feeling? We stay with the awareness of our physical-emotional reactions as long as it takes to reside in them. That means relaxing into them, as painful as they are. At some point we no longer need to push them away.

Let's say we've been criticized repeatedly by someone. Instead of sulking or lashing back in reactivity, we remember the practice path. First we feel the anger and resentment rising. Next we listen to and label our thoughts: "Why do you always have to put me down?" "You're such a negative person." "No one should have to put up with this." Then we move from thinking and blaming into locating the resentment in our body. We feel the tightness in the mouth, the heaviness in the shoulders, the ache in the heart, the rigidity of the muscles. Staying with the physical experience, striving to avoid getting hooked into thoughts of self-justification and blame, we ask, "What is this?" We come back again and again to the physical reality of the moment. At this point we're not even entertaining thoughts of forgiveness; we're just bringing awareness to our suffering without trying to push it away. Once we can rest like this in our bodily experience, we're ready for the third stage.

The third stage of a forgiveness practice is to say words of forgiveness. It's important to realize that saying these words has nothing to do with condoning the actions of another. It's about forgiving the person, not what they did. It means seeing that the action came from the person's own pain. And the way we do this isn't by looking for the other's pain but by attending to our own. Once we've attended to our own, we're more open to truly seeing the other's. At this point, saying words of forgiveness helps us open into the heart. Trying to open to the other's pain before passing through the first two stages of forgiveness practice—clearly seeing our resistance and resting in our experience of it—won't work; then we're just adding cosmetic mental constructs over our suppressed feelings.

Only after we've experienced how our own emotional reactivity stands in the way of real forgiveness can we truly understand that the other was just mechanically acting, in the only way a person can, out of beliefs and conditioning. We can then say the words:

> I forgive you.
> I forgive you for whatever you may have done from which I
>   experienced pain.
> I forgive you because I know that what you did came from
>   your own pain.

In speaking of a poem he had written, the Vietnamese monk and Zen meditation teacher Thich Nhat Hanh recalled a letter about a twelve-year-old girl, one of thousands of Vietnamese boat people, who had thrown herself into the ocean after being raped by a sea pirate. This letter ignited so much rage in him that he wanted to get a gun and kill the pirate. At the same time he realized how easy it was to think only of the victim, not of the rapist. In no way was he condoning the sea pirate's act; he was pointing to the fact that when our hearts are closed, we're all capable of thinking, feeling, and doing horrible things. He called the poem "Please Call Me by My True Names," as a reminder that we must acknowledge all of our names, not just the ones we like to identify with. This is how we can access those closed-hearted parts of ourselves that we otherwise rarely encounter. In so doing, we can come closer to genuine compassion and forgiveness.

A few years ago I watched a TV documentary about the decision to drop the atomic bomb during World War II. My understanding had been that the decision was made to avoid losing over one hundred thousand men in a land invasion of Japan. Whether or not I agreed with this rationale, at least it had some merit. But the film pointed out that Japan had tried to surrender shortly before the bomb was dropped, approaching Russia as a third party to broker peace with the Allies. President Truman and his advisers decided not to negotiate, refusing even to hear the terms of surrender before they dropped the bomb. Dropping the bomb wasn't just about ending the war and saving American lives; it was also about showing Russia who carried the biggest stick. At that point in the program, I had such a strong reaction that I had to turn the television off. I felt tremendous self-righteous indignation against the people I had once believed were at least acting from some positive moral position.

In practicing with the rage—experiencing my own anger without the blaming thoughts—I remembered what Thich Nhat Hanh had said about his poem. I realized, experientially, that I was not so different from President Truman or his advisers. Nor was I different from those who dropped the bomb, or from the millions of people who cheered when they heard the news that a bomb was dropped on Japan. This was a sobering moment for me, considering that countless people were killed, and the suffering that was caused still reverberates. Whether or not the documentary had the facts straight, my self-righteous belief-based rage was as solid as a rock. In looking at my anger and opening to what had appeared to be so abhorrent, I saw that the fear-based, narrowly patriotic stance that had resulted in the death of so many wasn't really foreign to me at all. In fact, that conditioned trait was equally present in me.

This realization came from experiencing and seeing through my own anger. This is an important point. It's easy to comprehend intellectually that others are acting from their own protectedness and pain, and that we share with them certain traits that we prefer not to see in ourselves. But such conceptual understanding doesn't really touch our lives. It can never lead to the compassionate and genuine forgiveness that's possible once we've practiced with our own closed-heartedness and seen through it.

In practicing forgiveness, it is possible to move from living in our own isolated pain—which usually manifests as anger and resentment—to experiencing the universal pain that we all share. This suffering is what we realize experientially when we're able to see that we're not essentially different from those we've been quick to judge. Experiencing the truth of suffering frees us to move into the universal heart: the essential fact of our basic connectedness. In this place, the illusions that lead us to think we are separate and protected selves naturally dissolve. We no longer view the world through the lens of "us" versus "them." We no longer perceive the other as an enemy. We no longer seek revenge for what we regard as wrongdoing. We no longer demand recompense.

To enter into the process of forgiveness at this level, where the illusion of separation between self and other begins to dissolve, is a profoundly transformative practice. It's also challenging, partly because we don't want to do it and partly because entering into our own pain is never easy. It is rare that the transformation of resentment occurs in just one or two sittings. If the resentment is deep, it may take months. Timing is also an important element. Sometimes the pain is too raw; we have to wait until the feelings are less intense.

It's sometimes said that you can't forgive others until you forgive yourself. While that sounds good, the formula is just a little too pat. It's a partial truth that misses the heart of the matter. What is this "self" that we must first forgive? There is no one solid self. This illusion of the self is the essence of the self-centered dream. Real forgiveness is our true nature; it's not about one "self" forgiving another "self." This experiential understanding becomes apparent when we no longer believe in the illusion of the self. So instead of formulating notions of forgiving ourselves before or after forgiving others, we simply direct our healing awareness toward what is. We focus on wherever we feel resentment and whomever we can't forgive.

Even though it's some of the most important work we can do, forgiveness is one of the practices we least want to work with. Remembering the words traditionally posted at the entrance of Zen temples can be helpful:

Let us be respectfully reminded:
Life and death are of supreme importance.
Time swiftly passes by
and with it our only chance.
Each of us must aspire to awaken.
Be aware: Do not squander your life.

These words point to the folly of our upside-down way of thinking, of the magnitude of our constant decisions to let emotional reactions like resentment close us down. As we feel the pain of our hardness, and as the consequences of our unwillingness to open really hit us, perhaps we'll be more motivated to begin the essential work of forgiveness.

After an Unspeakable Crime

Judith Toy

Judith Toy recalls her struggle to make sense of the murder of three family members, finding Zen and forgiveness along the way.

> How can there be laughter,
> How can there be pleasure,
> When the whole world
> Is burning? When you
> Are in deep darkness,
> Will you not ask for a lamp?
> —THE DHAMMAPADA

The first time I felt any relief from the sorrow that enshrouded me after three members of my family were murdered was six months later when I was meditating with Dai-En Bennage in the Endless Mountains.

Connie, my daughters' favorite aunt, and her teenage sons, Allen and Bobby, were bludgeoned and stabbed to death in their home by the boy across the street in an upscale Pennsylvania neighborhood in October 1990. The killer also raped Connie. After the shock waves that started with the phone call that brought the terrible news, the first feeling I can remember was one of culpability. What did I or my family do to bring this upon us? The guilt was subtle, but it lay there, in the dark pool of my grief.

The following April, exhausted, I sought solace at Dai-En Bennage's zendo, an apartment in a Quaker-built manor known as Mt. Equity, in Pennsdale. My husband and I were Quakers and had been introduced to Bennage through our Friends Meeting. I fell in love with her at first sight. She had just returned from more than twenty years in Japan, the first woman and the first foreigner to complete the advanced teacher training of the Soto Zen sect in that country. Her face beamed when she smiled. She was ebullient, smart, disciplined, and meticulous.

I told her that during meditation there were voices in my head uttering stern biblical warnings about false images. She responded by offering to put her Buddha statue in a drawer, and I became her first overnight student in America. It was the beginning of my journey from hatred to healing.

Twenty years later, even through the lens of Zen, it is still hard to tell this story, and I have changed some names and places to protect those involved. It feels like I'm peering through a telescope underwater: The way my daughter Rachel had said just weeks before the murders, "Mom, I don't know what I'd do without Aunt Connie. She's always there when I need her." The way I woke up from a dream the night after it happened, feeling a sharp blow to my head. The way I overheard neighbors talk about a young cop at the scene who got sick. The black four-inch headlines in the tabloids at the local grocery store. Photographers hiding behind trees at the funeral; the three coffins in a row.

Connie had felt a motherly concern for Charles, the latchkey kid across the street. After school, while Charles and her son Allen tinkered under the hood of Allen's Lumina, which had been left to him by his father, not long dead of cancer, Connie would appear in the doorway of the garage with a smile and a tray of snacks and ginger ale.

The night of the murders, Charles hid, crouched in the dark of the same garage, waiting for them to return from a trip to the seashore, to go to bed and sleep. There had been no angry words among the boys. Charles had been in the top 2 percent of his high school class the year before—a quiet, scholarly boy headed for an engineering major at Drexel University—until he dropped out three weeks before graduation. He stopped cutting his hair and stopped shaving. What happened that turned him into a monster? No one knew then that he had been stalking the neighborhood at night for a year.

When he was certain they were asleep, he crept upstairs and murdered them one at a time in their beds with a hammer and a knife. Then he slid into the seat of the Lumina, his getaway car. Charles took the family TV, some clothing, a cache of Connie's makeup, some jewelry, and Bobby's Nintendo set. The cash value of his take, the only motive anyone could ascribe to the murders, was about five hundred dollars.

With the bloody murder weapons in the trunk, he drove to Fort Lauderdale, Florida, to see friends, including his fifteen-year-old girlfriend, Leeanne. He told her the story of the murders in detail: how he had planned and carried them out, the order in which he had killed his victims, how Bobby had cried out to his mother for help—and how he was planning to return to Pennsylvania to kill his own parents and grandmother. Leeanne called the police. Officers took her to the Fort Lauderdale station and videotaped her as she recounted Charles's story and applied Connie's stolen lipstick to her own lips. Charles was arrested and brought back to the county seat in Pennsylvania, where the district attorney was obliged to beef up security to protect him from an angry mob when he arrived at three in the morning. How hatred begets hatred: the district attorney remembers a woman screaming, "Fry him! Fry him!" Charles's parents became instant pariahs.

Our family was unanimous in not wanting Charles dead—but not out of idealism or pacifism. We wanted him to suffer long and hard behind bars. For the rest of his days, we reasoned, he should face what he had wrought.

We were spared being in the same room as the killer and reliving over and over the horror of the murders when, during the first day of the trial, Charles confessed to all three. The judge gave him three consecutive life sentences with no chance of parole.

That was December, and the following April, I went to see Dai-En Bennage at Mt. Equity Zendo. I had stumbled into meditation in the seventies through the Hermann Hesse book *Siddhartha* but hadn't the slightest idea what I was doing. Bennage showed me how to hold my body and what to do with my breath and my tongue and my chin and my mind. She told me, "What you feel is damning you, can set you free." She told me the story of the monk on the side of the cliff—with a growling tiger above him and a spitting tiger below him—peacefully eating his strawberries. I began to believe that buried somewhere within me was the equanimity of that monk. One afternoon, among the green rolling hills at Mt. Equity, she offered me a cassette tape of a talk by Thich Nhat Hanh. The moment I heard his voice I knew I would follow him.

Can tragedy seed miracles? Perhaps—if we plow the ground. Sometimes, though, it takes a hit on the head, a shock, or a deep loss to crack us open just enough for understanding to grow. Five years after the fact—five years of daily sitting and breathing and bells and sitting and breathing and walking—I was still trying to understand. It was the autumn, around the anniversary time. I was working on a poem about the murders, and suddenly I inhabited Charles. That is, I lost any feeling of separation between us. There was no guilt, no sorrow, only what Thich Nhat Hanh calls "interbeing." The poem told me what I did not know I knew. In that moment of understanding and compassion, I knew in a profound way that Charles was not a monster but a boy in whom something had gone terribly wrong. This is because that is.

I wanted to tell him how I felt, but I hesitated. Perhaps part of me was still afraid. Before I could, he took a laundry bag and hanged himself in his prison cell. This brought everything back to me, and I was disconsolate. If I had gone to him, could I have saved his life?

Shortly after I was ordained by Thich Nhat Hanh as a member of his Order of Interbeing in 1997, a friend approached me. Her husband, Carl, was in a medium-security prison after being busted for growing marijuana in his attic in an effort to make enough money to keep his two girls in private Quaker schools. Carl had strong Buddhist leanings, and she asked whether I would visit him. After several months of visiting Carl in a closet-like space with a window in the door, inviting the sound of a small bell, smiling and breathing, he asked whether we could start a sangha.

Since I had just been ordained, I had the necessary credentials. The prison chaplain was a Methodist, my childhood tradition, and we saw eye to eye. We put up a poster that said "Still Your Mind and Open Your Heart," and fifteen guys signed up for our first gathering. My husband, Philip, said to me, "You're not going in there alone; I'm coming with you." Our Zen gig was wildly popular. Every week we would walk through several metal gates with a flower. Both the guards and the inmates would make fun of us. Charles had been held in the same facility, and, it turned out, some of the men had known him. We met there weekly for two and a half years before moving to North Carolina in 1999. The men came to call themselves Fragrant Lotus Petal Sangha. We always hugged at the end.

One of the inmates took to the practice like a monk; he called us after he was released and asked to receive Buddhist precepts. He secured permission from his halfway house, borrowed money from his grandmother for a Greyhound ticket to North Carolina, and arrived heavily dosed on antipsychotic meds. When I saw this great big, really scary-looking guy prostrate himself during the Order of Interbeing ceremony to receive the Five Mindfulness Trainings, my story came full circle. I felt absolved for not telling Charles I'd forgiven him. What Charles did was unforgivable. But he was forgivable. He had not become a monster in a vacuum.

The founder of Christian Science, Mary Baker Eddy, translated "Forgive us our trespasses as we forgive those who trespass against us" from the Lord's Prayer as "Love is reflected in love." That's the best explanation I can offer of what happened. Didn't the Buddha say it, too? Hatred never ceases through hatred: hatred only ceases through love.

The Practice of Forgiveness

Jack Kornfield

Forgiveness does not mean that you condone what happened. In fact, it often means that you will do whatever is necessary to make sure it never happens again—to yourself or anyone else. In the end, says Jack Kornfield, forgiveness simply means not putting anyone out of your heart. Those who practice forgiveness know it is an act of courage.

As human beings, we are guaranteed at one time or another to suffer from betrayal, conflict, loss, and physical and emotional pain. We suffer betrayal and conflict in our families and communities. At times, these difficulties can feel insurmountable and we long for a way out of the suffering and conflict. The first step we need to take is to protect ourselves and others, to set limits, to minimize harm. Then what is also necessary for us to move forward through our pain is forgiveness—of ourselves and others, and of the events that have caused our suffering.

It's important to remember that forgiveness doesn't happen all at once. You can't achieve forgiveness by covering up your genuine hurt feelings. There are times when it is important to fully experience feelings of grief and rage and despair and pain before we can move on. Sometimes there are also events in your life that you believe to be absolutely unforgivable. But sooner or later, for your own good, your heart will realize that it needs to let go. As my friend and teacher Maha Ghosananda, the Gandhi of Cambodia, said to the Cambodian refugees who had suffered enormously, "Remember these teachings from Buddha, 'Hatred never ceases by hatred, but by love alone is healed. This is the ancient and eternal law.'"

This instruction appeals to the nobility of our hearts. To find peace we must first bring an end to hatred through love. "Oh nobly born," say the Buddhist texts, "remember who you really are. Know that a great and forgiving heart lies within you too." There is an awareness inside of us— even in those who experienced the horrors of the Khmer Rouge and the killing fields in Cambodia—that as long as we harbor anger and resentment in our hearts we will never find peace. Without forgiveness, we are trapped in the past, carrying forward and repeating the sufferings we've experienced, from generation to generation. Without forgiveness, the Northern Irish Protestants and Catholics have continued their battles for centuries. Without forgiveness, the Hutus and Tutsis in Rwanda, the Bosnians and Serbs and Croats, the Palestinians and Israelis, will continue to sentence their children and their children's children to generations of suffering and conflict. To free ourselves, each of us will have to say, "These cycles of suffering and retribution stop here, with me. I refuse to pass this suffering on to my children."

In this way, forgiveness is not primarily for others but for ourselves. It is a release of our burdens, a relief to our hearts. A story I like to tell is about two ex–prisoners of war who met again years later. One said to the other, "Have you forgiven our captors yet?" And the second one answered through gritted teeth, "No, never." With this the first one looked at him kindly and said, "Well then, they still have you in prison, don't they?" When we learn to forgive, we can let go of what is holding us back and move on with our lives. Forgiveness means giving up all hope for a better past.

Forgiveness is not a single act but a practice that one undertakes, sometimes over a long period of time. When one of my teachers taught me forgiveness practice, he said, "Why don't you try it twice a day for five minutes, then after six months, let me know how it's going." I found that my understanding of this practice changed and deepened month by month. By the time the six months were completed, I realized that my teacher had asked me to practice forgiveness over three hundred times before I evaluated its effects.

What I discovered by practicing forgiveness over this period of time was that sometimes I felt true forgiveness in my heart, and sometimes I felt its opposite: deep resentment that I refused to let go. Sometimes I experienced pain, and at other times I was overcome with rage and anger. But eventually tears would come that brought emotional healing. And little by little, the way water wears away a stone, the pain in my heart melted.

It is important to understand that forgiveness does not mean that you condone what happened. In fact, it often means that you have to do what is necessary to make sure it never happens again—to yourself or anyone else. But in the end, forgiveness also means not putting anyone out of your heart. Those who practice forgiveness know it is an act of courage. As the *Bhagavad Gita* says, "If you want to see the brave, look to those who can forgive."

I remember some years ago riding on the train from Washington, D.C., to Philadelphia to attend my father's memorial service. I sat down next to an elegantly dressed man who told me in our conversation that he had quit his work for the State Department to work with youth in the inner city. His main project was to work with young men who were accused of murder.

Then he told me a story.

One young boy, just fourteen years old, wanted to become part of an inner-city gang. In order to initiate himself into the gang, he went out and shot another teenager his own age. He was subsequently caught and arrested for the murder and, after a time, was brought to trial. He was convicted, and just before he was taken off to prison, the mother of the young man who'd been murdered stood up in the courtroom, looked him square in the eye, and said, "I'm gonna kill you." And then he was led off in handcuffs.

While he was incarcerated, the mother of the young man who had been killed came to visit him. He was shocked and surprised. During her first visit she talked to him for a little while, and later she came back and brought him some things he needed—a little money to buy things in prison, some writing materials—and began to visit him regularly. And over the next three or four years, as he served his sentence, she would come visit him regularly.

When the time came for him to be released, she asked him what he planned on doing when he got out of jail. He had no idea. "Where are you going to work?" she asked him. He didn't know. So she told him, "I've got a friend who has a little business—maybe you could get a job there." And then she asked, "Where are you gonna live?" And he said, "I don't know. I didn't have much of a family even before I came in here." And she said, "Well, you can come and stay with me. I've got a spare room." And so the young man moved into her home and began to work at the job that she had found for him.

After about six months, she called him into the living room, sat him down, and said, "I need to talk to you." He said, "Yes, ma'am." She looked at him and said, "Remember that day in court when you were convicted of murdering my only child?" He said, "Yes, ma'am." She said, "Remember I stood up and I said, 'I'm going to kill you'?" He said, "Yes, ma'am." "Well, I have. I set about changing you. I came to visit you over and over and brought you things, and made friends with you. And when you got out, I took care of you and got you a job and a place to live, because I didn't want the kind of boy who could coldly murder my son to still be alive on this Earth. And I've done it. You're not that boy anymore. But now I have no son and I've got no one and here you are and I wonder if you'd stay with me and live with me for a time. I can finish raising you as my son and I'd like to adopt you, if you'd let me." And she became the mother of her son's killer, the mother he never had.

For most of us, forgiveness will not be so dramatic, but in small ways and large, we all need to find the healing waters of forgiveness. We must start where we are: our own body and spirit and heart. However we can, we need to forgive, to wash away the anger and guilt and blame that we carry. And once we've learned how to forgive ourselves, we will be able to ask forgiveness from others for the ways we've harmed them out of our ignorance and suffering. And then we will be able to look with the genuine eyes of mercy upon those who have hurt us out of their own pain and ignorance, their anger and confusion. In that moment we will understand the true gifts and purpose of forgiveness—that it is never too late to forgive, that forgiveness is the only medicine that can release us from the past and allow us to truly begin anew.

Meditation Practice

Sit in a comfortable position. Allow your eyes to close gently. Rest for a moment and allow yourself to relax. When you are ready to begin, become aware of your breath and breathe for a few minutes as if you were breathing gently in and out of your heart. Now let yourself feel the emotions you still carry and the barriers you've erected within your heart because you have not forgiven. Some are the result of not forgiving others, and some are from not yet being able to forgive yourself. Let yourself feel the pain and constriction that comes from keeping your heart closed. As you breathe gently, follow the three steps of the practice of forgiveness.

First, asking forgiveness from others:

Reflect: "There are many ways that I have hurt and harmed others, betrayed them, abandoned them, caused them suffering or pain, knowingly or unknowingly. I remember these injuries now."

Let yourself visualize and remember the ways you've caused harm to others—one or two particular incidents or any number of them. Take as much time as you need to picture whatever memories burden your heart. Remember as well how much of your actions came from your own pain and confusion, your hurt and fear. Now allow yourself to feel the genuine sorrow and regret and pain you still carry. When you are ready, realize that you are finally able to release this burden and ask for forgiveness. After a few more breaths, silently repeat to yourself, "In the ways that I have caused sorrow for you, knowingly or unknowingly, out of my own fear and confusion, out of my anger and hurt and suffering, I ask your forgiveness. Forgive me. Please forgive me." As you ask for this forgiveness, gradually let yourself receive the blessing of forgiveness. Allow yourself to make amends, to let go, to move on with a heart freed from this burden. Sense that you can be forgiven.

The second direction of forgiveness is forgiveness for harming yourself:

Just as we have caused suffering to others, there are many ways that we have hurt and harmed ourselves. We hurt ourselves at the same time we hurt others. And in many other ways we also abandon and betray ourselves. Now remember the many ways that you've caused pain and suffering to yourself. You have harmed yourself, knowingly and unknowingly, in thought or word or deed. Feel the cost of this self-betrayal. Sense the ways you judge yourself about what you've done, recognize the pain, the sorrow, and the shame that you still carry in your body, heart, and mind. Realize that you are ready to release these burdens.

As you remember them, extend forgiveness for each act of harm in this simple way: "For the ways I've hurt myself, betrayed or abandoned myself, caused myself pain as I have to others at times, through action or inaction, out of fear, confusion, hurt, anger, and ignorance, I now extend forgiveness to myself. I hold myself with mercy and tenderness. I forgive myself." If it's helpful, you can place your hand on your heart to literally hold yourself with forgiveness at this point. Then continue to repeat, "In the ways that I have caused pain and suffering out of my ignorance and fear, out of hurt and confusion, I offer myself forgiveness."

Let the healing balm of forgiveness touch every part and cell of your body. Let it wash over every story and feeling you hold in your heart. Ease your mind into the great heart of forgiveness. Breathe gently and continue this practice as long as you need to.

The third direction of forgiveness is forgiveness of those who have hurt or harmed you:

In this practice, it is very important not to be hurried, nor to expect that you can or should forgive others right away. For a time, the practice of forgiveness can bring up its opposite. You can experience layers of grief and rage and tears and sorrow and shame. Hold whatever happens during this part of the meditation with tenderness and forgiveness and mercy. And let this practice be a process of purification that will, little by little, cleanse your heart so that when you are ready, you will be able to release the past and forgive even those who have harmed you, so that you can move on freely with your own life.

Begin this practice by repeating silently, "There are many ways that I have been hurt or harmed by others, abused, abandoned, and betrayed—knowingly and unknowingly. I remember these occasions now." Visualize the times in the past that you have been hurt by others, and feel the pain and sorrow you still carry. Then sense the burden of this pain you carry and resolve to release it by gradually extending your forgiveness to others as your heart is ready. When you are ready, repeat silently, "I remember the many ways in which you have hurt or wounded or harmed me, abandoned or betrayed me. I know that you acted this way out of your own fear and pain, out of your hurt and anger and confusion. I've carried this pain in my heart long enough. To the extent that I am ready, I offer forgiveness to you who have caused me harm. I release you, I forgive you. As best as I can, I will not put anyone out of my heart. I will release the past and start anew. While I cannot condone what you did and will do everything in my power to make sure no one is harmed by you again, now in this moment, I release you. I offer you forgiveness, so that I can move on."

Breathing gently into the area of the heart, continue with this third practice of forgiveness as long as it is helpful to you. Again and again, in a gentle and courageous way, liberate your heart, as you liberate others.

A Lesson for the Living

Stan Goldberg

As a hospice volunteer, Stan Goldberg comes face-to-face with the pain of someone who desperately wants forgiveness before he dies. Life doesn't last forever, Goldberg learns. If we've done something to hurt others or if others have hurt us, now is the time to ask for forgiveness.

There's a presumption when you're asking for forgiveness that you did something wrong. Until getting cancer, I was reluctant to ask for forgiveness. I might halfheartedly admit that I "misinterpreted," said something "without thinking it through," or any of a dozen other rationalizations that allowed me not to use the words, "Please forgive me." I didn't realize what asking for forgiveness really meant until I met Jim.

My first shift as a hospice volunteer was scheduled for Thanksgiving at the Zen Hospice Project's Guest House in San Francisco. It was the Tuesday before Thanksgiving when I received an e-mail from the volunteer coordinator. Jim, one of the residents, was becoming confused, restless, and anxious. The coordinator asked if any volunteers could stay the night with him. Volunteer shifts normally end at 10:00 P.M., and with only one attendant on the floor at night, someone needed to be at his side from 10:00 P.M. to nine in the morning, when volunteers returned.

Since I'd already be there, I thought a few more hours wouldn't be a big deal. When I discussed it with my wife, Wendy, she asked if I was sure I wanted to do that, as this was my first hospice experience since completing my training.

"Of course," I responded. "What difference would a few more hours make?" I was still minimizing the lingering effects I felt from my cancer treatments. I could tell Wendy was concerned, but given our history (she usually wanted to discuss my feelings about the cancer and I usually refused), she didn't persist. I called the hospice attendant to let her know I would take the Thursday overnight shift.

"What can you tell me about Jim?" I asked.

"He's sixty-seven and was a heroin addict on and off since age seventeen," she said. "The last time he was using was about five years ago." There was a pause and I could hear her turning pages.

"I'm looking at his chart and see he doesn't get along with most people. Scares them actually. He's quiet during the day," she continued, "but at night he becomes a different person. We think it's the toxic chemicals his liver is producing. You know, he has hepatitis C."

I didn't expect that my first patient would be contagious and I'd need to use every universal precaution I had been taught. Unfortunately, I didn't remember all of them. How do you take the gloves off? Do you turn them inside out with a free pinky, or was it a thumb? What do you do if there is contact? Until then, dealing with a contagious person had been theoretical. Now it was someone with a name, and the only thing separating us would be a thin layer of latex and as much physical distance as I could create without being embarrassed.

"After ten, he enters another world," the attendant said. "Two things happened last night. The first was he left his room, yelling 'Deuce.'"

"Who's Deuce?"

"When I asked him, he said Deuce was his drug dealer. Then it got really strange. After I got him back into bed and left the room, he called me back and pleaded that I ask them to let him go."

"Who?" I asked.

"He said the bakery workers wouldn't let him leave because he hadn't finished baking something. In a loud voice I said, 'Let Jim leave!' It didn't help. He kept repeating that they wouldn't let him leave until his bread was baked."

She continued talking, but I heard little. Her story of Jim and the bakery had reminded me that I'd offered to bake bread for the Thanksgiving dinner.

I drove to the House in the afternoon on that warm Thanksgiving day. The Guest House was a Victorian home that maintained its 1850s splendor while surrounded by similar houses that had seen their prime decades before. There was nothing on its exterior that hinted about the remarkable things occurring inside. The only sign was a small bronze plaque next to the front door that stated this was a historical building.

I opened the unlocked door and smelled roasting turkey. I saw about ten people, each doing something related to dinner. The living room was transformed into a festive dining area with a large table in the center, covered with a purple tablecloth that shimmered as you passed by it. In the center was a beautiful flower arrangement, and on the mantel were at least forty cards with names written in calligraphy. Forty? I didn't realize there would be that many at the meal. As I wondered if I'd baked enough bread, people greeted me. Some I knew, others were staff I'd seen but never met. An older woman, wearing a colorful vest that was probably vintage 1970s, offered to take the bread into the kitchen. It was still warm, and the smell stunned her. She called other people over to share the experience. One was a resident who had non-Hodgkin's lymphoma. He was a huge man with letters tattooed on each of his fingers, from when he had been in San Quentin; sideburns down to his jawline; and a straggly mustache. I expected a deep rumbling to come out of his mouth, but his voice was amazingly soft as he told me his name, Paul, and then he introduced me to June, his wife. Although shorter than Paul, June blocked out his silhouette when she stepped in front of him. She immediately embraced me in a bear hug, kissing me as if I were a favorite nephew.

When June released me and moved to the side, I saw someone insisting on walking down from the second floor. His gaunt face was covered by a gray mustache and beard, his long thinning hair was tied in a ponytail, and his jeans were bunched in the front so they wouldn't fall off. After four steps, he couldn't move. Exhausted, he slowly sank onto a stair. It brought back memories of walking down the stairs in my house for the first time after having surgery for cancer, each step sending a sharp pain through my body.

"Jim, would you like help coming down?" the woman in the vest asked from downstairs.

With his eyes closed and his upper body held upright by two volunteers, he nodded his head yes. They raised him and using a fireman's carry brought him down the remaining ten steps. After they gently lowered Jim into a wheelchair, he rested his chin on his chest. When his breathing slowed, he was wheeled into the dining room, and a chair next to where I sat was removed. The table had twelve place settings precisely laid out as if on a grid. I wondered where the other twenty-eight people were and where they would sit. I waited for Jim to turn in my direction, but he didn't.

"Hi, Jim," I finally said. The disease had so ravaged him, he was unable to move his head. He turned his upper body to see me, and our eyes met. He stared without blinking, without expressing anything. I thought his look was imploring me to say or do something. But what? The best I could say was, "I'm Stan. I'll be staying with you through the night. This is my first shift at the House, so if I screw up, please let me know."

He leaned toward me and in a barely audible voice said, "There's no way you can make as many mistakes as I have. Don't sweat it."

Shortly afterward, the remaining ten people sat down and someone suggested we remember those who had died at the Guest House over the past few months. He gestured toward the place cards on the mantel. During the silent meditation period, I didn't think about the names. Instead, memories of my parents' deaths flashed back, along with frightening images of what my own might look like. After we finished, Jim turned back to his food and tried to pick up a fork. Although he could hold it, his fingers didn't have the strength to grasp it firmly, and it dropped to the floor. The person next to him, who was talking to someone across the table, took another fork without stopping his conversation and picked up a small amount of sweet potatoes. As he raised it, Jim opened his mouth and smiled at the volunteer. I looked around the table and saw that nobody showed any interest in what was occurring, as if this were common.

After eating a few bites of sweet potatoes and ice cream, Jim slowly hunched over. Was he dying right here in front of me? No one seemed concerned until someone casually asked him if he'd like to go back to his room. He nodded yes and was wheeled to the steps.

It was about eight when dinner was over. Everyone left except the attendant, Evan, and one other volunteer, Gary. Evan went upstairs to be with the residents while Gary and I finished cleaning. When we were done, we were expected to go upstairs and spend time with the residents. When I asked the volunteer coordinator before my shift began what I should be doing, she said, "Just be present." Although I nodded, signaling that I understood, I didn't.

I realized I was repeatedly vacuuming the same spot on the rug, dragging out the cleaning as long as I could. Downstairs, there was distance between Jim and me. It felt safe. Upstairs, well, I didn't know how I was going to be "present."

As I climbed the stairs, the food odors faded, gradually overpowered by the smell of disinfectant. I asked Evan for the notes kept on each resident. I read that Jim only left his room when he had the strength. Since the prior week, he'd been downstairs just once. Only a few people had come to visit since he'd arrived two months ago. And he was becoming combative and increasingly incontinent. Bowel movements were loose because of the colitis, and he often couldn't get to the commode in time, or when he was delirious, he forgot to take off his pants and diaper.

I entered Jim's room and saw him sitting on a recliner with his eyes closed. According to Evan, Jim hadn't slept in his bed for two days. He preferred to sleep fully clothed on the recliner. I looked at the bed with its quilt and puffed-up pillows, trying to imagine how many people had died in it over the seventeen-year existence of the Guest House.

"Hi Jim," I said, sitting in a chair three feet away from him. He said something, but I couldn't hear what it was. I moved the chair closer and said, "Is there anything I can get you?"

He shook his head no. "Anything I can do for you?" Again, a no. I noticed he was wearing dress shoes covering socks whose elastic tops were indenting his skin. "Those shoes and socks look uncomfortable. Would you like me to take them off?" I asked.

He shook his head no, then slowly turned to me and waited until I moved even closer. Reluctantly, I placed my ear a few inches from his mouth and wondered if he'd spray me with saliva.

"They pinch my toes," he said, barely above a whisper.

"If they pinch your toes, why don't you want them off?"

"It keeps me awake."

I didn't know if he wanted to stay awake because he feared dying if he fell asleep or because he wanted to talk. If it was the first, I didn't think

I was ready for it. If it was the second, I'd be less concerned but unsure how to talk to him. Despite the role-playing we did in training, I felt like a teenager on a blind date. Our conversation began easily enough with my asking him how long he'd been at the House. He said three months. He asked me how long I'd been doing this. I said, "Since dinner." He laughed. But as his laugh changed into a cough, I held my breath. When he finally stopped, I inhaled.

For a while, the easy talk continued. I asked how he liked the food. He said, "It depends upon who's cooking." He asked me how old I was. I said almost fifty-eight. Then after some more small talk came a shift in the conversation's tone when I asked him how old he was. "I'm sixty-seven and won't see sixty-eight." I tried changing the direction of the conversation. As a new hospice volunteer, I still wasn't comfortable talking about death. I asked how long he lived on the streets. "More than anyone should have to," he said. He was as persistent as a telemarketer trying to get you to buy penny stocks. I realized that no matter what I would say, he would pull me back to what he wanted to talk about, not just the facts of his life, which on their own were frightening enough, but how he was feeling about his dying. Reluctantly, I gave in and asked about his pain. He told me that with enough morphine, even the worst eventually went away. I nodded my head, agreeing.

"How do you know about morphine?" he asked.

"I have prostate cancer. They gave it to me last year after surgery."

Jim wanted to know if I had family. Yes, I said. A wife and two adult children. I was no longer holding my breath as he spoke, and my chair was now touching the recliner. We were speaking with just inches separating our heads when he fell asleep. Earlier, I read in the notes that he often did this—fell asleep, eyes wide open, then started speaking when he woke as if there had never been an interlude. I sat and waited.

Ten minutes later he said, "How old?"

"My son's twenty-two and my daughter's twenty-six."

"How did you tell them about the cancer?" Although it had been a year, I still wasn't comfortable talking about those conversations.

"It was hard," I said.

Jim kept looking at me as if he were waiting for more. I saw that his eyes were glistening.

"Do you have any kids?" I asked. One girl, he told me, who hadn't visited. Jim didn't think his daughter knew he was dying.

"I haven't seen her in five years. She's in Illinois."

"Would you like to see her?"

As he nodded his head yes, the hints of moisture cascaded down his cheeks.

"Can anyone get in touch with her?"

"Her mother, but she won't do it. They don't speak. We don't speak." There was a long pause, and then he said, "I need to ask her to forgive me."

I asked him if he would like us to see if we could contact his daughter. With closed eyes he nodded his head yes, then slowly exhaled. When he fell asleep, I went outside the room and asked Evan if Jim ever talked about his daughter.

"No," he said. "This is significant. I'll see what I can find out after my shift is over. Then we'll try to call her."

I went back into the room and sat next to Jim as he slept. I thought about the times when I could have sabotaged my relationship with my children. I remembered when my son was nine and I was under stress. I was directing a university program and enlarging my private practice. Between the two, I had little time for my family. As my son and I were walking together on a busy street near our house, he reached up and grabbed my hand. My thought was to withdraw it and lecture him that nine-year-olds don't hold their father's hand in public. When I looked down at his face, I realized he was using a physical connection to compensate for the emotional one I was denying him. I held his hand tighter and turned away before he saw my tears. What if I'd withdrawn my hand? Would Justin have become as distant as it appeared Jim's daughter was from him? And if I'd rejected him, how would I ask Justin, as an adult, to forgive me? I wondered how Jim would do it. What could have happened to make a daughter not want to have contact with her father for five years? And would the knowledge that her father was dying be enough to overcome it?

Jim woke again, and for the next three hours we talked as if we were lifelong friends sitting at a bar, delighted just to be with each other. Maybe this is what "being present" meant. He told me how he loved to sing classical music but that he could barely breathe anymore. I told him about my love of fly-fishing in remote areas, but because of my hormone treatments for the cancer I was too weak to go alone. Climbing steep canyons was no longer possible. Walking was even painful since I fractured my pelvis playing handball. I asked him if he'd like me to make French toast in the morning from the bread I baked. There was a long pause, and then he slowly turned so he was looking directly at me.

"You bake bread?"

"Yes, I do."

"What kind?"

"Well, for tonight's dinner I baked challah, egg bread."

"Can you get me the recipe?"

"Sure, I'll bring it in next week."

He leaned back on the recliner, remaining silent for about a minute. Then he inhaled as much as he could to complete another sentence. "I want to make that bread, but I know I can't."

"We'll do it together," I said with a quivering voice.

He closed his eyes, smiled, and quickly fell asleep. As I watched him, death became more real and frightening. It was in front of me in a body that was winding down and a brain that couldn't tell delusion from reality. I wondered if this was how I would die: watching my abilities fall away to the point where I couldn't even feed or wipe myself. My apprehension stopped when he woke.

"I'm hungry," Jim said.

Thank God! At least here's something simple. After all, how difficult can it be to feed someone?

"What would you like?" I asked.

"Ice cream."

"I'll go downstairs and see if there's any left."

The mantra at the Guest House was there are no emergencies in hospice. I was told people were there to die, not recover. In a hospital there's a sense of urgency when a life is in jeopardy. Here, everything moved slowly, deliberately, as if each moment was to be savored. But I forgot the mantra and painfully bounded down the stairs, each step reminding me that my reduced bone density was putting me at risk for another fracture. In the freezer were quart containers of chocolate and vanilla. Plenty to satisfy the small amount I thought he'd eat. I ran back up.

"There's chocolate and vanilla. Which do you want?" "Both." I went back down and put a large scoop of each in a bowl and again climbed the stairs. "I have both in this bowl. Which one would you like to start with?"

"Both."

I took a small portion of each on a spoon. "I'm going to feed you, so let me know if the amount is too large."

He nodded his head, and I slowly placed the spoon into his open mouth. He closed it, allowing the ice cream to slide off as I pulled out the spoon. His eyes closed, and he slowly moved his tongue from side to side. With each movement of his tongue, his smile grew. Sometimes it took thirty seconds before the ice cream was gone and he was ready for the next spoonful. It was something so simple, so pleasurable, I couldn't understand it. Pleasure for me had always been complicated. I felt it when I made a perfect cast to a fish hidden behind a rock as I stood in my favorite stream in Wyoming. I experienced it completing a poem in which I merged thoughts into a unified line. But that night, it was just the taste of ice cream that seemed to bring more joy to someone than I could have ever experienced through complex manipulations of either my body or my mind. We repeated the sequence for the next ten minutes until the bowl was empty.

"More please," he whispered.

I went downstairs, refilled the bowl, and we began again. After he finished, I sat next to him and tried to sleep when he did, propping my feet on a second chair. Shortly after one o'clock I felt a tapping on my shoulder. Irma, the late-night attendant, introduced herself. She gave Jim a dose of Roxanol, a liquid derivative of morphine.

"Lie down on the couch," the tiny older woman then said to me. She was less than five feet tall, and she spoke quietly, with a South American accent. "You sleep. He'll go to sleep now." I later learned that Irma had come to San Francisco from Bolivia forty years earlier, when she was in her midthirties. Most of us at the hospice thought of Irma as the caring grandmother we all dreamed of having.

"But if I sleep over there," I said, pointing to the couch on the other side of the room, "I won't hear him if he wakes."

"Don't worry. I'll be here," she said.

She pulled a blanket and pillow from a second bed in the alcove and placed them on the floor between the recliner where Jim slept and the door. She had been doing this since the previous week when Jim began wandering. He would often wake and try to walk quietly down the stairs. Irma couldn't watch him and take care of the other residents by herself. That's why people had volunteered to stay with him throughout the night—every night until he died.

"Sleep, sleep," Irma said to me. I didn't need any encouragement. She lay on the floor and I crunched sideways on the couch with a blanket pulled up to my head. I immediately fell asleep.

"I need your help," Irma said in a whisper, as she gently tapped my shoulder. I looked at the clock. It had been less than an hour. "I'm sorry, but he's had an accident."

Although I was groggy, I knew what she meant. I reached into my back pocket and pulled out the gloves. Across the room I saw Jim.

"I'm sorry, I'm sorry," he said, standing next to the recliner. "Goddamn it. Look what I did," he said, staring at his soiled jeans.

Earlier in the evening I wondered how I'd react to cleaning another person, especially someone contagious. Worse, would it be a preview of my future? Looking at Jim apologizing over and again, my fears and the odor that filled the room both disappeared. In their place, I saw someone devastated by one of the most embarrassing things an adult can do in the presence of other people.

"I'm sorry, I'm sorry. Look what I did," he repeated.

"It's all right Jim," I said. Irma and I helped him to the bed, where it would be easier to clean him. He stopped apologizing as she told him where to move his legs and what we'd be doing. Irma directed each of my movements like a choreographer preparing a child for his first dance recital. When I hesitated, she'd gently take my hands and place them where she wanted them.

It took almost thirty minutes to clean him, change his clothes, and replace the bed linens. When we began, my hands moved hesitantly, almost as if my fears pulled them back. But when I stopped trying to analyze everything and just let my concern for him lead me, a flowing rhythm developed. I didn't have to wonder if I was rubbing him too roughly or too lightly. It was as if I were transported back to when I changed my children's diapers, and my hands instinctively knew what to do.

Finally done, I slept on the couch until six, when Jim woke. He asked to go back to the recliner, and I gently led him there. He turned his body so he could look out the window on the other side of the room. It was a typical gray San Francisco morning.

"It's going to be a good day," he said, then fell back to sleep.

Evan came to the House at 8:00 A.M. even though his shift didn't start until late afternoon. He stood outside Jim's room and motioned to me. We walked down the hall so Jim wouldn't hear us.

"I asked the house manager about Jim's daughter," he whispered.

"Can we contact her?" I asked.

"No."

"Why not? He wants to see her."

"She said she died five years ago."

"But we talked about a daughter in Illinois. Are you sure there isn't another one?"

"No. That was Jim's only child. She's buried there. The family blames him for his daughter's death. Nobody here knows how it happened, and the family didn't want to talk about it."

At 9:00 A.M., after spending eighteen hours at the Guest House, I left to go home. The street seemed cleaner, the sky bluer, and I was becoming less afraid of my emotions. I confronted my fears of contagion and death that night, not by talking but by doing. I was experiencing Jim's dying, and I was imagining what might happen to me. I wondered if he agreed with his family and blamed himself? I was so overwhelmed by my experiences that I had to concentrate on remembering to stop at traffic lights and stay on the right side of the road as I drove. I felt as if I were dropped from a sensory deprivation chamber into the middle of a Rolling Stones concert. Only ten minutes more, then I'd be home.

"How was it?" Wendy asked as I walked through the door.

I couldn't speak. I started to cry and hugged her as my grown children looked on. After my night with Jim, I felt more alive than I ever had. During my shift, there wasn't time to think about the past or future. My mind remained in the present, unlike the previous six months, which I'd spent wallowing in the past, trying to relive experiences that I'd never have again, or leaping into the future, creating goals that would affirm a long life—one that I might not have.

For the next three weeks, I stayed overnight every Thursday after the end of my shift. One week, I stayed overnight on two consecutive days. Although there were peaceful times, Jim was acutely agitated at least half of the time. One night, he even tried to punch Irma when she was giving him morphine.

"Is that the best you can do?" he shouted as I caught a left hook before it could hit her face. I don't remember ever reacting so fast.

"Jim, it's me, Irma," she said to him sweetly, not flinching. Their faces were inches from each other as I struggled to hold back his arm. Instead of moving away, Irma kept talking. "Remember? You said I was like a grandmother to you. Remember?"

He looked at her intently. Finally, there was a look of recognition, then he said, "Hey, Irma. How are you, darling?" A smile came over his face, and I felt his muscles relax. Then I watched his eyes close.

This pattern repeated itself for the next few weeks. Jim became agitated, believing he was on the streets again, ready to fight all comers, whether they were imaginary street people trying to steal his stash or the little Bolivian grandmother who was trying to comfort him. When the delusions stopped, and if he was conscious, he apologized profusely, repeatedly asking everyone in the room to forgive him. As he ate less, his body began consuming its own fat, revealing a wiry, muscular physique. If you didn't know his condition, you might assume he was an aging boxer. Then, with little fat left, his muscle started breaking down.

Volunteers agreed to stay at his bedside twenty-four hours a day. The nurse told me the toxic chemicals his dying liver was producing caused the agitation. I thought it was more than chemistry. He struggled constantly with things that needed finishing before he died. His comment at Thanksgiving dinner that I could never make as many mistakes as he had was the first sign. Then came the conversation about wanting to reestablish a connection with his daughter. As our friendship developed, he talked about wanting to ask for forgiveness from scores of people he had hurt. Some had already died; others he didn't know about. Family, other than his brother, wouldn't speak to him.

Whatever mistakes Jim had made in the past didn't appear correctable, or if they were, I couldn't seem to help him find a way to do it. Perhaps I didn't have the experience or the wisdom or the willingness to open myself even more than I had already. The only thing I could do was listen. Other volunteers were more successful at calming Jim than I was. One woman got in bed with him when nothing helped the pain and restlessness. She caressed him until he fell asleep, the way a mother caresses a frightened child. I was humbled watching her, wondering if I could ever become as compassionate. But even with her, Jim's agitation stopped only for short periods. Few friends visited. After repeated phone calls from Jim to his brother, he agreed to come and stay with him for two days. When he heard his brother would be visiting, we talked about forgiveness. He wanted to ask for it but was afraid to.

I never saw Jim's brother smile, and I never saw him talk to any of the volunteers or staff. During the first day of his stay, I heard their conversation through the open door of his room. It started pleasantly, with both of them recollecting their childhoods, then adolescence, and finally adulthood. As they progressed through the years, joviality was gradually replaced by accusations. He reminded Jim of every thoughtless thing he ever did, using words that sounded to me as if they were burning the inside of his mouth. Jim sank lower into the recliner as his brother vividly described painful events for twenty minutes.

Tearfully he said, "I'm sorry, Rick, please forgive me. I'm sorry for the pain I caused you."

"Really? You should have thought about it before you went back to using."

"I know."

"Even if I forgive you, your daughter is still dead because of you."

I didn't hear any words indicating that he was shocked. I'd wondered since our first night if he really believed his daughter was still alive. When he started crying, Rick left the room. I entered quietly and sat next to him.

"It didn't work," he said. "I've done some terrible things in my life," he continued.

"We all have."

"No, you don't understand. You can't. Not bad things. Terrible things. There are things I can't be forgiven for. I know that when I die, people will celebrate. And they should. I wanted my brother to forgive me, but I didn't think he would. Actually, I knew he wouldn't, but I had to try."

As he cried, I put my arm around him. I'd never done that with Jim. Hugging and cradling were things he always wanted from female volunteers. Firm handshakes were for men. As I held him, he leaned toward me. This was the closest we'd ever been physically. I started thinking about things I'd done throughout my life that I was sorry for. The list seemed endless. Eventually he became quiet.

Looking at me, he said, "You're a sweetheart."

"That's not something I'd expect to hear from a street-smart guy like you. I don't even hear that from my wife," I lied. He laughed. We were both becoming more comfortable expressing our feelings. "Is there anything I can do for you, Jim?"

In a clear voice, he said, "Shoot me."

"Sorry. Anything but that," I said. He smiled and leaned back in the recliner, waiting for the morphine to take effect.

I knew he'd be in physical and psychological pain until he died. I didn't admit it to anyone, but I hoped it would happen soon. I saw aspects of Jim's life in my own. I looked back on times when I wanted to ask for forgiveness but didn't. I wondered if my father's death twenty-five years ago would have been any different if I'd been able to ask him to forgive some spiteful things I said years before he died. Would his last few hours have been more peaceful if I'd been able to express gratitude for all he gave me? I was slightly better with my mother's death. I always wondered if she knew how important she was to me. I knew I should have told her, but I wasn't able to then.

I was spending Tuesday and Thursday overnights with Jim. But one Thursday in December, all the volunteers were required to attend a training session at another location. The first presentation was by a nurse who had been working in hospice for fifteen years. As she described her interactions with patients, I realized I still wasn't able to deal with an idea that had been presented during my training: being able to fall in love with those I served and then let them go without regrets. I wouldn't say I'd fallen in love with Jim. Maybe I felt the type of friendship that occurs when you share experiences so wrenchingly authentic that they create a bond that defines the relationship forever. I knew I'd miss him like a crotchety old uncle who, years after his death, is only remembered for his good qualities.

"How do you accept the loss when someone you love dies?" I asked.

She immediately replied, "Love can take many forms. The love I experience for my patients involves feeling that I've done everything I could have to make their death as peaceful as possible. I knew every one of the thousands I cared for would die within six months. If I focused on that, I'd go crazy or quit. But when you know you're helping them on a journey, your love is different. So is your sense of loss. Yes, I miss the patients I've worked with, but that's minor compared with what I think I gave them."

There was another speaker, but at the end of the nurse's presentation, I began feeling intense pains in my abdomen. Even though my surgeon had told me that when the cancer returned it wouldn't give me dramatic pain, I excused myself and left anyway, feeling a little panicked.

The next morning I received an e-mail announcing that Jim had died at nine o'clock the previous night. I realized my pains began shortly afterward. I'd never believed in prophetic feelings. When other people would tell me about theirs, I'd listen politely and think, "Give me a break! Who could believe that?" Now I don't question them.

The e-mail said his body would be removed from the House at eleven in the morning. Anyone who wanted to say good-bye could sit with him until then. I arrived at nine and sat alone at the side of the bed. It was the first time I saw him looking peaceful. I felt I was looking at the face of a sixty-seven-year-old baby, content to just be. When I went home, I reread one of my favorite passages from the Buddha's teachings:

> This existence of ours is as transient as autumn colds. To watch
> the birth and death of beings is like looking at the movements of
> a dance. A lifetime is like a flash of lightning in the sky, rushing
> by, like a torrent down a steep mountain.

After Jim died, I asked my wife and children to forgive me for a number of thoughtless things I'd done. Fortunately, they weren't in the same league with the death of Jim's daughter, but I often ask myself, What if they were? How could I ask for forgiveness for something that was "terrible"? I'm not sure I could, although after Jim, I was inspired to help other people do the same thing. I helped one woman write a letter asking for forgiveness from her adult daughter, whom she felt she'd neglected as a child. For another patient, a phone call to an answering machine was all he could do. It seems to me that asking for forgiveness is redemptive, not necessarily in any religious sense, but it seems to remove something that makes the dying process more difficult.

There's an old Buddhist story about a monk who'd walk around with two bags of pebbles tied to his waist. One bag contained white pebbles and the second, black ones. Whenever he did something virtuous, he took out a white pebble and put it in his pocket. Whenever he did something that was hurtful to someone, he took out a black one. At the end of the day he looked at the number of white and black pebbles in his pocket. If the whites outnumbered the blacks, it was a good day. Since seeing the pain of someone who desperately wants forgiveness before they die, I understand how important it is to ask now—and to forgive others now, too. I've found that when I ask for forgiveness for something I did that was thoughtless, some of my black stones magically become white.

Forgiveness Is a Gift

Elaine Pierce

From Japanese-occupied Malaya to her life as an immigrant in the United States, Elaine Pierce's mother was on a journey of forgiveness. This is her moving story.

My mother was born in 1922 in Kuala Lumpur, the capital of what was then the British colony of Malaya. As the only daughter of a prosperous Chinese merchant family, she enjoyed many luxuries, such as her personal *amah*, or servant, and the delicacies that were served at every meal. Her own mother was a formidable character. Although in my grandmother's youth women were still purchased like property, she managed her own finances and routinely traveled to the commercial district to make deals on commodities with the menfolk. She also delivered food and medicine to community members in need, her daughter in tow.

At age thirteen, the first blow in Mom's life occurred when her much-revered mother became ill with diabetes. Mom dropped out of school for several months to care for her until she died. Soon afterward, her father took a young second wife, and in time, Mom acquired seven half siblings. These events, however, did not interrupt her life of privilege; on a typical Saturday evening she'd gather up her girlfriends in her stylish convertible on their way to an elegant dance at the British embassy, all of them attired in French shoes and custom-tailored silk cheongsam dresses with thigh-high slits on one side.

Then came World War II. The British woefully underestimated both the resourcefulness of the invading Japanese troops, who nimbly commandeered bicycles to carry out reconnaissance missions in the jungle, and the quantity of heavy artillery and tanks that the Japanese had brought with them. Within seven weeks of landing on the coast, the Japanese military advanced into Kuala Lumpur, beginning an occupation of the country that would last almost four years. Of the country's three major ethnic groups—the Malays, Indians, and Chinese—the Japanese persecuted the Chinese most cruelly, due to long-standing enmity between their two countries. Around fifty thousand Malay Chinese were massacred during the occupation.

Suddenly, Mom's family was plunged into insecurity and scarcity, having to subsist on vegetables that they grew in their backyard. Her father built a platform hidden in a dense rubber plantation where the women could hide to avoid being raped when Japanese soldiers marched through town. One night, Mom was huddled there with her female relatives and house staff when she saw tiny lights coming down the hill. "They've found us!" She shuddered, only to realize with profound relief that she was looking at fireflies.

At the time, my grandfather owned a row of shops with living quarters above. The Japanese, coveting the building materials, told him that he had twenty-four hours to tear down the building or be beheaded. This forced him to throw his tenants and their possessions into the street with no advance notice.

Mom loathed having to kowtow to the Japanese and learn their language. Her school was among the many that were disbanded. Just before the war started, Mom's college entrance exam papers had been sent by ship to Great Britain for grading. For the duration of the war, she did not know the fate of those papers or whether she'd ever be able to go to college. At long last, she received the good news that she not only had passed but had also been awarded a scholarship. When asked if she'd like to go to England to study, she sniffed, "Not to the country that abandoned us to the Japanese!" Instead, she boarded a ship for San Francisco, where she knew no one, and set out to build a life for herself.

As the years went by, her war stories were recounted less frequently, with less acrimony. Mom had no prejudice toward Japanese people in general. But clearly, her wartime experience was the pivotal force that determined her trajectory in life and her dominant personality characteristics: her drive; ambition; and blunt, confrontational nature, as well as the fiercely protective energy she focused on her family. It probably also contributed to her irreverent sense of humor and her love for sharing a sumptuous home-made banquet with close friends.

Although there was always an altar with a diminutive ivory Kwan Yin statue in our home, I didn't think my mother was a particularly observant Buddhist when I was young. It turns out I was wrong. Going through her papers after she died, I found decades of receipts for offerings made to the various Buddhist temples that she encountered during her well-traveled life. Eventually, she became a long-term member of the Hsi Fang Temple in San Diego, and when she talked about the nuns who calmly and capably conducted the weekly services and charitable work of this temple, I detected a note of pride and admiration in her voice— Mom always did get a kick out of seeing strong women in charge. Their dharma talks and meditation guidance were of great comfort to her both when my father became terminally ill and when her own health began to falter.

Last fall, Mom became confined to a wheelchair and was unable to speak above a whisper because of metastatic breast cancer. Did it slow her down? Barely. Every day that she could physically manage it, she and one of her caregivers were out and about playing dominoes at the senior center; going for a drive by the ocean; getting a massage; or visiting restaurants, movie theaters, casinos, orchid shows, or her hair salon. She refused to miss one minute of her life, and in the company of others her smile could still light up a room.

The last movie she and I saw together was *Gone with the Wind.* Even though she was somewhat confused by that time, I could see her intently watching the TV. It occurred to me then that the tale of Scarlett O'Hara was a fitting metaphor for Mom's life, minus Scarlett's ruthless conniving and cruelty. There's a scene after Scarlett returns to find Tara destitute and her father insane. She's digging through the earth with her bare hands, looking for some roots to eat, when she stands up, silhouetted against the sky, and raises a clod of dirt in her fist. "As God is my witness," she exclaims, "I'll never be hungry again!" Yep, that's Mom, I thought.

Two days before she died, Mom asked her young caregiver, Angie, to take her to a sushi restaurant, even though she'd never before been interested in Japanese food. Mention sushi to her and she'd always wrinkle her nose—"Ugh, raw fish." But that was her request, to go out for sushi.

One of Mom's pleasures was giving Angie first-time experiences, so she suggested some items for Angie to order, yet only nibbled a few grains of rice herself. I don't know how she kept from fainting that day, because by then choking prevented her from taking all but the tiniest sips of the smoothies we gave her, and she was making virtually no urine. She also had very poor control of her hands, which were weak and tremulous. At the end of the meal—with great concentration—she took more than ten minutes to write carefully and legibly on the receipt, "Thank you. That was very good. Helen Pierce."

What I infer here is that, despite a resentment that had long ago ebbed, Mom decided that there was one vitally important final thing that she needed to do; she needed to formally forgive the Japanese soldiers for what had happened to her family during the war and somehow transmit her forgiveness. Writing her note was the intimate, personal ritual that she devised to accomplish this.

The Buddhist monk Thanissaro Bhikkhu writes, "The Pali word for forgiveness—*khama*—also means 'the Earth.' A mind like the Earth is nonreactive and unperturbed. When you forgive me for harming you, you decide not to retaliate, to seek no revenge. You don't have to like me. You simply unburden yourself of the weight of resentment and cut the cycle of retribution that would otherwise keep us ensnarled in an ugly samsaric wrestling match. This is a gift you can give us both, totally on your own, without my having to know or understand what you've done."

The dignity and wisdom of my mother's small act of kindness feels to me like a blessing we are all invited to learn from. It makes me wonder, what burdens can *I* release through forgiveness during the relatively short time I have left on this planet? What exactly am I still hanging on to and why?

PART FIVE

Opening to Compassion

Developing the Compassionate Heart

Sharon Salzberg

Compassion is not at all weak. It is, rather, the strength that arises out of truly seeing the nature of suffering in ourselves and in the world. According to Sharon Salzberg, compassion allows us to name injustice without hesitation and to act strongly with all the skill at our disposal.

I teach one thing and one only: that is, suffering and the end of suffering.
—THE BUDDHA

M any years ago, when I was living in India and practicing meditation in Bodh Gaya, I had gone with a friend to spend a few days in Calcutta. When it was time to leave, we found we were running late to catch our train back. The only way we could get to the train station on time was to take a rickshaw. In many other places in India, rickshaws are pulled by people on bicycles or motorbikes, but in Calcutta they are actually pulled by people running on foot. So, even though we hated the thought of being carried by another human being in this way, we caught a rickshaw to the station.

The rickshaw man took us by shortcuts through dark streets and down back alleys. At one point, suddenly out of nowhere, an extremely big man approached the rickshaw driver and stopped him. Then he looked at me, grabbed me, and tried to pull me off the rickshaw. I looked around the streets for help. There were a lot of people everywhere, as there often are in India, but I did not see a single friendly face.

I thought, "Oh, my God, this guy is going to drag me off and rape me. Then he's going to kill me, and nobody is going to help me!" My friend who was sitting with me in the rickshaw managed to push the drunken man away and urged the rickshaw driver to go on. So we escaped and got to the station.

I was very shaken and upset when we arrived in Bodh Gaya. I told Munindra, one of my meditation teachers, what had happened. He looked at me and said, "Oh, Sharon, with all the loving-kindness in your heart, you should have taken your umbrella and hit that man over the head with it!"

Sometimes we think that to develop an open heart, to be truly loving and compassionate, means that we need to be passive, to allow others to abuse us, to smile and let anyone do what they want with us. Yet this is not what is meant by compassion. Quite the contrary. Compassion is not at all weak. It is the strength that arises out of seeing the true nature of suffering in the world. Compassion allows us to bear witness to that suffering, whether it is in ourselves or others, without fear; it allows us to name injustice without hesitation and to act strongly with all the skill at our disposal. To develop this mind state of compassion, the second of the brahma-viharas, is to learn to live, as the Buddha put it, with sympathy for all living beings, without exception.

The feeling we call compassion is often misunderstood, however. The first time I was teaching meditation in the Soviet Union, I talked a lot about compassion. As the words were being translated into Russian, I kept getting the funny feeling that I was not conveying my meaning clearly. I finally asked the interpreter, "When I say 'compassion,' what do you say?" He answered, "Oh, I describe a state of being terribly overcome by somebody's sorrow, like having a stake through your heart and having the burden of somebody's pain burdening you as well." I just sat there thinking, "Oh, no."

It is easy to understand how the meaning of compassion could be taken to include this state of being overcome by the suffering of another. When it is translated literally from the Pali and Sanskrit word *ka-*

runa, compassion means experiencing a trembling or quivering of the heart in response to a being's pain. But compassion is not debilitating, as suggested by the state described by the interpreter. To be overwhelmed by pain can lead us into despair, grief, aimlessness, even anger. This is not compassion. Ram Dass and Paul Gorman, in their book *How Can I Help?* write: "It's one thing to have one's heart engaged, and another to have it overwhelmed or broken. Here lies our aversion to suffering." If we feel that our hearts will break, that we will be overwhelmed, that we cannot bear what is going on, we find it difficult to open to pain—yet that is the basis of compassion.

The first step in developing true compassion is being able to recognize, to open to, and to acknowledge that pain and sorrow exist. Everywhere, absolutely everywhere, in one way or another, beings are suffering. Some suffering is intense and terrible; some is quiet and small.

W. H. Auden wrote:

About suffering they were never wrong,
The Old Masters: how well they understood
Its human position: how it takes place
While someone else is eating or opening a window or just
    walking dully along

While suffering is not all there is in life, it is a thread that needs to be recognized clearly if we are to develop true compassion.

If we look at our own experience, it comes as no big surprise that suffering exists. We have our ups and downs, we have pain or loss or sorrow, times when we do not get what we want, or we do get what we want but it goes away or proves to be not what we wanted after all. We all experience this pattern. Because we know this experience as real, not receiving external confirmation of our perception is actually far more painful than a frank acknowledgment would be.

Yet we are brought up with the feeling that suffering is somehow wrong or to be avoided. We get the idea that suffering is unbearable and should not even be faced. So we create a society that accommodates our need to deny pain as best we can. We use material consumption and painkillers to avoid suffering. We take people who are different, people who are in trouble, people who are old, people who are dying, and put them out of sight in institutions. These are forms of suffering we all share, but there is so much humiliation and bitterness about getting sick or growing old or dying that we feel we have to hide our pain. One striking example of this pervasive denial occurred when Ronald Reagan was first running for president. The media were filled with images of the American family, which at that time was almost a sacred entity. According to the social myth being propagated, there were many issues the courts would no longer have to decide or the legislatures consider, because "the American family" was going to take care of them. This was a picture of the American family without suffering or conflict. All of its members were communicating and taking good care of one another. There was so much familial respect and closeness that no intervention on the part of government agencies would be necessary.

When I read these descriptions in the newspaper or heard them on the radio or television, I would think, "What families are they talking about?" They were not talking about any that I had ever met or heard of. They were not talking about the families with violence and alcoholism, or even the ones where people hadn't really talked to each other for many years.

I do not mean to imply that there is no happiness in family life. There can be great happiness in family life, but how often is it so very perfect as this political vision implied? No wonder people feel terrible about their own situations! Look at what is being held up as real.

Thus we live like children growing up in a dysfunctional family, where there is conflict but no one ever speaks about it. The pain is denied, as if the children could be spared the awful truth. But they always know what is going on, though they are never given any validation for this understanding and its attendant feelings. This is how people learn not to trust their own experience. Through denial, a tremendous disparity is created between inner reality and the circumstances of the external world.

A story from the great Hindu epic the *Mahabharata* illustrates this human drive to deny. Yudhistara is asked, "What is the most wondrous thing in the entire world?" He replies, "The most wondrous thing in the entire world is that all around us people can be dying and we don't believe it can happen to us." It is as though we live our lives with a big surprise waiting at the end. Many times when I have stood in line at the checkout counter of the supermarket, I have seen the tabloid headlines telling about Elvis Presley, who is still alive and has been sighted somewhere. "ELVIS SPOTTED IN FLORIDA!" or California, or even once on Mars. Why can't he have died? People do die. Why is that so impossible to accept?

When we deny our experience, we are always moving away from something real to something fabricated. To live by this web of legend will always harm us. The truth may be difficult to open to, but it will never hurt us. What a tremendous relief to have the actual truth openly spoken: "There is suffering in this world." Everything is up-front. There are no games, no pretense, no denial. To acknowledge the truth of suffering allows us to feel our unity with others. The goal of our spiritual practice is to be able to understand, to be able to look without illusion at what is natural in this life, at what is actually happening for others and for ourselves. This willingness to see what is true is the first step in developing compassion.

More difficult than acknowledging pain, however, is opening to it. This is the second step in developing compassion: opening to pain and establishing an appropriate relationship to it. In order to genuinely open to pain, we may have to do so a little bit at a time. If our opening is forced or contrived, our sense of purpose may shatter.

Sometimes, when we begin to open to suffering, we displace it, so that even though we see it, we also have the sense of being able to control it, as if we could turn it off and on. This tendency to displace may be why people can so avidly read about violence in newspapers or magazines or watch it constantly in movies or on TV. We look at tragedy with the hope that we can control it by turning the dial.

When we do not feel in control, very often we feel righteous anger, fear, or grief. In Buddhist psychology these are known as compassion's near enemies because they may disguise themselves as compassion. Compassion's far enemy, cruelty, is so clearly the opposite state that it is easy to detect. It can be harder to distinguish when we are lost in aversion. We may feel angry at injustice or outraged to see or hear of misuses of power, whether in families, communities, or political systems. We may become afraid ourselves when we witness the fear of others. We may feel sorrow and grief over the losses suffered by others. All of these feelings are similar to compassion, "the trembling of the heart." But compassion is quite different, in fact, from anger, fear, and grief. These states of aversion can drain us, perhaps destroy us. This is not to say that it is wrong to feel them, but we must be able to look at our experience truthfully and see the consequences of one set of responses as opposed to another.

Once I gave a talk on the differences between aversion and compassion. Someone came to speak to me, quite upset. He told me about his sister who was severely brain-damaged and in a nursing home, all too often receiving substandard care. He insisted that only his repeated, infuriated interventions were keeping her alive in that institution. His whole body was trembling as he spoke. After some moments, I asked him, "What is your inner reality like?" He replied, "I'm dying inside. The anger is killing me!" Certainly there are injustices to be named in this world, and hate-filled situations to be changed, and inequities to be remedied. There is appropriate treatment to be demanded, without prejudice or fear. But can we do these things without destroying ourselves through anger?

The state of compassion as the trembling of the heart arises with a quality of equanimity. Can you imagine a mind state in which there is no bitter, condemning judgment of oneself or of others? This mind does not see the world in terms of good and bad, right and wrong, good and evil; it sees only "suffering and the end of suffering." What would happen if we looked at ourselves and all of the different things that we see and did not judge any of it? We would see that some things bring pain and others bring happiness, but there would be no denunciation, no guilt, no shame, no fear. How wondrous to see ourselves, others, and the world in that way!

When we see only suffering and the end of suffering, then we feel compassion. Then we can act in energetic and forceful ways but without the corrosive effects of aversion.

Compassion can lead to very forceful action without any anger or aversion in it. When we see a small child reaching toward a hot burner on a stove, we instantly take action! Our response is born out of the compassion we feel: we move to pull the child back, away from harm. We do not reject or condemn the child.

To be compassionate is to wish that a being or all beings be free from pain. To be compassionate is to sense from within what it must be like to experience someone else's experience. I had such an opening at the end of my first visit to the Soviet Union. In the airport, just as I was leaving, I had to go through Soviet passport control. This inspection was done quite formally because, I imagine, they did not want Soviet citizens leaving the country with falsified foreign passports. So passport control was something of an ordeal. Smiling, I handed my passport to a uniformed Soviet official. He looked at my picture, and he looked at me, and he looked at my picture, and he looked at me. The look he gave me was, I think, the most hateful stare I have ever received from anybody in my life. It was an icy rage. It was the first time in my life that I had experienced that kind of energy so directly and personally. I just stood there, shocked. Finally, after quite a long period of time, the official handed me back my passport and told me to go.

I went to the transit lounge of the airport, where my traveling companions were waiting for me. I was very upset. I felt as though the man's energy had poisoned my being. I had absorbed his hatred, and I was reacting strongly to it. Then, in one moment, everything shifted. I thought, "If being exposed to his energy could make me feel so terrible after ten minutes, what would it be like to live inside that energetic vibration all the time?" I realized that this man might wake up, spend much of the day, and go to sleep in a state quite similar to the one I had just experienced from him. A tremendous feeling of compassion came into me for him. He was no longer a threatening enemy but, rather, someone in what seemed to be intense suffering.

To view life compassionately, we have to look at what is happening and at the conditions that gave rise to it. Instead of looking only at the last point, or the end result, we need to see all of the constituent parts. The teachings of the Buddha can be distilled into an understanding that all things in the conditioned universe arise due to a cause. Have you ever had the experience of feeling resentful toward someone and then having an insight into what in their history might have caused them to behave in a certain way? Suddenly you can see the conditions that gave rise to that situation, not simply the end result of those conditions.

Once I knew two people who had both suffered from abuse in childhood. One, a woman, grew up to be quite fearful, while the other, a man, grew up to be quite angry. The woman found herself in a work situation with the man, disliked him intensely, and was trying to have him fired from his job. At one point in the process, she got a glimpse into his background and recognized how they both had suffered in the same way. "He's a brother!" she exclaimed.

This kind of understanding does not mean that we dismiss or condone a person's negative behavior. But we can look at all of the elements that go into making up that person's life and can acknowledge their conditioned nature. To see the interdependent arising of these impersonal forces that make up our "selves" can provide the opening for forgiveness and compassion.

Compassion means taking the time to look at the conditions, or the building blocks, of any situation. We must be able to look at things as they are actually arising in each moment. We must have the openness and spaciousness to see both the conditions and the context. We may, for example, hear a statement such as "Heroin is a very dangerous drug." This is undoubtedly true. But is it necessarily true for someone who is terminally ill, in excruciating pain? What is the context of the reality of the moment? If we can look in that way, we are not held to rigid categories that may close off our compassionate understanding.

How do we put compassion into action in our lives? The Buddha gave a teaching known as "the precious human birth" in which he described how rare and precious it is to take birth as a human in the vast cosmological scheme, and how as a human it is so rare and precious to experience just the right mixture of pleasure and pain to undertake deep spiritual inquiry. If there is too much pain in our lives, then we are overcome, perhaps needing to concentrate solely on how to survive each day. If there is too much pleasure, then we may get lazy and not have the motivating spark to look for meaning in our life.

This teaching fosters compassion in two ways. First, we can commit ourselves to creating for all others the kind of environment in which there is space and time enough for a spiritual opening, so that people can live according to the knowledge that they will die and find that truth which goes beyond this body and mind, which does not die. Second, if we see people, no matter what their worldly circumstances, squander the precious opportunity for awakening in this brief human life, we can be moved to compassion for them. Living with this awareness, every aspect of our lives can be an opportunity for compassion. Even a very simple action may be an extraordinary expression of the compassionate heart. Sometimes we think that to be compassionate we all have to be Mother Teresa. But we can look at the very simple things we do in our lives in order to see: What do they reflect about our relationship to pain? Do they reflect an understanding of pain? Are we looking at the various conditions making up a given situation, and are we looking at it in context?

Even very simple actions can make a big difference. We may not be able to take away the mass of somebody's suffering, but we can be present for them. Even if through our small act of being present, somebody does not feel as alone in their suffering as they once did, this will be a very great offering.

I was in a bad car accident in the late seventies. I arrived at Insight Meditation Society on crutches to teach a long retreat, and I was having difficulty getting around. That was the year His Holiness the Dalai Lama came to visit. The preparations for his visit were intensive, because we had to arrange a great deal of security for this man who is considered a head of state. Our peaceful, rural retreat center became a stronghold. Pleasant Street was barricaded off, and state policemen patrolled the roof with guns. There were video cameras and a lot of excited activity. I was feeling dismal on crutches, especially when I ended up in the back of the huge crowd waiting to greet the Dalai Lama when he arrived. The car with His Holiness in it pulled up at last and was greeted by the cameras, the people, and the armed policemen. The Dalai Lama got out, looked around, and saw me standing way in the back of the throng, leaning on the crutches. He cut straight through the crowd and came up to me, as though he were homing in on the deepest suffering in the situation. He took my hand, looked me in the eye, and asked, "What happened?"

It was a beautiful moment. I had been feeling so left out. Now I suddenly felt so cared for. The Dalai Lama did not have to make the pain go away; in fact, he could not. But his simple acknowledgment, his openness, helped me feel included. Every act can be expressive of our deepest values.

Whatever life presents to us, our response can be an expression of our compassion. Whether someone speaks truthfully to us or deceitfully, harshly or gently, we might respond with a loving mind. This is also an act of compassionate service.

The Buddha himself expressed compassion in many different ways. His compassion was measureless, reaching from the most personal level to the most absolute. His service to beings ranged from caring for the sick to teaching a path of liberation. To him, the two were not distinct from each other.

Once a monk in the Buddha's time came down with a terrible disease that had some very unpleasant manifestations. He had, according to the text, oozing sores that looked and smelled so horrible that everybody avoided him completely. This monk lay helpless in bed, dying a grisly death with no one to care for him. When the Buddha became aware of this situation, he himself went into the monk's hut, bathed his wounds, cared for him, and gave him reassurance and spiritual instruction.

Later, the Buddha addressed the monastic community, saying that if somebody wanted to serve him, the Buddha, they should look after the sick. Those words seem so like ones spoken nearly five hundred years later by another compassionate spiritual teacher: "Whatsoever you do unto the least of these, so also you do unto me."

According to the Buddha, to develop compassion it is important to consider the human condition on every level: personal, social, and political. Once the Buddha described a king who decided to give over his kingdom to his son. He instructed him to be both righteous and generous in his new role as king. As time went on, although the new king took care to be just, he neglected to be generous. People became much poorer in his kingdom, and thievery increased. The king tried to suppress this thievery by instituting many harsh punishments. In commenting on this story, the Buddha pointed out how unsuccessful these punishments were. He went on to say that in order to suppress crime, the economic conditions of the people needed to be improved. He talked about how grain and agricultural help should be provided for farmers, capital should be given to traders, and adequate wages should be given to those who are employed.

Rather than responding to social problems through taxation or punishment, the Buddha's advice was to see the conditions that have come together to create a context in which people behave in a certain way, and then to change those conditions. The text states that poverty is one root of theft and violence and that kings (or governments) must look at such causes in order to understand the effects. It is much easier to be moral if one's life is secure in some way, and much more difficult to refrain from stealing if one's children or parents are hungry. Thus our commitment should be to create conditions so that people can more easily be moral. The very pragmatism of this teaching of the Buddha reflects the depth of his compassion.

The Buddha's teaching is never removed from a sense of humanity. He described the motivating principle of his life as dedication to the welfare and the happiness of all beings, out of sympathy for all that lives. He also encouraged the same dedication in others: to see our very lives as vehicles to bring happiness, to bring peace, for the benefit of all beings.

This teaching dictates no particular expression of compassion. You can take up your umbrella with all the loving-kindness in your heart and hit somebody over the head. Or you may renounce the worldly life and live as a monastic, which does not mean renouncing love for all beings or a feeling of connectedness. There are many possibilities. A compassionate act does not have to be grandiose. The very simple action of love, of opening to people, of offering somebody some food, of saying hello, of asking what happened, of really being present—all are very powerful expressions of compassion. Compassion enjoins us to respond to pain, and wisdom guides the skillfulness of the response, telling us when and how to respond. Through compassion our lives become an expression of all that we understand and care about and value.

To develop a compassionate heart is not just an idealistic overlay. It arises from seeing the truth of suffering and opening to it. Out of this arises a sense of purpose, a sense of meaning so strong in our lives that no matter what the circumstances, no matter what the situation, our goal or our greatest desire at any moment is to express genuine love. Our inherent capacity for love can never be destroyed. Just as the whole earth cannot be destroyed by someone repeatedly hurling themselves against it, so too a compassionate heart will not be destroyed in an onslaught of adversity. Through practicing the brahma-vihara of compassion, we develop a mind that is vast and free from enmity. This is boundless, unconditioned love.

Survival of the Kindest

Yongey Mingyur Rinpoche

We all know that we're biologically programmed to avoid threats to our survival and grasp for opportunities to enhance our well-being. Modern science, however, is now proving that altruism is also a vital biological drive of human and even animal life. "Compassion is the spontaneous wisdom of the heart," says Yongey Mingyur Rinpoche. "It's always with us. It always has been and always will be."

Imagine spending your life in a little room with only one locked window so dirty it barely admits any light. You'd probably think the world was a pretty dim and dreary place, full of strangely shaped creatures that cast terrifying shadows against the dirty glass as they passed your room. But suppose one day you spill some water on the window, or a bit of rain dribbles in after a storm, and you use a rag or a corner of your shirtsleeve to dry it off. And as you do that, a little of the dirt that had accumulated on the glass comes away. Suddenly a small patch of light comes through the glass. Curious, you might rub a little harder, and as more dirt comes away, more light streams in. Maybe, you think, the world isn't so dark and dreary after all. Maybe it's the window.

You go to the sink and get more water (and maybe a few more rags), and rub and rub until the whole surface of the window is free of dirt and grime. The light simply pours in, and you recognize, perhaps for the first time, that all of those strangely shaped shadows that used to scare you every time they passed are people—just like you! And from the depths of your awareness arises an instinctive urge to form a social bond—to go out there on the street and just be with them.

In truth, you haven't changed anything at all. The world, the light, and the people were always there. You just couldn't see them because your vision was obscured. But now you see it all, and what a difference it makes!

This is what, in the Buddhist tradition, we call the dawning of compassion, the awakening of an inborn capacity to identify with and understand the experience of others.

THE BIOLOGY OF COMPASSION

The Buddhist understanding of compassion is, in some ways, a bit different from the ordinary sense of the word. For Buddhists, compassion doesn't simply mean feeling sorry for other people. The Tibetan term— *nying-jay*—implies an utterly direct expansion of the heart. Probably the closest English translation of nying-jay is "love"—but a type of love without attachment or any expectation of getting anything in return. Compassion, in Tibetan terms, is a spontaneous feeling of connection with all living things. What you feel, I feel; what I feel, you feel. There's no difference between us.

Biologically, we're programmed to respond to our environment in fairly simple terms of avoiding threats to our survival and grasping for opportunities to enhance our well-being. We only need to flip through the pages of a history book to see that the story of human development is very frequently a tale of violence written in the blood of weaker beings.

Yet it seems that the same biological programming that drives us toward violence and cruelty also provides us with emotions that not only inhibit aggression but also move us to act in ways that override the impulse for personal survival in the service of others. I was struck by a remark made by Harvard professor Jerome Kagan during his presentation at the 2003 Mind and Life Institute conference, when he noted that along with our tendency toward aggression, our survival instinct has provided us with "an even stronger biological bias for kindness, compassion, love, and nurture."

I have been told many stories about the number of people who risked their lives during the Second World War to give refuge to European Jews hunted by the Nazis, and of the unnamed heroes of the present day who sacrifice their own welfare to help the victims of war, famine, and tyranny in countries around the world. In addition, many of my Western students are parents who sacrifice an enormous amount of time and energy shuttling their children between sports competitions, musical activities, and other events while patiently putting money aside for their children's education.

Such sacrifices do seem, on an individual level, to indicate a set of biological factors that transcend personal fears and desires. The simple fact that we've been able to build societies and civilizations that at least acknowledge the need to protect and care for the poor, the weak, and the defenseless supports Professor Kagan's conclusion that "an ethical sense is a biological feature of our species."

His remarks resonate almost completely with the essence of the Buddha's teachings: The more clearly we see things as they are, the more willing and able we become to open our hearts toward other beings. When we recognize that others experience pain and unhappiness because they don't recognize their real nature, we're spontaneously moved by a profound wish for them to experience the same sense of peace and clarity that we've begun to know.

THE AGREEMENT TO DISAGREE

From what I've learned, most conflicts between people stem from a misunderstanding of one another's motives. We all have our reasons for doing what we do and saying what we say. The more we allow ourselves to be guided by compassion—to pause for a moment and try to see where another person is coming from—the less likely we are to engage in conflict. And even when problems do arise, if we take a deep breath and listen with an open heart, we'll find ourselves able to handle the conflict more effectively—to calm the waters, so to speak, and resolve our differences in such a manner that everyone is satisfied and no one ends up as the "winner" or the "loser."

For example, I have a Tibetan friend in India who lived next door to a man who had a bad-tempered dog. In India, unlike in other countries, the walls surrounding the front yard of a house are very tall, with doors instead of gates. The entrances to my friend's yard and his neighbor's yard were very close, and every time my friend came out of his door, the dog would tear out of his neighbor's door, barking, growling, fur bristling—an altogether scary experience for my friend. As if that weren't bad enough, the dog had also developed a habit of pushing through the door into my friend's yard, again barking and snarling, making a terrible disturbance.

My friend spent a long time considering how to punish the dog for its bad behavior. At last he hit on the idea of propping open the door to his front yard just a bit, and loosely piling a few small, heavy objects on top of it. The next time the dog pushed open the door, the objects would fall, teaching him a painful lesson he would never forget.

After setting his trap one Saturday morning, my friend sat by his front window, watching and waiting for the dog to enter the yard. Time passed and the dog never came. After a while my friend set out his daily prayer texts and started chanting, glancing up from his texts every once in a while to look out the window into the yard. Still, the dog failed to appear. At a certain point in his chanting, my friend came to a very ancient prayer of aspiration known as the Four Immeasurables, which begins with the following lines:

> May all sentient beings have happiness and the causes of happiness.
> May all sentient beings be free from suffering and the causes of
>   suffering.

In the middle of chanting this prayer, it suddenly occurred to him that the dog was a sentient being and that in having deliberately set a trap, he would cause the dog pain and suffering. If I chant this, he thought, I'll be lying. Maybe I should stop chanting.

But that didn't feel right, since the Four Immeasurables prayer was part of his daily practice. He started the prayer again, making an earnest effort to develop compassion toward dogs, but halfway through he stopped himself, thinking, No! That dog is very bad. He causes me a lot of harm. I don't want him to be free of suffering or to achieve happiness.

He thought about this problem for a while, until a solution finally came to him. He could change one small word of the prayer. And he began to chant:

May SOME sentient beings have happiness and the causes of
  happiness.
May SOME sentient beings be free from suffering and the causes of
  suffering.

He felt quite happy with his solution. After he'd finished his prayers,
eaten his lunch, and forgotten about the dog, he decided to go out for a
walk before the day was over. In his haste, he forgot about the trap he'd
set, and as soon as he pulled open the door to his yard, all the heavy
things he'd piled up on its edge fell on his head.

It was, to say the least, a rude awakening.

Yet, as a result of his pain, my friend realized something of great
importance. By excluding any beings from the possibility of achieving
happiness and freedom from suffering, he had also excluded himself.
Recognizing that he himself was the victim of his own lack of compassion, he decided to change his tactics.

The next day, when he went out for his morning walk, my friend
carried with him a small piece of *tsampa*—a kind of dough made of
ground barley, salt, tea, and lumps of butter that Tibetans usually eat for
breakfast. As soon as he stepped out his door, the neighbor's dog came
rushing out, barking and snarling as usual, but instead of cursing the
dog, my friend simply threw him the piece of tsampa he was carrying.
Completely surprised in midbark, the dog caught the tsampa in his
mouth and began to chew—still bristling and growling but distracted
from his attack by the offering of food.

This little game continued over the next several days. My friend
would step out of his yard, the dog would come running out and in midbark would catch the bit of tsampa my friend threw him. After a few days
my friend noticed that even though it kept growling while chewing on
the tsampa, the dog had started to wag its tail. By the end of a week, the
dog was no longer bounding out ready to attack but instead ran out to
greet my friend, happily expecting a treat. Eventually the relationship
between the two developed to the point where the dog would come trot-
ting quietly into my friend's yard to sit with him in the sun while my
friend recited his daily prayers—quite contentedly now able to pray for
the happiness and freedom of all sentient beings.

Once we recognize that other sentient beings—people, animals, and
even insects—are just like us, that their basic motivation is to experience

peace and to avoid suffering, then when someone acts in some way or says something that is against our wishes, we're able to have some basis for understanding: "Oh, well, this person (or whatever) is coming from this position because, just like me, they want to be happy and they want to avoid suffering. That's their basic purpose. They're not out to get me; they're only doing what they think they need to do."

Compassion is the spontaneous wisdom of the heart. It's always with us. It always has been and always will be. When it arises in us, we've simply learned to see how strong and safe we really are.

Loving Loving-Kindness

Brian Haycock

Between the road ragers and the self-absorbed creeps, the bad drivers and the drunk passengers, it's hard making a living behind the wheel of a cab. That can seem like a good excuse to look out just for number one, says Brian Haycock. But it's not. We're always better off when we're helping others.

Driving a cab, you meet a lot of people. In a typical twelve-hour shift, a driver will load twenty fares, about thirty or forty people in all, and spend about fifteen minutes with each of them. You talk about the weather, sports, good places to eat, what's going on this weekend. You don't talk about politics. Or religion. You don't get to know any of these people. It's all pretty impersonal. You just pick them up and drop them off, and you never see them again.

This gives us a great opportunity to have a positive—or negative—effect on the lives of people without being drawn into the ongoing psychodramas that can turn day-to-day life into such an emotional minefield. For drivers on the Eightfold Freeway, this is where right action comes into play. This is where the Golden Rule rules.

The Buddha taught compassion for all beings. In Buddhism, compassion is generally thought of as an active feeling of empathy, a willingness to share in the suffering of others. It grows from the realization that we are not really separate from each other. We are all part of a much greater pattern. In other words, we're all in this together. To hurt others is to hurt ourselves. And in daily life, that's not just a saying. It's reality.

Compassion and empathy are central to all religions. In Christianity there is a great emphasis on the practice of forgiveness. When Pope John Paul II forgave the man who shot and nearly killed him, it was a great spiritual lesson for the world. And the selflessness of such leaders as Mother Teresa and the Dalai Lama is an inspiration for people of all faiths.

Right action means to have compassion for all beings, not just the ones who deserve it. The bad drivers, the self-absorbed creeps, the road ragers, the crackheads—they'll all pay a heavy price for their actions. The toxic passengers will run into real trouble down the line. They're looking for it, and they'll find it. There's suffering in their lives as well. We don't need to add to it. And we don't have to add to anyone else's burdens either.

It's hard making a living behind the wheel of a cab. The drivers have to hustle long hours and handle a heavy load of stress to make it all pay. That can seem like a good excuse to act out. It's not. We're always better off when we're helping others.

I'm at the airport, second up at the cabstand in front of the terminal. I've been waiting in line for almost two hours, and I just want to get going. In front of me is a driver named Ray who always works the airport. He's standing at the back of his cab with the trunk open, a vacant smile on his face. He looks at me, shrugs, looks back at the terminal, fidgets a little. He's watching the stragglers from the previous flights, people who've been using the restrooms, waiting for luggage. They're coming out a few at a time, mostly heading for the parking lots.

I know what he's thinking. He's watching the people as they come out, trying to guess which ones want a cab, how far they'll be going. Some of the drivers have the variables all worked out: the number of people in a group, the way they're dressed, the amount and type of luggage, a long list of factors. Sometimes they'll stand there in the cab line, debating the possibilities, arguing about the people coming out. Sometimes they even bet on it. Ray's thinking about it now, deciding which ones he wants, which he doesn't. He's been in line for a long time, and he's been thinking about the big fare he's going to get, getting attached to the idea of it. He thinks he deserves a good one just for waiting.

Not that it matters. Whoever comes out next and wants a cab, that's who he's getting.

It takes a few minutes. Then a woman comes up, in her fifties, well dressed, trailing an overnight bag on wheels. I'm thinking she's going to a hotel, probably downtown; not a long trip. He's thinking the same but he keeps the smile on, says hello. He picks up the bag, puts it in the trunk, and I can read his lips as he says, "Where would you like to go?"

Apparently, he doesn't like the answer. The smile drops away. He reaches up, slams the trunk. Walks around the car with his lips moving, a nasty look on his face. Pounds a fist into the roof as he opens the door and gets in. The poor woman is still standing there, at the back of the cab, looking shocked. She's wondering what she did wrong. She's probably wondering if she should get in the cab with this guy. He might be dangerous. Or crazy. Finally, she goes around, opens the door, and gets in.

Welcome to Austin, ma'am. Enjoy your stay.

Familiar, isn't it? We get so wrapped up in ourselves that we lose all connection with the people around us. It happens all the time. I know Ray a little, and he's got some issues. He's actually a pretty nice guy, but he keeps to himself most of the time. He's a little on edge. And like most of us, he didn't see himself sitting in the cab line at the airport when he graduated from high school.

Part of living the dharma is connecting with other people. Seeing the connections that unite us. It's hard to do sometimes. Out on the streets, it's a hard life, and that makes for a great excuse. It's easy to just look out for number one.

This teaching of compassion is one of the cornerstones of all Buddhist practices. In Mahayana Buddhism, compassion is expressed as part of the bodhisattva ideal of living for the benefit of all beings. The practice of *tonglen* involves taking on the suffering of others in a very real way. For some schools, compassion is the main focus of the practice. One school, called Vipassana, or Insight Meditation, emphasizes the development of compassion through rigorous introspection. This practice is called *metta,* or loving-kindness. *Loving-kindness*—all one word, said with a soft, hopeful smile.

The practice of loving-kindness includes meditations aimed at the development of personal qualities such as serenity and a sense of personal safety that lead in turn to a great compassion for others. For example, we might chant "May I be safe from physical harm" over and over, like a mantra. With sufficient practice, we attain a feeling of safety and personal security. Once that is achieved, it's easier to be open to the needs of others.

It seems like a lot of work. After all, the point is simply to be a decent human being. That doesn't seem so hard. But these are difficult times, and it's easy to find excuses to let this aspect of our practice slide. We have to take care of ourselves, and we may not have much left over for others.

Loving-kindness doesn't come easily to me, which probably means I should take it up and work extra hard on it. There's a book on the Buddhist shelf at the library, *Gentling the Heart*. When I see the title, I know it's not for me. People who would want to read a book like that probably don't need to be that much more loving toward others. And the people who need it the most—like me, or Ray, out at the airport—won't read it.

You don't see much loving-kindness out on the streets these days. Everyone's battling the traffic, trying to get ahead of everyone else. We could use a few real bodhisattvas out here. People who can help calm things down and show the rest of us how it could be. I'd like to do that myself, but I've got a ways to go. I'm working on it. And I'm learning.

I pull up at the Greyhound station on a Tuesday afternoon, second in the cab line. Business is bad, even for a Tuesday. Midsummer in Austin. It's been slow for weeks. People with money are all vacationing somewhere that's cooler than the surface of the sun. The rest of us are stuck here chasing dollars. There's nothing coming out on the cab radio. I'd go out to the airport and sit in line there, but that hasn't been turning over either. Besides, this is closer. I keep the air conditioner running, engine on, burning gas.

Nothing happens at the bus station until a bus comes in, and there aren't that many buses. Drivers who work it regularly know the schedule. I don't. I figure I'll just sit there until something happens. I might get a long fare, something to make my afternoon. Some good fares come out of the bus station. Or I might wait two hours for a five-dollar ride. It seems like the best of a long list of bad bets.

I've got those midsummer cabdriver blues. I've got 'em bad.

After a while, I shut off the engine and get out. I'd sit in the shade, but there isn't any. I walk over to the back of the station, where the buses load. There are a few people on the benches there, waiting for the next bus. They all look like they're going to nod off or dissolve in the sun. I'd go inside and check the schedule, which would be the smart thing to do, but I don't want to know.

There's a woman at the back of the station with a little girl. They look lost. She loads some suitcases and a taped cardboard box onto a small cart and sits the girl on top, pushes the cart out to the sidewalk. The girl enjoys the ride, but it's a short one. The woman stands there looking around.

They don't look like they can afford a cab.

Finally she takes the girl by the hand and walks over. "Excuse me, do you know where the Salvation Army is located?"

It's downtown, four or five miles from the bus station. I tell her that.

She looks troubled. The little girl is looking at her reflection in the door of the cab. She can't see much, but she seems entranced. In this heat, she'll be wailing soon enough. The woman thinks it over and asks, "Where can I catch a bus?"

If I were king of the world, or just the head of Capital Metro, I would put a bus stop right next to the Greyhound station. After all, it is a bus station. But there isn't a stop anywhere near here. I start describing the route she'll have to take to the closest bus stop, which is at Highland Mall. I glance over at the suitcases, the cardboard box sealed with duct tape. I look at the woman. She looks like she has a black eye. Not a bad one, but it's there. I can't do this.

"Come on, I'll give you a ride over there."

"Are you sure? I can't afford to pay you. I know you have to make a living out here."

"It's all right. I'm not exactly getting rich sitting here." I walk over and collect the cart with the suitcases and the box, wheel it over to the cab. I load the trunk. The little girl stands on her toes on the curb, studying the inside of the trunk.

I'm thinking I'm going to give her a ride to the bus stop, then get back in line at the station, but I'm picturing her trying to get the suitcases on a city bus. I make a turn and head for the interstate, downtown. I feel better already. I crank up the air conditioner.

On the way in, we talk. It's what I thought. She was in an abusive relationship, and she's getting out. She's here to start over. She asks if all the people in Austin are as nice as I am, and I tell her yes, most of them are, but I'm not usually this nice. I'm working on it.

When we get to the Salvation Army, I help her with her bags. The people there are expecting her. She won't be staying at the shelter. They're going to help her get a new start. As I turn to leave, the little girl looks up at me, gives me a beautiful smile, and says thank you. It's the first thing she's said since she left the back of the bus station. It's like the sun coming out on a dark afternoon.

From there, I head over to the Omni and load a fifty-dollar fare to Georgetown, and while I'm there, a call comes out on the radio and I load another coming all the way back downtown, and then . . .

No. Of course not. Life isn't like that. It's still a Tuesday afternoon in July. I pull up third in line at the Omni and wait there an hour to load a five-dollar fare going over to the capitol. But I feel good about it. That's what counts.

And a week from now, when I look back at what I've been doing, I'll realize that that was the best afternoon of my week. That was the one time I felt like I belonged in this world, like I had something real and important to do in this life.

Three Lessons in Compassion

Joanna Macy

When Joanna Macy spent a summer with Tibetan refugees, she saw first-hand how they operated as if every being were their mother in a former life. "I cannot emulate that reach of compassion," she says, "but I have seen it.... I know now that it is within our human capacity. And that changes for me the face of life."

I thought I knew what compassion was—it is a familiar concept, common to all religions. But in that first summer I spent with the Tibetans, it appeared in dimensions new to my experience. I wasn't a student of Buddhism then, when I lived in India with my husband and children and first encountered Tibetan refugees in the foothills of the Himalayas. Nor was it, I thought, interest in the dharma that drew me back to them the following summer—back to that ragtag collection of monks and lamas and laypeople who, with their leader Khamtrul Rinpoche, had come out from Kham in eastern Tibet. I simply wanted to be around them. I felt a kind of wild gladness in their company and imagined I could be of some use.

Despite their colorful, stirring ceremonies, they were in difficult straits. Prey to diseases unknown in Tibet, they were living hand to mouth, crowded into rented, derelict bungalows in the hill station of Dalhousie. With no remunerative livelihood or land of their own, they were at risk of being separated from each other and shipped off by Indian government authorities to different work projects, road gangs, camps, schools, orphanages, and other institutions being set up for the thousands of refugees from Chinese repression in Tibet. So, along with an American Peace Corps volunteer, I worked to help them develop an economic base that would enable them to stay together as a community. When my children were free from school in Delhi, we moved up to Dalhousie for the summer.

Our goal was to help the refugees draw on their rich artistic heritage to produce crafts for sale, and to set up a cooperative marketing scheme. In the process, friendships took root that would change my life.

It was clear that the rinpoches, the incarnate lamas of the community, were great masters of Tibetan Buddhism, but I did not ask for teachings. Given the conditions with which they were coping, and the demands on their attention and health, that seemed presumptuous. I wanted to ease their burdens, not add to them. The precious hours when we were free to be together were devoted to concocting plans for the community; applying for government rations; or choosing wools, dyes, and designs for carpet production. Walking with four children between my rented cottage above Dalhousie's upper circle road and the Khampa community on a lower ridge a mile below, there was not time anyway for reading scriptures or learning meditation. But the teachings came anyway. They came in simple, unexpected ways. Three incidents live vividly in my memory.

One day, after my morning time with the children, I was walking down the mountain to meet with my Khampa friends. Before heading off, I had accompanied my oldest, eleven-year-old son to an impromptu dharma class for Westerners at a school for young Tibetan lamas. The English-speaking nun in charge was teaching, and she said, "So countless are all sentient beings, and so many their births throughout time, that each at some point was your mother." She then explained a practice for developing compassion: it consisted of viewing each person as your mother in a former life.

I played with the idea as I walked on down the mountain, following a narrow, winding road between cedars and rhododendron trees. The astronomical number of lifetimes that the nun's words evoked boggled my mind—yet the intent of this quaint practice, for all of its far-fetched fantasy, was touching. What a pity, I thought, that this was not a practice I could use, since reincarnation hardly featured as part of my worldview. Then I paused on the path as the figure of a laborer approached.

Load-bearing laborers were a familiar sight on the roads of Dalhousie, and the most heavily laden of all were those who struggled up the mountain with mammoth logs on their backs. They were low-caste mountain folk whose bent, gaunt forms were dwarfed by their burdens, many meters long. I had become accustomed to the sight of them, and accustomed as well to the sense of consternation that it triggered in me. I would usually look away in discomfort and pass by with internally muttered judgments about the kind of social and economic system that so exploited its own population.

This afternoon I stood stock still. I watched the slight, bandy-legged figure move slowly uphill toward me, negotiating its burden—which looked like the trunk of a cedar—around the bend. Backing up to prop the rear of the log against the bank and ease the weight of it, the laborer paused to catch his breath. "*Namaste,*" I said softly, and stepped hesitantly toward him.

I wanted to see his face. But he was still strapped under his log, and I would have had to crouch down under it to look up at his features— which I ached now to see. What face did she now wear, this dear one who had long ago mothered me? My heart trembled with gladness and distress. I wanted to touch that dark, half-glimpsed cheek and meet those lidded eyes bent to the ground. I wanted to undo and rearrange the straps that I might share his burden up the mountain. Whether out of respect or embarrassment, I did not do that. I simply stood five feet away and drank in every feature of that form—the grizzled chin, the rag turban, the gnarled hands grasping the forward overhang of log.

The customary comments of my internal social scientist evaporated. What appeared now before me was not an oppressed class or an indictment of an economic system so much as a distinct, irreplaceable, and incomparably precious being. My mother. My child. A thousand questions rose urgently in my mind. Where was he headed? When would he reach home? Would there be loved ones to greet him and a good meal to eat? Was there rest in store, and songs and embraces?

When the man heaved the log off the bank to balance its weight on his back again and proceed uphill, I headed on down the mountain path.

I had done nothing to change his life or betray my discovery of our relationship. But the Dalhousie mountainside shone in a different light; the furnishings of my mind had been rearranged, my heart broken open. How odd, I thought, that I did not need to believe in reincarnation for that to happen.

The second incident occurred soon after, on a similar summer Dalhousie afternoon. It was one of the many teatimes with Khamtrul Rinpoche, the head of the refugee community from Kham, and two of his younger tulkus, or incarnate lamas, when we were devising plans for their craft production center. As usual, Khamtrul Rinpoche had a stretched canvas propped at his side, on which, with his customary, affable equanimity, he would be painting as we drank our tea and talked. His great round face exuded a serene confidence that our deliberations would bear fruit, just as the Buddha forms on his canvas would take form under the fine sable brush in his hands.

I, as usual, was seized by urgency to push through plans for the craft cooperative and requests for grants. I could not know then that this work would eventuate in the monastic settlement of Tashi Jong, where, in a few years, the four-hundred-member community of Khampa monks and laypeople would sink their roots in exile.

On this particular afternoon a fly fell into my tea. This was, of course, a minor occurrence. After a year in India I considered myself to be unperturbed by insects, be they ants in the sugar bin, spiders in the cupboard, and even scorpions in my shoes in the morning. Still, as I lifted my cup, I must have registered, by my facial expression or a small grunt, the presence of the fly. Choegyal Rinpoche, the eighteen-year-old tulku who was already becoming my friend for life, leaned forward in sympathy and consternation. "What is the matter?"

"Oh, nothing," I said. "It's nothing—just a fly in my tea." I laughed lightly to convey my acceptance and composure. I did not want him to suppose that mere insects were a problem for me; after all, I was an experienced traveler in India, relatively free of Western phobias and attachments to modern sanitation.

Choegyal crooned softly, in apparent commiseration with my plight, "Oh, oh, a fly in the tea." "It's no problem," I reiterated, smiling at him reassuringly. But he continued to focus great concern on my cup. Rising from his chair, he leaned over and inserted his finger into my tea. With great care he lifted out the offending fly—and then exited from the room. The conversation at the table resumed. I was eager to obtain Khamtrul Rinpoche's agreement on plans to secure the high-altitude wool he desired for the carpet production.

When Choegyal Rinpoche reentered the cottage, he was beaming. "He is going to be all right," he told me quietly. He explained how he had placed the fly on the leaf of a branch by the door, where his wings could dry. And the fly was still alive, because he began fanning his wings, and we could confidently expect him to take flight soon.

That is what I remember of that afternoon—not the agreements we reached or the plans we devised, but Choegyal's report that the fly would live. And I recall, too, the laughter in my heart. I could not, truth to tell, share Choegyal's dimensions of compassion, but the pleasure in his face revealed how much I was missing by not extending my self-concern to all beings, even to flies. The very notion that it was possible gave me boundless delight.

My third lesson that summer also occurred casually, in passing. In order to help the Tibetans, I wanted to tell their story to the world—a story I was just beginning to discover. I had stunning photos of the Tibetans in exile, of their faces and crafts and the majestic lama dances of their lineage. I envisaged an illustrated article for a popular periodical, like the *National Geographic*. In order to hook Western sympathies and enlist Western support, such an article, I figured, should include the horrors from which these refugees had escaped. Stories of appalling inhumanity and torture on the part of the Chinese occupation had come to me only peripherally, in snatches, from laypeople and other Westerners. The rinpoches themselves were reluctant to describe or discuss them.

I presented my argument to Choegyal Rinpoche, the most accessible and confiding of the tulkus. He had been a mature thirteen-year-old when the soldiers invaded his monastery, and he had his own memories to tap of what they had done to his monks and lamas. I suspected a voyeuristic element in my eagerness to hear the ghastly tales—a voyeurism bred by the yellow journalism of Sunday supplements in my New York childhood and by horror movies of arcane Chinese torture. Still I knew that such accounts would arrest the attention of Western readers and rally support for the Tibetan cause.

Only when I convinced Choegyal that sharing these memories with the Western public would aid the plight of Tibetan refugees did he begin to disclose some of what he had seen and suffered at the hands of the

Chinese before his flight from Tibet. The stories came in snatches of conversations, as we paused outside the new craft-production center or walked over to the monastery in its temporary, rented quarters. Then only did he divulge some elements of what had occurred. Many of these elements, the forms of intimidation, coercion, and torture employed, have become public knowledge by now, although reports from Amnesty International and the International Council of Jurists may not have the heart-churning immediacy of Choegyal's words. The lesson I learned, however, and that will stay forever with me, is not about the human capacity for cruelty.

I was standing with Choegyal under a rhododendron tree, the sunlight flickering on his face through the leaves and through blossoms the color of his robes. He had just divulged what must have been the most painful of his memories—what the Chinese military had done to his monks in the great prayer hall as his teachers hid him on the mountainside above the monastery. I gasped with shock and breathed hard to contain the grief and anger that arose in me. Then I was stilled by the look he turned on me, with eyes that shone with unshed tears.

"Poor Chinese," he murmured.

With a shudder of acknowledgment, I realized that the tears in his eyes were not for himself or his monks or for his once great monastery of Dugu in the land of Kham in eastern Tibet. Those tears were for the destroyers themselves.

"Poor Chinese," he said, "they make such bad karma for themselves."

I cannot emulate that reach of compassion, but I have seen it. I have recognized it. I know now that it is within our human capacity. And that changes for me the face of life.

Kindness Changes Everything

Noah Levine

When we practice loving-kindness, says Noah Levine, we change for the better—and so does our world.

The Buddha first taught loving-kindness to a group of monks who had been practicing meditation in a forest. The monks were fearful that the spirits of the forest did not want them there and that the spirits were going to attack them. Although the monks were probably just afraid of the dark, their fear became anger toward the forest, and their anger became hatred. And, of course, when one is feeling angry, unsafe, and resentful, it becomes more and more difficult to meditate. So the group of monks went to the Buddha, asking for advice on how to deal with the perceived threat.

The Buddha's advice was the teachings of the Metta Sutta (the Loving-Kindness Lecture). He went into detail about the necessity of forgiving everyone for everything, and he taught the monks how to live a life of kindness, with the desire and willingness to protect others and not cause harm.

The practical meditation technique for developing kindness, according to the Buddha, is focusing the mind on certain phrases by re-peating them. Some of the common phrases are "May all beings be at ease," "May all beings be safe and protected from harm," "May all beings be met with forgiveness," "May all beings be free from suffering," and "May all beings be happy."

It is said that after receiving the teaching on *metta* the monks went back to the same place in the forest but with a new outlook. As they re-cited the phrases of kindness, the forest began to feel safe. The fear of being attacked left them and all of the beings of the forest began to appear friendly. Birds seemed to be singing sweet songs just for them; the mos-quitoes seemed to leave them alone, but when a mosquito or other bug did bite one of them, they were happy to offer some sustenance to that life-form. As their hearts became kind, their environment became safe.

When we are coming from a place of kindness ourselves, we natu-rally experience kindness from others. Kindness is the antidote to fear as well as to many other forms of suffering. My own experiences have veri-fied this teaching. In my early life I was filled with anger. I was almost constantly dishonest; I caused harm to many people and wished harm upon many others. I was living in the opposite way from what is sug-gested in the Metta Sutta. I had no humility, no integrity, and no wish to protect anyone but myself. Living that way had me going in and out of jail regularly, addicted to drugs, and—most important—always looking over my shoulder to see if anyone was going to attack me. I felt com-pletely unsafe. Of course, crack cocaine has a way of making you para-noid, but it was also true. Having stolen from so many people, I was always worried about getting caught. Living a life of drugs and crime, I was afraid of the police. I was often in physical altercations, and the threat of violence on the streets was a real one. I knew nothing about being kind or loving and was met with a great amount of violence. I was so delu-sional that I often felt like a victim, and I justified the ways I was hurting people by blaming it on the people who had hurt or betrayed me.

I now know that I created the whole thing. It was my unskillful reac-tion to the pain of my life that led to the suffering of crime, drugs, and violence. But as I came to the dharma and trained my mind with metta phrases, I slowly began to change my way of thinking and acting. It was not an overnight transformation but a very gradual change that is con-tinuing to take place even now, twenty-two years into the practice.

That said, kindness does not result in safety for everyone, at least not on a physical level. I can't help but think, for example, of all the truly kind and loving people who must have been tortured and killed in Nazi concentration camps, in Communist Chinese reeducation prisons, in the cities and villages of civil war–torn countries on the African continent, and during the genocide of the native people of North America. I am also thinking of the millions of homosexuals who have been met with violence and hatred for no reason other than their natural sexual orientation, and the millions and millions of truly kind people who've been beaten and killed just for the color of their skin or their religion or gender or political views. This leaves me with the conclusion that perhaps part of what the Buddha was pointing to in this teaching was not always physical safety but more of an inner safety.

I am thinking of a Tibetan Buddhist nun who is beaten and raped by Communist soldiers. Her body is violated and made unsafe; it is the greatest trauma possible. But her years of kindness and compassion practice allow her to access an internal place of safety, a source of loving-kindness that allows her to extend mercy and love to herself and meet her attackers with forgiveness and compassion. She understands the deep state of ignorance that these men are in, and she understands the karmic hell they are creating for themselves. In such circumstances, metta does not protect us against being physically hurt, but it does have the potential to protect us from hatred and all of the suffering that comes with such hatred. Kindness has the power to protect us from the extra layer of suffering we create through greed, hatred, and delusion, and in that way it makes the world a safer place.

Kindness is a general term. I'm defining kindness as that which will end suffering in each situation, meaning that what is kind will depend on the circumstances. For instance, when it comes to pleasurable experiences, the kind relationship to pleasure is almost always nonattached appreciation. If we can enjoy pleasurable moments without clinging to them or getting caught in craving for them to last forever, then we can avoid the typical suffering we often create around pleasure. So the kind thing to do is not to get attached. And if we are not able to meet pleasure with nonattached appreciation and we become attached, then the kind thing to do is let go. And the next level of kindness that is called for is being patient with ourselves in the process of learning to let go. When we start judging ourselves for not being good at letting go, we respond with forgiveness. Forgiveness is also an act of kindness. Get the picture? The kind thing to do depends on the situation. It does not mean being fake nice all the time. It means being real and responsive.

When it comes to painful experiences, the kind thing to do is to meet the experience with compassion. Compassion ends suffering. It does not end pain, but it takes care of the extra level of suffering we tend to layer on top of our pain. In that way, the kindest thing we can do is to cultivate tolerance and compassion toward pain. One of the situations where kindness becomes tricky is when we are faced with the possibility that our seemingly kind actions could actually be causing harm—that we could be enabling someone to suffer through our intentions to be kind. For instance, in the case of dealing with a friend or family member who is addicted to drugs, a strong boundary needs to be set. While lending money to a friend is usually a generous and kind act, with the addict it could cause more harm than good. Most of us face this dilemma on some level or another on a regular basis, such as when we're asked for money on the street by someone who seems to be homeless and is obviously intoxicated. Is giving in a way that may lead to further addiction and suffering really an act of kindness? In some cases, the kindest thing we can do is kindly say no. Sometimes kindness means telling someone something, some truth, they may not like hearing. At times kindness may even hurt. Kindness doesn't have the intention of causing pain, but in some situations it is unavoidable.

Some of the kindest things I have ever done for myself have been the most difficult and painful experiences of my life. When I first started meditation, I found the retreats to be excruciatingly boring, and my body was in agony much of the time. Looking back, taking up meditation was the kindest thing I have ever done for both myself and others. What at the time truly sucked, eventually led to a radical change in my heart and mind. And the positive changes in my life have allowed me to inspire and encourage thousands of others to take the hard and transformative path of meditation retreats. The point is that kindness comes in many different forms. It is situational: there is no way of saying that generosity is always kind or that causing pain is always unkind.

If you wish to respond with kindness in all situations in your life, it is important to have a daily and disciplined meditation practice that includes the heart-mind trainings of metta. It can start with a few minutes a day of offering kind and forgiving phrases to yourself and others. Eventually the practice will need to be incorporated into all aspects of your life. Walking down the street, you can say, "May all beings be at ease." Driving down the freeway, you can say, "May all beings be met with forgiveness." And sitting at work, you can say, "May all beings be happy, peaceful, and free." The wisdom and compassion that are developed with the practice of metta offers us access to spontaneous, appropriate response-ability. It will not always look the same, it may not always feel good, but kindness will become the filter through which we sift our responses to every situation. With this increased ability to respond skillfully to each situation in our lives, the world will become a safer and safer place.

Biggest Love

Judy Lief

It doesn't matter if we start small; we can find a way to hold the whole world in our heart. Judy Lief on cultivating a love that is unfettered and pure—a love that touches everyone.

The human realm is said to be the realm of passion. Passion is what holds us together; confused passion is what entraps us, and transformed passion is what can liberate us. Although our passion is often tainted by the tendency to grasp or possess, in essence it is accepting of others. Passion is attraction, whereas aggression is rejection.

In the traditional Buddhist iconography of the six realms of being—the hell realm, hungry ghost realm, animal realm, human realm, jealous god realm, and god realm—each realm is associated with a particular buddha. In the human realm, the buddha carries an empty bowl, a poignant statement of the experience of emptiness, longing, and incompleteness so many of us experience. When I think of the early monks and nuns going about their daily begging rounds, I think of the two sides of human passion: our insatiable hunger and the power of connecting with one another.

There seems to be a continuum of passion, extending from a pinched passion rooted in emptiness, desperation, and neediness, on one extreme, to an open and free-flowing passion rooted in fullness, confidence, and appreciation on the other. But there is never a moment in which passion is absent; we are swimming in it. The challenge is to figure out how to spend less of our time trapped in the constricted form of passion and more of our time in the loving-kindness form of passion. If we can do that, then the love inside us will extend until it embraces the world.

GROUNDWORK

It is good to start small and simple. What touches your heart right now? What do you love? Who do you love? Maybe you feel you love lots of things, or maybe you feel that you really don't love anything or anyone. It could be that your focus is more on how to make others love you and worrying that they don't or that you will never find your "one true love." What does reflecting on such questions evoke in you? What emotions? What bodily sensations? What story lines?

Going further, it is worthwhile to explore the feeling of loneliness. Can you stay with that experience? Loneliness can feel like a big emptiness inside us that we are desperate to fill. But can anything really suffice to make it go away? Does it come and go, or is it always a part of us? What if we don't try to make it go away or to cover it up? How would that change how you view others?

Speaking of others, how do you divide them up? Which beings and things are "worthy" of your love and affection, and which are not? What are the boundaries of your affection? How limited does your supply of affection seem to be, and how do you parcel it out? When you reach into your little stash of loving-kindness, do old memories and hurts arise? Are you afraid of getting hurt?

By asking yourself these kinds of questions, you can make a kind of assessment of your heart and lay the groundwork for cultivating the capacity to love. It is important to know where you stand, so you know what you have to work with. The idea is not to get caught up in your ideas about what you are supposed to feel about this or that, him or her, this group or that group, this type or that type. Instead, it is to find a starting point that is not theoretical but realistic.

If you are trying to open your heart and cultivate greater loving-kindness and compassion, it is good to look deeply at your own situation and to really try to figure out where you are with all of this. As you look around, you might find only one thing that evokes a feeling of love or kindness in you right now, and that's okay. Rather than trying to develop some grand vision of universal compassion for all beings, which is tempting and sounds great, you could begin modestly with what is right in front of you, something immediate and particular. Even if what you love right now is on the more pinched end of the spectrum, you can start with that. The underlying seed of kindness may be masked by your fixation or neediness, but it is still there. Similarly, if you have slightly scary flashes of openheartedness, which are intriguing but make you feel like scrambling to secure your boundaries and protect yourself, you could start with that.

Mothers and Teachers

To help us move along the continuum from pinched or distorted loving-kindness to true kindness and compassion, the Buddhist tradition presents us with examples to emulate and learn from. The first example is that of a mother with her only child. This primary bond is simple and natural, powerful and true. There are many stories of the way ordinary mothers are willing to put their children's needs before their own. If there is too little food, the child gets fed first; if there is danger, the mother shields her child even at the risk of her own life. Of course, there are counterexamples, but the idea of the loving mother still rings true. The bottom line is that someone took care of us when we were babies; otherwise, we would not have survived.

In contemplating the example of the loving mother, it could be helpful to reflect on what distinguishes this kind of love and why it is a good model to emulate. The example of motherly love reminds us that kindness is a natural human capacity essential to our survival as a species. It shows us that it is possible to put another person's needs ahead of our own. The example of a mother's selfless love for her children has inspired countless people throughout time. We long for love that is unfettered and pure. We long to be held in our mother's loving arms and to be able to give love freely without hesitation or self-regard. All of this is expressed in the powerful image of a mother and child. You see it in painting and sculpture; you hear it in song.

Another example of kindness is said to be the genuine teacher or spiritual guide. Genuine teachers do not use their students as foils or gather students to build up their own power and esteem. Instead, they put their students' interests first and are willing to do whatever it takes to awaken their students and guide them on the path. Although you may be trying to get something from the teacher, the teacher is not trying to get anything from you. In our usual tit-for-tat world, when you offer something in a relationship, you expect something back. There is a bargaining component. But with the teacher-student relationship, since the teacher doesn't need anything from the student, that teacher cannot be bribed or conned, so bargaining is out of the question. No matter how many strategies you may cook up, whatever you put out is simply reflected back, as if by a giant mirror. This is great teaching, for the contrast between love with hooks and love that just is becomes painfully apparent. It also becomes apparent that there is no limit to love once we drop our attachment. In the encounter with the teacher, we are given a glimpse of a kind of love that is present and atmospheric, possessed by no one, and completely free of agendas and strategies.

The idea of reflecting on this human realm of passion is to be realistic. In this realm we can experience the pain of destructive or obsessive love, but we can also be inspired by examples of selfless love. By observing love with an agenda, we can begin to glimpse what love without an agenda might be. And sometimes, oddly, the strongest ground for the development of loving-kindness is to realize how often our first impulse is not all that kindly.

Deliberate and Spontaneous Compassion

Once we have assessed our situation and thought about examples we might emulate, how can we begin to expand our capacity for love? When we are deep into one particular relationship, it is easy to create a kind of love bubble, a little world that feeds on itself and is cut off from the world around us. But we don't have to do that, and in fact, though nice, it can quickly become claustrophobic. Instead we could view our closest relationships as stepping-stones for learning how to view larger and larger aspects of the world with the same kind of interest and delight.

This may be easier said than done, of course. What isn't? But compassion and kindness are not foreign to our nature. They are in there somewhere, and the good news is that we can uncover them and cultivate them.

There are said to be two kinds of compassion: deliberate and spontaneous. Deliberate compassion is the practice and spontaneous compassion is the result. Learning to be more compassionate is like learning to drive a car. At first it feels scary, unnatural, and awkward. We have to keep thinking about what we are doing and what we should do next. But as we get more experience, it is as if our body and reflexes automatically know how to go about it.

Deliberately trying to cultivate kindness and compassion can feel forced and even hypocritical. It means doing things we do not necessarily feel like doing. But that is the point. Instead of waiting to feel kind, we should go ahead and act kind anyway. We should pretend. One way to work with this practice is to try to do one kind gesture each day, whether you feel like it or not. It can be something as small as picking up a sock or putting the slightly better morsel of food on your spouse's plate rather than on your own. Minipractices like that are great opportunities for really getting to know the pain of the habit of always looking out for No. 1.

Spontaneous gestures of love or compassion surprise us from time to time. When you experience these moments of spontaneous compassion, it is natural to want to hold on to them, but like thoughts in meditation, it is better simply to note them and let them go.

BABY STEPS TO KINDNESS

Mahayana Buddhism is all about stretching. What are we stretching out from? From our small-mindedness and self-absorption. To do so we need to engage in the world. But it is amazing how often we think we are out in the world interacting with others, while actually, we are simply robotically acting out our preconceived internal story line. Our vision is clouded, and we can only take in what feeds into our plot line.

One way to begin to soften this kind of pattern is by exploring some basic steps that can lead us in the direction of kindness. Instead of trying to will ourselves to be kind—presto! all at once—we can create an atmosphere congenial to the development of loving-kindness. The following are five small steps you can practice that may be helpful in this regard:

Settle Down

There has to be a here to be a there, and a connection between the two. So the first step is to slow down and let your mind settle enough that you are able to drop from the heights of conceptuality back into your body, a simple form in space. Can you really feel present, in your body as it is, right where you are?

Be in the Moment

Now that you are more solidly somewhere, you can let yourself be more clearly sometime. When your thoughts drift from the past or the future, from memories and regrets to plans and dreams, you can gently bring yourself back to the present moment.

Drop Escape Routes

Stay put in this particular place and time, just the way it is.

Pay Attention to Space

Notice the quality of space within you and around you. Pay attention to the boundaries of your physical body and the space in front, behind, and on each side of you. Also pay attention to the mental-emotional space that accommodates the comings and goings of sensations, thoughts, moods, and emotional upheavals. With whatever arises in your perception, on an outer or inner level, notice the space in which both you and your perception rest.

Share the Space

Explore what it is like to share this quality of space with whatever or whoever is there with you. Notice the power of accommodation, acceptance, and nonjudging. When you sense the arising of territoriality and fear, accommodate that, too, in greater spaciousness.

You can explore these steps singularly or in combination, it is up to you. The idea is that if you create the right atmosphere, compassion naturally arises. It is already present, just waiting for your invitation.

ALCHEMY

What ordinary people see as lead, alchemists see as gold in disguise. Like alchemists, we can learn to uncover the gold hidden within our human condition—no matter how conflicted and unpromising we humans often seem to be. Our dramas and fascinations, our obsessions, our loves gained and lost, may captivate us, but they are fundamentally ephemeral. However, anything that awakens and touches our hearts even a little bit can open us to the possibility of something more. Within the fluctuating passions of the human realm, we can discover the unwavering force of selfless compassion and loving-kindness.

Contributors

After graduating with a degree in philosophy, EZRA BAYDA became a carpenter and builder, an occupation he worked at for thirty years. He is married to Elizabeth Hamilton, the author of *Untrain Your Parrot*, and together they teach at Zen Center San Diego. Bayda's most recent book is *The Authentic Life: Zen Wisdom for Living Free from Complacency and Fear*.

TARA BENNETT-GOLEMAN is a psychotherapist and the bestselling author of *Emotional Alchemy*. She integrates insights from mindful awareness training with those from her postgraduate studies in Schema Therapy, a branch of cognitive therapy. Bennett-Goleman is also a lover of the arts. She's a longtime student of Japanese tea ceremony and flower arranging, and her love of dance first blossomed when she studied Kathak, an Indian dance form.

Until forced to retire by illness, TONI BERNHARD was a law professor at the University of California, Davis. Today she's the author of *How to Be Sick: A Buddhist-Inspired Guide for the Chronically Ill and Their Caregivers* and *How to Wake Up: A Buddhist-Inspired Guide to Navigating Joy and Sorrow*. Her blog, *Turning Straw into Gold*, is hosted by *Psychology Today*.

SYLVIA BOORSTEIN studied chemistry and mathematics at Barnard College, then went on to earn a master's degree in social work from the

University of California, Berkeley, and a PhD in psychology from Saybrook University. A teacher of vipassana and *metta* meditation, she is the author of *Happiness Is an Inside Job* and *That's Funny, You Don't Look Buddhist: On Being a Faithful Jew and a Passionate Buddhist.*

KAREN CONNELLY is the author of the award-winning *Burmese Lessons,* a memoir about her experiences in Burma and on the Thai-Burma border. Her first novel, *The Lizard Cage,* was compared in the *New York Times Book Review* to the works of Orwell, Solzhenitsyn, and Mandela, and hailed in *The Globe and Mail* as "one of the best modern Canadian novels."

MARK EPSTEIN received his undergraduate and medical degrees from Harvard University and is now a psychiatrist, in private practice in New York City, who frequently lectures on the value of Buddhist meditation for psychotherapy. He's the author of a number of books, including *The Trauma of Everyday Life* and *Thoughts without a Thinker.* His articles have been published in *Tricycle, Yoga Journal,* and *O: The Oprah Magazine.*

CHRISTINA FELDMAN is the author of *The Buddhist Path to Simplicity: Spiritual Practice for Everyday Life.* She's a member of the international board of the Buddhist Peace Fellowship; a cofounder of Gaia House, a Buddhist meditation center in Devon, England; and a senior teacher at the Insight Meditation Society in Barre, Massachusetts. What she teaches, she says, is a reflection of the constantly changing nature of her own practice.

NORMAN FISCHER is the founder and spiritual director of the Everyday Zen Foundation and a former coabbot of the San Francisco Zen Center. In the 1970s and '80s, Fischer was a member of a lively group of Bay Area poets and participated widely in readings, publications, and poetry performances. His books include *Training in Compassion: Zen Teachings on the Practice of Lojong.*

CAROLYN GIMIAN is a senior teacher in Shambhala International and a senior editor of the works of the late Chögyam Trungpa Rinpoche, including *The Collected Works of Chögyam Trungpa* and *Smile at Fear:*

Awakening the True Heart of Bravery. She's also the founding director of the Shambhala Archives, the archival repository for Chögyam Trungpa's work in Halifax, Nova Scotia.

STAN GOLDBERG is a professor emeritus of communicative disorders at San Francisco State University and the author of *Leaning into Sharp Points: Practical Guidance and Nurturing Support for Caregivers*. For eight years he was a bedside hospice volunteer at Pathways, Hospice by the Bay, George Mark Children's House, and Zen Hospice Project. Goldberg is a devotee of the *shakuhachi* (Japanese bamboo flute).

THICH NHAT HANH is a Vietnamese Zen Buddhist monk and peace activist who was instrumental in founding the Engaged Buddhism movement. He lives at Plum Village, the practice center he established in France in 1982, but he also has centers in the United States, Germany, Thailand, Hong Kong, and Australia. He's the author of *Anger: Wisdom for Cooling the Flames* as well as many other titles.

In 2007 JULES SHUZEN HARRIS received dharma transmission from Pat Enkyo O'Hara, becoming her second dharma successor. As a psychotherapist, he has found creative ways to synthesize Western psychology and Zen to achieve dramatic results with his patients. He holds black belts in iaido, the art of drawing and cutting with a samurai sword, and kendo, Japanese fencing. He has founded two Japanese swordsmanship schools.

SHOZAN JACK HAUBNER is an onanist, or so he claims, living out his remaining days in an iron lung in his parents' basement. He likes Italian food, *Seinfeld* reruns, and long walks on the moonlit beach where he's buried most of his victims. But Shozan Jack Haubner is a pen name. He's actually suspected of being a Zen practitioner living in New York. He's the author of *Zen Confidential: Confessions of a Wayward Monk*.

BRIAN HAYCOCK is a former cabdriver and the author of *Dharma Road: A Short Cab Ride to Self Discovery*. He also enjoys writing neo-noir crime fiction, and his work has been published in *Thuglit, Yellow Mama, Menda City Review, Swill, Pulp Pusher,* and (as he puts it) other highly reputable publications.

SISTER CHAN KHONG is the author of the book *Beginning Anew: Four Steps to Restoring Communication* as well as *Deep Relaxation: Coming Home to Your Body* and *Learning True Love: Practicing Buddhism in a Time of War.* For more than fifty years, she has worked closely with Thich Nhat Hanh and is recognized as a major force in helping him develop his community.

Born in India to Tibetan parents, DZIGAR KONGTRÜL grew up in a monastic environment and received extensive training in Buddhist doctrine. He is the founder of Mangala Shri Bhuti, his teaching organization, as well as Longchen Jigme Samten Ling, a mountain retreat center in southern Colorado. His books include *Uncommon Happiness.*

JACK KORNFIELD holds a PhD in clinical psychology and trained as a Buddhist monk in the monasteries of Thailand, India, and Burma. He cofounded the Insight Meditation Society in Barre, Massachusetts, and the Spirit Rock Meditation Center in Woodacre, California. His books have been translated into twenty languages and have sold more than a million copies. They include *The Wise Heart* and *After the Ecstasy, the Laundry.*

NOAH LEVINE is the author of *Dharma Punx* and *The Heart of the Revolution: The Buddha's Radical Teachings on Forgiveness, Compassion, and Kindness.* He's the founding teacher of the Against the Stream Buddhist Meditation Society, with a center in Los Angeles and more than twenty affiliated groups around North America. He has a master's degree in counseling psychology and teaches meditation internationally.

JUDY LIEF is the author of *Making Friends with Death: A Buddhist Guide to Encountering Mortality.* She is also the editor of many of Chögyam Trungpa Rinpoche's books, including the three-volume set *The Profound Treasury of the Ocean of Dharma,* which gives a penetrating overview of the three-yana journey from beginning to end.

JOANNA MACY is a scholar of Buddhism, general systems theory, and deep ecology. In the face of overwhelming social and ecological crises, her work helps people transform despair and apathy into constructive, collaborative action. Macy's book credits include *World as Lover, World as Self: Courage for Global Justice and Ecological Renewal* and *A Year with Rilke,* a collection of poetry and prose she translated in collaboration with Anita Barrows.

KAREN MAEZEN MILLER began studying Zen with Maezumi Roshi. Now she teaches at the Hazy Moon Zen Center in Los Angeles and is the author of *Paradise in Plain Sight: Lessons from a Zen Garden.* Miller and her husband and daughter have a century-old Japanese garden in their backyard. She does a lot of weeding, raking, and picking up after the dog.

YONGEY MINGYUR was born in 1975 in Nepal. He was sixteen when he completed his first three-year retreat, and he was appointed master of the next one, making him the youngest known lama ever to hold this position. In 2011 he left his monastery in India to begin a solitary retreat as a wandering yogi. He is the author of *Joyful Wisdom.*

RACHEL NEUMANN is the editorial director of Parallax Press, the publishing arm of Thich Nhat Hanh's community, and the author of *Not Quite Nirvana: A Skeptic's Journey to Mindfulness.* She lives in the Bay Area and writes regularly on the intersections of mindfulness, parenting, politics, and the mess of daily life. Her work appears in *Shambhala Sun, The Village Voice,* and other publications.

For twenty years, ROSHI PAT ENKYO O'HARA taught at the Tisch School of the Arts at New York University. She received priest ordination from Maezumi Roshi and dharma transmission from Bernie Glassman. She's the abbot of the Village Zendo, in New York City, and a founding teacher of the Zen Peacemakers Family, a spiritual and social-action association.

ELAINE PIERCE is a public health physician specializing in the prevention and treatment of sexually transmitted diseases. She has practiced vipassana meditation for seventeen years and says that her *sangha* has given her the opportunity to share experiences with the most honest, courageous, and principled people she knows.

An anthropologist and social activist, MITCHELL RATNER is a founder and senior teacher of the Still Water Mindfulness Practice Center in Silver Spring, Maryland. He's been a lay member of the Tiep Hien Buddhist order since 1993 and in 2001 received the *dharmacharya* (meditation teacher) transmission from Thich Nhat Hanh. Ratner's classes and retreats focus on integrating mindfulness meditation with work, meaningful relationships, and the challenges of everyday life.

SHARON SALZBERG is celebrated as the bestselling author of books such as *Faith, A Heart as Wide as the World,* and *Real Happiness.* In 1976 Salzberg, Joseph Goldstein, and Jack Kornfield established the Insight Meditation Society in Barre, Massachusetts, which has become one of the most important Buddhist centers in the United States.

JOAN SUTHERLAND is the founder of the Awakened Life community, which forms the center of the Open Source, a collaborative network of Zen communities and practitioners. She's also a translator and a cofounder of the Pacific Zen Institute, a koan school with an innovative approach. Before becoming a Zen teacher, she worked for nonprofit organizations in the feminist antiviolence and environmental movements and as a scholar and teacher of archaeomythology.

JUDITH TOY was ordained as a member of the Order of Interbeing by Thich Nhat Hanh in 1997, and along with her late husband, Philip Toy, she founded several *sangha*s in that tradition, including one in a men's prison. The name given to her by Thich Nhat Hanh is True Door of Peace.

B. ALAN WALLACE, a scholar and practitioner of Buddhism since 1970, has taught Buddhist theory and meditation worldwide since 1976. Ordained by the Dalai Lama, he devoted fourteen years to training as a Tibetan Buddhist monk. He then went on to earn an undergraduate degree in physics and the philosophy of science at Amherst College and a doctorate in religious studies at Stanford. He's the author of *Buddhism with an Attitude* and *The Four Immeasurables.*

Credits

About the Editor

Andrea Miller is deputy editor of the *Shambhala Sun* magazine and the editor of the anthologies *Buddha's Daughters: Teachings from Women Who Are Shaping Buddhism in the West* and *Right Here with You: Bringing Mindful Awareness into Our Relationships*. Miller holds an MFA in creative writing from the University of British Columbia, and her writing has appeared in various publications, including *Mindful* magazine, *Buddhadharma: The Practitioner's Quarterly,* and *The Best Buddhist Writing* series.